Duck and Cover

Confronting and Correcting
Dubious Practices in Education

Rick Ginsberg
and Yong Zhao

TEACHERS COLLEGE | COLUMBIA UNIVERSITY
NEW YORK AND LONDON

Published by Teachers College Press,® 1234 Amsterdam Avenue, New York, NY 10027

Front cover design by adam bohannon design. Image is from P.S. 58 in Brooklyn, NY, 1962, courtesy of the New York World-Telegram and the Sun Newspaper Photograph Collection (Library of Congress) Repository.

Library of Congress Cataloging-in-Publication Data

Names: Ginsberg, Rick, 1952- author. | Zhao, Yong, 1965- author.
Title: Duck and cover : confronting and correcting dubious practices in
    education / Rick Ginsberg and Yong Zhao.
Description: New York, NY : Teachers College Press, [2023] | Includes
    bibliographical references and index.
Identifiers: LCCN 2022051786 (print) | LCCN 2022051787 (ebook) | ISBN
    9780807767917 (hardcover) | ISBN 9780807767900 (paperback) | ISBN
    9780807781500 (ebook)
Subjects: LCSH: Education and state. | Curriculum planning—Evaluation. |
    Education—Aims and objectives. | School improvement programs. |
    Education—Moral and ethical aspects.
Classification: LCC LC71 .G48 2023 (print) | LCC LC71 (ebook) | DDC
    379—dc23/eng/20231229
LC record available at https://lccn.loc.gov/2022051786
LC ebook record available at https://lccn.loc.gov/2022051787

ISBN 978-0-8077-6790-0 (paper)
ISBN 978-0-8077-6791-7 (hardcover)
ISBN 978-0-8077-8150-0 (ebook)

Printed on acid-free paper
Manufactured in the United States of America

Contents

PART III: SYSTEMIC AND ANALYTIC CONUNDRUMS

Acknowledgments

A book like this consists of, in essence, our reflections on educational policies and practices. These reflections have been inspired by many people: our colleagues at the University of Kansas and other higher education institutions, teachers and education leaders we have met in schools, and policymakers and administrators we have interacted with. It is impossible to list and thank all of those who have inspired us. We are especially grateful for those whose work inspired and directly influenced us. Professors David Berliner and Gene Glass wrote the wonderful book *50 Myths & Lies that Threaten America's Public Schools: The Real Crisis in Education,* which inspired us to think more about the dubious policies and practices that have been promoted and implemented in schools. Professor Diane Ravitch's numerous historical recounts of American schools, in particular *The Death and Life of the Great American School System: How Testing and Choice Are Undermining Education,* inspired us to think more deeply about the policies and practices in our schools. Professor Pasi Sahlberg's Finnish education and analyses of educational reforms around the world made us look beyond our own familiar systems. Professor Barnett Berry shared insights about teaching and teacher reform as well as valuable research related to several of our arguments. Our KU colleague Professor Kelli Feldman read drafts and shared insights regarding teaching. We are grateful for their work and support.

We are also thankful for the support of our families. In particular, Rick wanted to thank his wife Lauri, who as a parent, former teacher, and teacher educator offered wonderful insights and feedback that improved the book. Yong thanks his wife Xi Chen, also an educator, who has similarly provided great conversations and feedback that improved the book. We both dedicate the book to our children—for Rick, his son Matt and daughter-in-law Urszula, daughter Alexandra, son Noah, and baby grandson Benny; for Yong, his son Yechen, and his daughter Athena.

Introduction

We humans do a lot of dumb things. Sometimes for good reasons, often with the best of intentions, but dumb nevertheless. Sometimes we do things we just like or things that make sense despite the risks involved. Consider, for example, bungee- or base-jumping, the Pamplona Running of the Bulls, sky-diving, not getting a protective vaccine in the midst of a pandemic. Most of us go to airports and jump into tin cans called jets speeding through the sky at over 500 miles an hour just to get someplace fast. Think about how unnatural that is. Certainly, many people eat foods they know are unhealthy, but gosh, that Whopper® sure tastes good! We all have our moments.

Organizations are made up of individuals who may collectively decide on a course of action that seems right, but in actuality was either initially misguided or, after a period of time, its usefulness waned, though the practice persisted. Of course, some things organizations do are just plain strange. That is what this book is about. We focus on policies and practices in schools that were initially well-meaning but wrong, that persist beyond their useful shelf-life, or were dubious from their inception.

We titled this book *Duck and Cover*. Those of you old enough might remember that Americans in the 1950s were gripped with rising fears about the threat of the Soviet Union and potential for nuclear war. Schools weren't spared from this sensation, and actually crafted what became known as "duck-and-cover" policies to protect kids in the event of a nuclear attack. The practice was simple. If there was imminent fear of a bomb hitting a school or landing in its vicinity, students were trained to dive under their desks and cover their heads with their hands. Do that and you would be safe. That was the fix. Implied, of course, was that this act of kneeling under the desk would offer a level of protection against the impact of the bombs.

Perhaps other than the symbolic act of doing something, this has to be one of the most stupid educational policies ever enacted. While neither of us ever experienced living through an atomic or nuclear explosion, we conclude with some level of confidence that even the fanciest and costliest of student classroom desks provided no protection if an atomic bomb happened to land on or near a school. Of course, all kids growing up at the time knew this. But children were more compliant and less critical beings back in the 1950s and 1960s, so the practice endured. Perhaps such ridiculous

1

types of duck-and-cover policies inspired children to eventually challenge the decisions and authority of teachers and school leaders in later years. In the face of such absolute stupidity, kids had to grow up skeptical.

To give educators their due, the "duck-and-cover" plan evolved from President Truman's Federal Civil Defense program, and a film was developed in consultation with the Safety Commission of the National Education Association. The film *Duck and Cover*, created for schools in 1951, had Bert the turtle diving inside his shell to avoid the potential for harm in an explosion. The film narrator set out the plan very clearly: "Be sure and remember what Bert the turtle just did, friends. Because every one of us must remember to do the same thing." Students were told to duck under their desks, then ball up with their knees tucked under their chin into their chests and cover their heads with their hands. That was "duck and cover," derived from a fictional cartoon turtle. We poor humans had to do this, of course, because unlike Bert, we don't have one of those nuclear-protective shells connected to our bodies!

Though we've seen no data on the impact of the great "duck-and-cover" anti-nuclear prophylactic act, it pretty clearly was foolish and offered no protection—unless, of course, the bomb fell in a distant other country, in an ocean, or on another planet. More likely, the practice raised the level of panic students felt about the potential for nuclear war. The message was clear—be worried, bombs are coming, you don't have a protective shell, take cover, put your hands behind your head and dive under your desk!

Why would education policymakers and educators, ostensibly smart and well-trained people, develop and implement such a seemingly silly and useless policy? Its potential for being effective in the case of a nuclear bomb was zero. But something had to be done, so policymakers and educators made a plan and implemented a policy. Well intended, perhaps with some symbolic value (e.g., "We're in charge and we are doing something to protect you"), but nothing of any real worth.

Sadly, in PK–12 schools, we create duck-and-cover types of policies and practices all the time to address a multitude of issues and concerns. Typically these are well meaning, other times absurd, but such policies and practices often aren't well thought through. After a period of full implementation, these policies characteristically take on a life of their own and persist well beyond any sensible shelf life. Once firmly in place, the durability of such policies and practices is challenging to dismantle.

Why education policymakers, school leaders, and educators continually implement these duck-and-cover policies or cling to them is curious. We believe there are multiple factors at play driving the proliferation of duck-and-cover policies and practices. Part of it stems from the honorable desire to serve students well. School board members are typically elected, and they want to show something for their efforts. It is logical behavior for them. But elected officials, similar to any politician, undertake behaviors to seek ways to maximize votes, what Anthony Downs (1957) described in his "Economic Theory of Democracy" as optimizing behaviors.

Superintendents, however, are hired hands, who can lose their jobs with a majority vote of one by the school board. Years ago, Raymond Callahan (1962) referred to this as the vulnerability thesis. The highest levels of school leadership need policies and accomplishments they can highlight and laud. The pressures are real. Clearly, school leaders are faced with pressures all the time, operating in a climate of needing to show action and success, so implementing such programs in some respects is rational behavior. But left unchecked, adopting such policies leads to poor outcomes. Ironically, it may also lead to potential adoption of some new highly and publicized remedy with similar faults. Duck and cover: The practice feeds on itself!

We acknowledge that in the environment school leaders occupy, trying different approaches or innovations to improve performance or organizational effectiveness clearly makes sense. But what we find sad is the inability of many school leaders to accept that failure is a necessary ingredient for success, with a hesitancy to move on to other approaches if adopted policies and practices aren't working. Don't just adopt new approaches; there is a need to assess and evaluate whether they work. Incorporate some kind of feedback loop to determine impact of policies and practices. Commenting about the fear of failing, Ramirez (2013) explained it in scientific terms:

> In STEM, failure is a fact of life. The whole process of discovery is trial and error. When you innovate, you fail your way to your answer. You make a series of choices that don't work until you fine the one that does . . . Scientists fail all the time. We just brand it differently. We call it data. (p. 36)

Schultz (2010) also drew from the scientific revolution in making much the same point as she focused on wrongness, "The advancement of knowledge depends on current theories collapsing in the face of new insights and discoveries . . . errors do not lead us away from the truth. Instead, they edge us incrementally towards it" (p. 30).

One might think that if something isn't working, using Ramirez's and Schutz's scientific explanation, it would be reasonably expected to try something new. We believe what often leads to duck-and-cover policy implementation and longevity is not only a reluctance or difficulty to evaluate and assess, but a propensity for sticking with what is familiar, even in the face of contrary evidence.

Consider some of the pressure on school leaders. Parents of students to some degree are all armchair educational experts, having experienced schools for themselves. They all also pay taxes. Few parents really want their kids to be guinea pigs for approaches they don't necessarily understand, but instead they want what is familiar. Sadly, this makes it hard to change too much. So the simple belief that if something isn't working, educational leaders should find something that does, faces an array of obstacles. And in the real world of schools—where job performance and positions of staff members may be at risk—switching around and choosing the right interventions, and then making adjustments along the way, is easier said than done. Jobs may be at risk, reputations, too. We think of it as "trial without error." Once the reform or innovation is adopted, it is hard to retract. Analyzing it this way, in Ramirez's and Schultz's terms, the approach in schools is unscientific.

What also supports and empowers leaders keeping with policies and practices is what economists refer to as the sunk-cost bias. If leaders have invested in a particular reform or approach, whether financially or just professionally, it gets rather difficult to admit that the policy or practice doesn't perform as advertised. It is hard to pull up roots and move on when you commit to an approach, no matter its real value.

But the persistence of duck-and-cover policies goes well beyond the realities of school leadership's comfort and survival. The system impacting schools includes local, state, and federal political actors who build platforms on improving schools. Consider this—does any gubernatorial candidate ever campaign for office with a pledge to weaken the performance of schools? Of course not, that would likely guarantee defeat. At the federal example, a plethora of pieces of legislation, for example the renowned 2001 No Child Left Behind Act, are enacted to address perceived shortcomings in American education. Policies at the local, state, and federal levels are put into place in the hope of improving educational practice and outcomes. And why not, considering that all children must go to school and all taxpayers pay for them? Leaders feel an obligation to act to improve schools, and they do so through policies and new practices.

As such, there is a need for generating policies and practices to strengthen school performance. For school leaders tasked with making decisions, some level of certainty and closure is also paramount. Closure offers predictability and a base for action (Webster & Kruglanski, 1994). However, problems emerge because this need for closure often leads to a level of certainty in policy decisions and practices that is unwarranted. As Kruglanski, Peri, & Zakai (1991) described it, "Many persons under high need for closure satisfy their motivation by abstaining from further informational search" (p. 145). In other words, find something that meets the immediate needs and don't consider all the potential ramifications or consequences. Or put more simply: Don't look back!

Tied to this, school leaders are like most everyone else, and intuitively shy away from feeling they are wrong. As Kathryn Schultz (2010) put it in her book *Being Wrong*, "a whole lot of us go through life assuming we are basically right, basically all the time, about basically everything . . ." (p. 8). She refers to this as error blindness.

An added complication is that the educational world, like most human endeavors, is complex and cloudy. The great philosopher of Science,

Sir Karl Popper (1966), had an influential essay called "Of Clouds and Clocks," decrying the levels of determinism and certainty that were driving thinking. Indeed, a whole branch of science focusing on complex adaptive systems (Waldrop, 1992) critiques notions of linearity and predictability so ingrained in human practices and human systems. So in a world where many desire certainty and closure, where complexity pervades the system, many will fall back on explanations and practices that Trout (2002) suggested might be intuitively satisfying, but not necessarily accurate.

Anyone involved with schools appreciates the ways that schools drive for certainty to satisfy environmental demands for outcomes from parents, politicians, and the public in general. While the core of schooling is noticeably resistant to change, described as the "grammar of schooling" by Tyack and Cuban (1995), changes occur all the time, and successful implementation must contain several essential characteristics (Cohen & Mehta, 2017). But the pressure on leaders to be successful and keep up is potent. For example, for decades PDK International has conducted polls of public perceptions of schools, where letter grades are assigned to the performance of local schools. Under the George W. Bush administration's "No Child Left Behind" legislation, schools not performing well were considered failing, labeled as "in need of technical assistance." Obama's key education legislation was labeled as "Race to the Top," underscoring the pressure on those unable to successfully and quickly scale the mountain. We guarantee that no school leaders or school board members want their schools or districts showing up in the press as being at the bottom. Something has to be done!

There are multiple factors driving school leaders beyond better performance and stated goals. Other institutional and organizational pressures drive school leaders to conform and act without the requisite consideration of consequences. Institutional theorists highlight mimicking behavior of organizations that characterize fields and often shape behavior for the future. DiMaggio and Powell (1983) described this homogenization of fields as institutional isomorphism. In their words, "powerful forces emerge that lead them to become more similar to one another . . . in the long run, organizational actors making rational decisions construct around themselves an environment that constrains their ability to change further in later years" (p. 148). This isomorphism plays out through three processes. The first DiMaggio and Powell (1983) labeled as forced isomorphism, which derives from mandates or the desire to gain the respect of others. The second they called mimetic isomorphism, where uncertainty prevails so modeling of other organizations is appropriate. Finally, normative pressures often hold sway making individuals behave in similar ways. What DiMaggio and Powell (1991) later referred to as cognitive sunk costs (an expanded version of the economic sunk costs described earlier), impede changing direction because such efforts, "threaten individuals' sense of security, increase the cost of information processing, and disrupt routines" (p. 194).

Schools, of course, are no different from people across our culture who move around and change all the time. Think, for example, of the fashion industry. People started wearing baseball caps backwards, the masses started getting tattoos, women's styles seem to change with each new season. In the food industry, new foods pop up that nobody heretofore ever heard of. Only the truly nutrition-conscious knew that quinoa and kale existed until a few years ago. Did anyone really know what acai was ten years ago, or how to properly pronounce it? Nobody wants to be on the outside when a new craze hits. In education, think back to the varying reform efforts over the decades, what historically were labeled as "fads and frills" (Tower, 1932) that dominated the educational discourse for a period of time. Whether it was school effectiveness, restructuring, site-based management, value-added testing, more recently socio-emotional learning and college and career readiness, no school or district can afford to ignore the powerful forces pushing leaders toward conformity. As Tyack and Cuban (1995) described it, crises, perceived or real, tend to trigger a burst of concern and cornucopia of fixes to address the identified needs.

A powerful phenomenon driving the duck-and-cover craze is the ongoing desire to grab the brass ring and find that one thing, the silver bullet, that will cure all the ills in education. Zhao (2018) referred to this as panacea thinking, something we describe in more detail in a later chapter. But systems and organizations like schools, given the environment they operate in, are especially vulnerable to the idea of a panacea. And sadly, there are hundreds of educational entrepreneurs—many well intentioned, others snake-oil salespersons—who take advantage of this school reality and push their wares typically without any science or logical basis for driving their particular reform other than fortune and glory. What Sperber (2010) described as the Guru Effect is all too often common in schools, where "individuals judge as profound what they have failed to grasp" (Sperber, 2010, p. 583). In practice, what emerges are sometimes well known and often highly credentialed charlatans spewing the brass ring gospel, pushing their wares and bottles of remedies to cure the failings in schools. Since the environment demands ongoing change to keep up, this may be inevitable. So there are a multitude of forces at play driving the duck-and-cover behavior we challenge. Sometimes it is individually driven, but most often organizational or institutional in nature. Typically, the intent isn't nefarious, but the outcomes are generally the same no matter the original idea. Policies and practices get put into place, and they persist no matter the efficacy or impact well beyond their natural shelf life.

Related to such institutional framing characteristics that organizations like schools experience, it is also true that groups often just behave in insipient ways. Writing from a Nazi prison, theologian Dietrick Bonhoeffer (De Gruchy, 2009) offered insights about what he labeled as stupidity. In describing this, he offered that "the impression one gains is not so much that stupidity is a congenital defect but that, under certain circumstances, people are made stupid or they allow this to happen to them" (p. 43). Of course, Bonhoeffer was describing the horrors that unfolded in Nazi Germany, but the underlying notion that individuals and then groups can act in unfathomable ways holds for multiple situations. For Bonhoeffer, stupidity was less a psychological than sociological matter. As he explained, "it is a particular form of the impact of historical circumstances on human beings, a psychological concomitant of certain external conditions" (p. 43).

The point isn't to individually denigrate school leaders, policymakers, and educators for doing what is common practice or to generate an array of rationales for implementing suspect policies and enact dubious practices. Whole fields of social science have explored these matters. Nor will we create a continuum of policies regarding their level of stupidity, though we see that as potentially having value, if nothing other than to expose the kind of faulty reasoning behind so many suspect practices and the continued stubborn faith and attachment to them. Rather, recognizing that school reforms emerge and proliferate for an array of reasons, we focus on the reality that the humans who make up organizations like schools can behave in bizarre ways due to a multitude of forces.

This doesn't suggest that educational leaders should do nothing when needs arise because the challenges they face and existing constraints are formidable. That would be as stupid as many of the policies that are adopted, though it is true that many policies should never have seen the light of day. Instead, the situation demands that leaders be cautious and thoughtful in devising policies for schools, that they follow up to determine effects and impact. That truly is why we wrote this book, to get leaders to think through new policies and examine the practices in place. But when they don't do this, when they just replicate what is fashionable, or when they allow outdated policies to continue, our caution is simple: Duck and cover!

We are ardent advocates for public schools. Between us we have five kids, and they all spent considerable time in public education. But as researchers, we recognized a pattern that needs to be addressed. In writing this book, we set out with the intention of providing school leaders and policymakers some ways to consider improving schools as they currently operate. The idea isn't to be critical so much as to help those in charge recognize policies and practices that need to be reconsidered, improved, or just dropped.

The purpose of this book, then, is to invite educational policymakers, researchers, and practitioners to question the common practices in the profession, to join us in the quest to uncover the duck-and-cover nature of many things being done that don't garner enough attention. Another purpose is to show the public that some of the commonly practiced and even sacred ideas in education are not scientifically sound or basically logical. Rather than hide in our shell, like Burt the turtle did in the original duck-and-cover promotions, we seek a shedding of shells to expose the thoughtlessness and true nature of much that is taken for granted.

We don't claim or even plan to offer an exhaustive list of all the dubious ideas that could be identified. There are too many, and no doubt many we never even considered. We also don't go into great detail or engage in a detailed analysis about each of the duck-and-cover policies and practices, as there are multiple studies defending and critiquing aspects of or all parts of these educational policies and practices. Instead, we attempt to list some of the most common poorly founded but persistent ideas in educational policy, research, and practice in K–12. We analyze these ideas, discuss their absurdities and fallacies based on evidence or common sense. While we leave the fuller academic debates to others, we hope that our identifying these practices helps policymakers, school leaders, and educators think about their behaviors, consider what they are doing from a new perspective, and ultimately, act in different ways.

In addition, we will raise some ideas for how to reconsider, remove, or replace these detrimental duck-and-cover policies and practices that pervade the educational landscape. We see our ideas as a starting point for educational leaders. We like to think of this approach as the new "3 Rs"—reconsider, remove, replace—understanding that change is always hard, dismantling current practice difficult, and examining long-standing practices uncommon. But what Scriven (1983) referred to as a "lack of self-reference" in academic practice is similarly problematic for schools. It is healthy to ask why we are doing what we do in the name of effective education. When questionable practices and policies are uncovered, they should be removed or changed. The old biblical admonition, "Physician, heal thyself," is equally appropriate to apply to schools in examining and correcting their policies. From our perspective, the duck-and-cover practices and policies we explore underscore the importance for stepping back and examining what is being done and why, with the goal of ultimately improving schools.

We would be naive to gloss over the difficulty in implementing changes in schools or any organization. The study of issues around implementation of policies began in earnest after the huge influx of federal dollars into social and educational programming in the 1960s and 1970s. Pressman and Wildavsky's (1973) classic study of an Economic Development Agency project in Oakland, California, utilized probability theory to underscore that the complexity of collective action tends to lead to poor likelihood of successful implementation. For decades, studies on change have underscored the tremendous difficulty of making substantive changes (Cohen & Mehta, 2017; Fullan, 2007; Marris, 1974; Watzlawick et al., 1974). Indeed, a whole field of implementation science has emerged to support the means for facilitating evidence-based practices, initially in health systems. The point is that change is difficult, takes time, and in the majority of cases, falls flat.

Related to this, Neustadt and May (1988) in *Thinking in Time*, showed how lack of historical knowledge often led to blunders in practice, repetition of past errors, something which our duck-and-cover thesis suggests is a real problem underpinning the ridiculous longevity of many policies and programs. Indeed, theories on confirmation bias (Nickerson, 1998) expose how many individuals search, interpret, or simply remember information that confirms current ideas and beliefs. We see this as part of the reason why so many leaders never question policies in place, allowing some policies to endure when they should simply disappear.

We also caution that our experience is not in K–12 administration, so our ideas for moving forward are from evidence gleaned from research, discussions with practitioners, and logic. We are sensitive to Fullan's (February, 2016) admonition that successful change is most likely when you let "the group change the group." Students in classrooms and teachers in schools are not passive players in the success of policies, but instead are intricately part of what happens. So depending on the specific policy or practice, we argue that students and/or teachers need be engaged in questioning current practice and fashioning appropriate remedies. We also want to caution that while much of what we write about is geared towards public schools, we suspect that private schools share many of these same duck-and-cover policies and practices, along with a host of others specific to their context.

The book is presented in three sections. The first we call Dreams, Fantasies, and Nightmares. It includes seven chapters dealing with issues including kindergarten readiness, college and career readiness, reading proficiency by 3rd grade, the achievement gap, social and emotional learning, foreign-language instruction, and educational technology. In each instance, the policy and practice started for a variety of laudable goals, but in each instance those goals were unrealistic, misguided, or have worn out their appropriate shelf life.

The second group of chapters we refer to as Operational Bugaboos: policies and practices that most every district has in place, all sound good, but in practice, these aren't always what they seem and create all sorts of questions and problems when considered in term of school and district impact and implications. In this section, we discuss professional development, class size, time, dress and grooming codes, teacher evaluation, and gifted and talented programs.

Finally, the last of the three sections considers what we call Systemic and Analytic Conundrums: practices that have often been in place a long time, but upon careful scrutiny, don't serve the schools particularly well. In this group we consider state standardized testing, governance by school boards, how teachers are paid, and meta-analysis.

The book exposes how America's schools are operating across a number of fronts, why those specified practices are problematic, and offers potential ways forward. We end with a conclusion drawn from the multiple chapters exposing duck-and-cover policies. It sets out the underlying assumptions that we derived from the analyses of the varying policies and practices, then identifies some key themes that transcend the chapters in the book. We also provide a guide for those leading schools to address the duck-and-cover policies and practices in schools or others being considered for implementation. We call this the duck-and-cover audit guide.

In the end, we hope we've exposed some things for school leaders and policymakers to consider in order to make schools better. If not, duck and cover, we'll all curl up under our desks, hands over our heads, waiting for the next bomb to fall.

Part I

DREAMS, FANTASIES, AND NIGHTMARES

CHAPTER 1

Kindergarten Readiness

Kindergarten is a big deal. It is the first level of formal schooling, required in most places for at least half a day, something most kids and their parents look forward to for a lengthy period before school actually starts. Late July and early August every year, advertisements start popping up on television and across social media with information on how to get the supplies, clothes, and other necessities for starting school. Schools send home lists of what the kids will need to be equipped for the school year ahead. For years, that is what kindergarten readiness actually referred to. Still today, the planning and tension of getting ready is built up as a yearly ritual across the country. Scan your Facebook account and you'll see picture after picture of young kids heading off to their first day of school, often holding signs marking their first day of kindergarten, with parents gazing at their little ones with tears of joy and trepidation. Kindergarten is the beginning of the formal school phase of nearly every child's life!

Most of us have some memory of our earliest experiences with formal schooling; in many cases, that meant kindergarten. Initially founded by German educator Friedrich Froebel in the first half of the 1800s, Froebel's kindergarten, or "garden of children," was to be a place involving play, self-activity, social participation, and motor skill practice, with a heavy dose of creativity—the keys for children's early education. To Froebel, kindergarten was "a place where children developed the personality, discipline, and social skills necessary to succeed in school and society" (Jeyne, 2006, p. 1938). If you attended kindergarten and think back to those days, no doubt it would be the play and fun activities that would spark your memories. Today, only 19 states and the District of Columbia require kindergarten in the United States, with a total of 39 states suggesting that it be offered with full or half day. In fact, 30 states require kindergarten-readiness assessments (Education Commission of the States, 2020).

The changes that have evolved trouble us. Parents want the best for their children. Think about when they take their child to see a pediatrician: They are told about their child's height and weight. There is often some added but quite useless information provided to show the pediatrician's knowledge. The information may be useless but can cause quite some anxiety. That information is the ranking of their child's height among all children of similar age in the nation. "Your child's height is at about 90%" makes parents happy but "your child's height is at about 5%" can cause great anxiety. The parents have likely already followed advice and fed the child only healthy food and provided care and love. What more can they do? Other than stretching the child every day, there is not a whole lot other than monitoring the anxiety-producing comparisons on future trips to the doctor's office. Who knows, perhaps adding a healthy dose of spinach or Wheaties™ might work? But what is certainly true is that variation in height is natural. Someone has to be taller than others. It is impossible for everyone to be at 90%.

Parents can choose not to be bothered by their child's height as long as the child does not have any disease or is malnourished. But when it comes to schooling, a practice for these same young children has evolved that falls into our conception of being duck-and-cover oriented. Parents have been subject to a true duck-and-cover policy that can affect them and their child. This is the kindergarten-readiness policy.

Kindergarten readiness has become a popular concept in America. States have developed kindergarten-readiness standards and assessments. As of June 2016, 26 states had either formally adopted or promoted through the state a definition of kindergarten readiness, while 6 of the states that lacked one were developing a definition (Pierson, 2018). More than half of the states have developed kindergarten-readiness assessments. Teachers are asked to assess and report their assessment outcomes to the state. The state then releases the assessments to the public.

Kindergarten readiness is a duck-and-cover policy because it seems useful from some perspectives, but upon scrutiny, it makes little sense. What happened to Froebel's notion of play, interaction, self-activity, and creativity? What happened to the child's garden? Kindergarten is grade 0. Why test for readiness for grade 0? No doubt it is the lure of potentially pumping up future educational performance—through a whole new world of assessment. But on the face of it, testing for kindergarten sounds like lunacy!

As to why a definition of kindergarten readiness is necessary, the State of Wyoming, one of the earliest states that developed kindergarten-readiness standards, has the following to say:

The Wyoming Early Childhood Readiness Standards have been developed to provide a more consistent definition of school readiness. Our goal is to provide early childhood educators with a framework to use in planning quality curriculum by identifying the skills (indicators) needed to maximize the potential for school success and promote a smooth transition to kindergarten. (Wyoming Department of Education, 2003)

The State of Oregon says

The Oregon Kindergarten Assessment is essential to understanding, and ultimately closing, the divide for our most underserved early learners. By providing a statewide perspective, the Oregon Kindergarten Assessment allows educators to track trends and measure progress and helps ensure that we are working together to give every child a great start in school and in life. (Oregon Department of Education, 2017)

Pierson of the U.S. Education Department's Regional Education Lab Northwest says that states use kindergarten readiness for one of the following purposes:

- To inform classroom instruction, curriculum planning, and professional development needs
- To identify students in need of specialized supports or interventions
- To provide a statewide snapshot of what children know when they enter kindergarten, monitor changes over subsequent kindergarten cohorts, and inform public policy and public investments in early childhood (Pierson, 2018)

The idea seems very attractive. Just like the original duck-and-cover mandates related to scooting under desks and covering heads with hands for protection from atomic bombs, kindergarten readiness sends a very soothing and comforting message to teachers and parents that an assessment would help them teach and parent better and therefore help the kids be ready to shine in school. After all, who does not want their child to be ready for kindergarten and guarantee their surging growth in the years that follow? In some sense, kindergarten has become less of a garden and more of a job, and all children have to be prepared for it. But in reality, kindergarten is not a job. It is a place for children to learn and grow.

Many parents buy into the rhetoric attached to kindergarten readiness. It is hard not to. As Cameron and Boyles (2022) explained it, parents are at a disadvantage, as they are impacted by the emphasis on accountability and measurement. The readiness discourse, in their words, "insists that education should immerse even the youngest child in a rigorous science, math, and technology curriculum, in anticipation of a future as 'college and career ready' citizens" (p. 108).

The idea of kindergarten readiness is simply a dubious concept for a number of reasons. First, kindergarten readiness is based on the idea that human beings develop the same way at the same speed. It is also based on the idea that every child has the same experiences to develop the same way at the same speed. Both ideas are wrong because human growth is an interaction between nature and nurture (Ridley, 2003). The innate abilities of human beings are not the same. They are born with great differences in intelligences (H. Gardner, 1983; H. E. Gardner, 2006), different desires (Reiss, 2000), and different personalities (John et al., 2008). Their home backgrounds are also drastically different. They have different socioeconomic status, different parents, different resources, different friends and relatives, and different cultures. When the differences in nature interact with the differences in nurture in some random way, human beings develop different abilities, interests, and personal qualities. Thus, when they enter kindergarten, it is inevitable that they are different. Expecting every child to have the same abilities in the few subject areas of the state assessments is simply a fantasy at best and a pure lie at worst.

Second, kindergarten readiness is an unnecessary concept. The idea that children should all be ready for kindergarten comes from the common laziness in education to dampen differences among us. Because the typical outcome of education is homogenization, education wants all children to be at the same level so that it does not need to deal with diversity and uniqueness. Educational institutions have been given an age-based curriculum and standard. They are expected to teach children to master the curriculum and meet the standard. If children could enter kindergarten at the same level, the teaching would be much easier. However, as discussed earlier, that is both simplistic and impossible. And the whole idea of kindergarten readiness alters the paradigm of education for these years. Whereas in the past, the idea was that adults will be ready to meet the needs of children, the current notion of readiness implies that students need to be academically ready for kindergarten (Jeynes, 2006; Johnson, 2019). It is a classic blame-the-victim approach.

Third, pursuit of kindergarten readiness hurts children from disadvantaged backgrounds as well as certain racial and ethnic backgrounds (Grodsky et al., 2017). Disadvantaged families have less monetary resources to help children develop the numerical and literacy capabilities expected by kindergarten than their more advantaged counterparts. In many cases, they haven't attended the fancy preschools that their wealthier counterparts had access to. As a result, it is no surprise that children from disadvantaged families do much worse in readiness assessments. Different races and cultures also have different views of how children should spend their time. Some pay more attention to academic experiences that better prepares children to be ready for kindergarten and school, but others may want their children to play, to experience nature, to participate in family and community culture, to learn things that are not directly related to academic outcomes. What some might say, to be kids. Consequently, children from academic-focused families are more ready than those from other backgrounds for the kindergarten-readiness tests. Attempting to force all children to be ready for kindergarten is in many ways a punishment delivered to people who are unable or unwilling to comply with the manufactured expectations of readiness. As Grodsky et al. (2017) concluded in their analysis of Wisconsin's Kindergarten-readiness situation, "serious attention to disparities in school readiness has largely been absent . . ." (p. 2).

Fourth, kindergarten readiness puts young children under great pressure. To test young children when they enter kindergarten on reading and math is not just silly, but more than that, it situates children as test takers early on. Whatever the test format is, it is often short, with time pressure. Typically, the assessment asks a child to read words or letters, or do some simple counting within a few minutes. They are expected to do well, but for those children who cannot do well or never had experiences taking tests, the time pressure and expectations likely make them anxious. The experience may not mean much to some children, but could be the beginning of a torturous journey with schools. It captures the concern (Elkind, 2009) warned against in *The Hurried Child*.

Fifth, the definition employed of kindergarten readiness has implications for what is taught. For example, should the focus be on math, reading, the ability to follow directions, getting along with others, or an array of other possibilities? Point is, exactly what kindergarten readiness means isn't necessarily clear. Weisenfeld (2017) found that the assessments used and their content isn't uniform due to different standards and expectations in the states. Other issues emerge. When should the assessments be administered in kindergarten? Early in the school year, midyear, end? Ackerman (2018), from ETS, identified an array of validity and reliability concerns that need to be addressed in these assessments: alignment with the purpose, population, and curriculum; individual items' measurement of the constructs intended; allowances for issues like language spoken or disability; sensitivity to students' skills; capacity of educators to administer these assessments; time pressures with sophisticated assessments; data access; and use capacity. Addressing all these issues adequately isn't currently guaranteed.

Related to this, Jeynes (2006) pointed out several other concerns. Schools often use tests like these to compare themselves with other schools. This can cause undue pressure to get scores up. Second, students often get compared to one another, causing undue stress for students in their formative years. Third, the tests may not be measuring what is really the essential knowledge for learners at this this age. He also identified that such testing programs lead to reducing recess, which prior studies show is important for kindergarteners given their developmental levels.

Children are naturally different. They come to kindergarten with their differences. Some of them will be quite good in literacy and math and thus meet the expectations of kindergarten readiness, but there are a large number of children who won't meet the expectations. Kindergartens should be able to teach all of them. In other words, kindergartens should be ready for all children. They should meet all children where they are instead of forcing children to be what they want. We appreciate that some will argue that having the assessment allows teachers to formulate curriculum to address their deficiencies. We counter that early learning should be about growth, and expression, and play, and interaction. The mindless push to ready children for a competitive test-based education likely will prove meaningless in the long term academically, and harmful emotionally.

Moreover, even for those who accept the idea of kindergarten readiness, there is very little we can do to help many children. They are born into and raised in homes. The significant and influential home environments cannot be changed by education. Social inequality and historical racism have long been the deep root of educational inequalities. When children come to kindergarten, their differences reflect an unequal society. Just expecting or requiring children to be ready for kindergarten is not going to change what children can do.

RECONSIDER, REMOVE, REPLACE

American education has come to a place where there is a test for all that ails a child. This obsession certainly hasn't proven to result in better outcomes even on the same kind of tests the government employs in key subjects at multiple grade levels. As diagnostic tools, tests, and assessments can certainly add value to the arsenal of information educators need. But when and at what grade levels should these tests be administered? We expect poor Froebel is turning over in his grave given what is being done to kindergartens across the United States.

In the case of kindergarten readiness, the assessments given to students are a duck-and-cover policy that can't perform what the developers intend. No doubt this practice started with the best intentions—test where kids are when they first arrive at school. Fashion curriculum to make them better if the tests show them deficient. What could be wrong with that?

But think about it: What is to be done with the information? You can't send the children back in vitro, so extra work on testable skills is the only answer. But this is kindergarten. Grade ZERO! Why do this to kids, label them in their formative years, and send early shivers up their parents' spines? This all comes from a place that implies a need for a dramatic alteration of what kindergarten was developed to do: to set the foundation for the formal schooling years. It directly aligns kindergarten with the assessment-obsessed education industry that has evolved in recent decades.

We suggest that kindergarten-readiness assessments end. If teachers identify some questionable or troubling behaviors among their students, bring in experts and utilize thoughtful diagnostic assessments related to the identified behaviors, ones that perhaps might guide the activities taking place in the classroom, or direct students for different kinds of supports. The issues the readiness assessments identify likely have nothing to do with school readiness, since kindergarten is to set the stage for later years by supplying that very readiness.

We recognize that psychometricians and many educators will flinch at our suggestion. But as we've shown, the tests provide little in supporting young students in their growth and education, place undue pressure on students and parents to "be ready" even before school starts, and likely produce emotional and other types of harm—especially taking students away from the kinds of things they should be doing in kindergarten. Unless and until there is sound evidence that adding this testing produces anything tangible, positive, and long lasting for children, it is time to take a step back and move on.

Interestingly, experts in early childhood education like David Elkind argue that the teaching done with young kids to get scores up creates risks for students' ultimate performance (Elkind, 2012). There is a difference between knowing what is typically tested and understanding. In early math and reading programs, children are often being taught only surface knowledge. Elkind warned, "young children get used to a learning style that will disadvantage them later." Worse, the approaches often used "can dull children's zest for learning" (p. 86). We leave it to the reading experts to debate these nuances. But the potential for harm is real.

The kindergarten-readiness assessments tell us a lot about student background, upbringing, prior educational experiences, or in some instances, legitimate medical or psychological needs that the system can support addressing. But kindergarten readiness for ultimate academic success? Duck and cover; this seems very far-fetched. We are reminded of the demands from infomercial guru Susan Powter's "Stop the Insanity" mantra in the 1990s, directed at limiting the fatty foods in everyone's diet. The insanity here isn't about food, but instead about testing for readiness for kindergarten. It is a duck-and-cover policy that needs to go away. Well intended, sure. Sadly, regarding those students labeled as unready, there is no Superman available here, "able to leap tall buildings in a single bound" and wipe away the test identified deficiencies. In the end, kindergarten readiness can't do what it purports to attempt, and likely will cause harm to those it intends to serve—the children labeled as unready. Instead, we suggest taking the funds dedicated to these misguided duck-and-cover assessments and apply them to teachers and strengthening classroom supports for students.

CHAPTER 2

College and Career Readiness

Going to college has always been the American ideal. Our high school curricula have a bias toward college preparedness as opposed to other vocational pursuits. For those who want to do well in life, going to college is held out as the key. Studies looking back at who earns more in this country show that having a college degree produces economic benefits. It is part of the American notion that anyone can move up the social mobility ladder.

Though recent data suggest this ideal of going to college may be slipping in popularity, the notion of being ready for a job or college after high school, or being career ready following college, is hard to challenge. Schools and colleges get assessed by these as measures. Despite the reality that few young men and women truly know what they want to do with their lives at age 18 after high school or age 22 after college, and the likelihood nowadays that most will be switching careers multiple times over their lifetime due to technology and other advances, in this country we cling to this idea of being ready for college (and a subsequent career) upon ending formal schooling as if it was number 11 on the tablets Moses brought down from the mountain. Amen! Few dispute the mantra.

As we suggested in the Introduction, people crave certainty, especially certainty for their futures. This is true in all facets of life. When people travel, they want to know their hotel has a certain level of service and certain facilities. They want to know the restaurant they are going to offers certain food. This is why hotel chains and restaurants have become popular. Kids, for example, want to know that they can get their Big Mac and french fries at any McDonald's establishment across the country. Everyone certainly wants the airplanes they travel on to take off and land safely and on time.

But people also want to know that their children, upon graduation from school, will have a good life. For many this means preparedness for college success or a well-paying job. CCR, or College and Career Readiness, has done exactly that, aimed at providing certainty where none exists. CCR has become the ultimate goal for all schools in the United States. It has become the guiding outcome for all school activities. Governments and schools want to do everything to make sure that our students, all of them, have CCR so that they can have a bright future. It is so seductive, no one can reasonably reject the idea. Just pop the CCR pill, and like magic, kids' lives will be grand and successful futures assured.

The effort to promote CCR started with the Common Core State Standards, an effort by the National Governors Association and Council of Chief State School Officers in 2010, with ample acknowledgement and support of many leading politicians, government agencies, advocacy and professional groups, think tanks, and foundations. Although the Common Core has not been adopted by all states, the concept of CCR has.

The Common Core, with the support of federal grants and private foundations such as the Gates Foundation, has been promoted to help students achieve CCR, to make them ready for the future. Achieve, the nonprofit organization created by bipartisan governors and business leaders in 1996, has made promoting CCR one of its core businesses. The U.S. Department of Education has also played a leadership role in promoting CCR. According to the Department of Education:

> Over the past several years, states have taken the lead in developing and adopting rigorous standards in English language arts and mathematics that build toward college and career readiness by the time students graduate from high school. Nearly every state now has adopted these college- and career-ready standards. (U. S. Department of Education, n.d.)

With federal and state initiatives, the idea of CCR has become widespread. In 2014, the American Research Institute (AIR) counted that at least 37 states had developed CCR definitions and standards (Mishkind, 2014). Schools developed or adopted curriculum and requirements that carry the state definitions and standards.

Not all states have the same definition for CCR, but a review of the definitions by American Institutes for Research (AIR) found that the state definitions typically include five categories of knowledge, skills, abilities, or capacities: 1. academic knowledge, 2. critical thinking and/or problem solving, 3. social and emotional learning, collaboration, and/or communication, 4. grit/resilience/perseverance, and 5. citizenship and/or community involvement. The AIR report concludes:

> State definitions included in this review reflect the recognition that readiness for college and careers is multifaceted, encompassing academic readiness, as well as knowledge, abilities, and dispositions that impact academic achievement. Research on this latter group is still emerging and, in some instances, is controversial as we have yet to conclusively determine the impact that instruction and educational supports can have on the development of these lifelong learning skills. (Mishkind, 2014, p. 6)

In many ways, CCR has become a dream that people in education believe will deliver hope and a successful future for all children. Education leaders, school administrators, teachers, students, parents, and the general public have been led to believe if our children meet the CCR standards, they will be ready for college, career, and life in the future. Who knows, likely they will all also win the lottery! Thus governments, educational institutions, and other organizations have been actively advocating CCR. For example, Achieve argues: "All students should graduate from high school ready for college, careers, and life, prepared to pursue the future of their choosing" (Achieve Inc., n.d.).

The lure of CCR is unimpeachable and its tentacles ubiquitous. For example, Malin et al. (2017) analyzed CCR in the Obama administration's Every Student Succeeds Act (ESSA), and found 21 discrete areas where CCR was evident in the legislation. They discerned four themes: advanced coursework including dual enrollment programming, cross-sector partnerships, STEM programing and teaching, and tailoring of programming to workforce needs. ACT (Mattern et al., 2014) summarized the basis for the urgency for achieving CCR as being the result of shortages of skilled workers, college graduates unprepared for the workforce, high school graduates unprepared for college, and large numbers of high school dropouts. They concluded, "The data clearly indicate that at every point along the K-Career continuum, students are falling off the track to being ready for college and work" (p. 10).

However, in our estimation, CCR is simply a myth at best and a big lie at worst. It is just another duck-and-cover idea. It sounds good but cannot be delivered. There are many reasons that CCR is only a fantasy, an idea that only exists in the mind of its advocates. There is very little reality that CCR is founded on evidence or is even possible to achieve. Moreover, even if it were achieved, it likely would not make students ready for college, career, and life.

First, there is no clearly agreed upon definition of CCR. Many states and schools have a set of CCR standards and there are some commonalities across these standards (Mishkind, 2014). However, the standards still differ quite a lot in different states and schools. All CCR standards have math and language competencies, for example. But not all standards agree upon on all other skills and abilities. And standards are simply estimates often distant or only loosely tied to any form of scientific rationale. As the eminent Harvard statistician Andrew Ho lamented, "This is the fundamental problem of standards, you can come up with a different and seemingly defensible standard every day over coffee" (Kamanetz, 2016).

Some have identified that the CCR definitions have a distinct college-focus bias, favoring college over directly entering a career (Malin et al., 2017). There certainly are many careers, especially in the trades, whose career needs may not necessarily jive with the college orientation of the standards. Do the standards and skills they represent apply to them? And for the 15–20% of high school students who never graduate, the CCR standards seemingly have little applicability or relevance.

Achieve defines CCR as "College- and career-ready (CCR) graduates should be able to enter and succeed in entry-level postsecondary courses without the need for remediation" and should have "mastery of rigorous knowledge and skills in core academic disciplines . . . the skills and dispositions necessary to be successful in charting their postsecondary path . . . successfully participated in postsecondary opportunities through advanced coursework" (Achieve Inc., n.d.). Achieve's CCR definition includes mastery of knowledge and skills in core academic subjects that include English, math, history, science, civics, history, art, and music. It also includes skills in effective communication, problem solving, critical thinking, and information and data analysis as well as collaboration, presentation, and making informed judgments. Furthermore, Achieve wants students to participate in postsecondary opportunities through advanced coursework such as AP, IB, and dual enrollment in addition to opportunities in career and technical education, work-based learning, and other possibilities for exploring interests, aptitudes, and goals.

Let's assume that Achieve's definition of CCR is representative of all CCR definitions. These definitions have not been empirically tested. Although Achieve has a fairly broad definition of CCR, there is no evidence that these standards actually work for students. It is also a very high standard as articulated; the small percentage of students who can meet these stiff comprehensive requirements might well find success, but for those who do, we question whether this can be attributed entirely to schooling or instead to family privilege.

No one has provided clear empirical evidence that mastery of these CCR standards means the students will be successful in colleges, jobs, and life. This is especially significant given that experts are suggesting that jobs will be changing rapidly in the future. For example, *Forbes* (Amdur, 2021) reported estimates suggesting that by 2025, 25% of America's jobs will be ones that didn't exist in 2021. So, the definitions of CCR are at best good guesses based on past experiences, which have not been supported with strong empirical evidence. For example, college entrance exams such as the SAT and ACT, together with high school grades (GPAs), have long been used for college admissions, but they hardly predicate students' success in college or life (Burton & Ramist, 2001; Geiser & Studley, 2001; Kobrin et al., 2008). There is no other study of how standardized tests of school subjects in elementary, middle, or high school predicate students' success in college. In fact, it is worse than that, as Nobel Laureate James J. Heckman and his colleague Tim Kantz (2012), explain, "A more relevant criterion is how well these tests predict meaningful outcomes, such as educational attainment, labor market success, crime, and health. No single measure of cognitive ability predicts much of the variance in these outcomes . . ." (p. 452).

Second, in reality, it is impossible to have one set of standards to get all students ready for college and career. There are thousands of different postsecondary educational institutions: elite private ones such as Harvard, Yale,

Princeton, and the other Ivy Leagues, as well as top public universities, state universities, regional colleges, private colleges, and community colleges. There are postsecondary-level technical schools geared towards preparing workers for the trades. These higher education institutions have tens of thousands of majors and programs. These universities, schools, and majors have different expectations of students and provide different experiences to students. Although there may be some very basic things that are common across all students, it is impossible that all the majors, schools, and universities want the same knowledge, skills, and abilities taught. It is difficult to imagine that Harvard or Princeton has the same expectations as community colleges. It is equally difficult to imagine that a drama major has the same expectations of abilities as an engineering or philosophy major, not even mentioned those who might major in physics!

Not only do colleges have different expectations, but so do careers. A computer engineering job does not expect the same set of knowledge and skills as jobs in the retail industry. Should electricians have the same knowledge and skills as those in the hotel or restaurant industries, auto repairmen the same as psychologists or physicians? And given that college graduates are expected to change careers multiple times over their working lifetime, what exactly might colleges or secondary schools do to prepare them for the diverse skills and assets likely needed? We're both college professors; we are pretty certain our administrators would be thrilled to mandate that due to career-readiness demands, every citizen must attend and never leave college. So amen to CCR for that, but we still question the viability of what is being suggested.

Conley (2013) offered a widely cited set of strategies for college and career readiness, including key cognitive strategies, key content knowledge, key transition knowledge and skills, and key learning skills and techniques. These are at such a high level of abstract and structure, it is hard to imagine how all the varying educational institutions, programs, majors, and offerings could possibly focus on these collectively in any meaningful way.

Third, as already suggested, the future is uncertain and unpredictable (McDiarmid & Zhao, 2022). Despite all the discussions about what the future might hold, no one actually knows. We know that technology will certainly continue to develop, but no one can be certain what new technologies might do and which directions they will take. No one predicted exactly the birth and influence of Google and Facebook. No one expected that automation would take away so many human jobs. A great example of this dynamic is that only a few people ever heard of Zoom before COVID-19 hit, but now we all know what "You're on mute" means. Zoom emerged due to the unpredictable pandemic and changed work and schooling, probably far into the future. Things change, and technology is changing jobs rapidly. The World Economic Forum (Whiting, 2020) estimated that by 2025, 85 million jobs may be replaced by a shift in the division of labor between humans and machines.

Moreover, geopolitics, politics in nations, and unforeseen events can force unpredicted directions in the long run. Consider, for example, the impact of COVID-19 on the workforce, as it is causing what is currently referred to as the Great Resignation, with large numbers of people leaving jobs. What about the worldwide impact of the recent volatility spurned on by the war in Ukraine? Those are two recent and clear examples of the point. Economies change as well, so do societal values and cultural traditions. Human beings also migrate for better lives. These shifts have accelerated societal changes, making uncertainty and unpredictability the unshakable features in the future. So how can an assembly of ideas from the past prepare students for an uncertain and unpredictable future?

Fourth, it is important to remember that the future is not pre-made for our youth. About 100 years ago when the world was much more isolated and changed much more slowly, it was perhaps possible to expect that children would enter a world (the future) much like the one they were born in. It was possible then to define skills and knowledge for this world. Students could then be prepared to enter this world they inherit from their parents. But today is drastically different from 100 years ago. Students in today's schools experience drastic changes while they are in school. Everyone is going through changes as they grow up. The future is being made and remade constantly. Educators and policymakers continuously lament the learning loss created by COVID-19, but rarely emphasize the ability to change, the growth in resilience and creativity that so many students exhibited during the worst circumstances fostered by the unprecedented pandemic. Thus, what we need to do in education is to prepare children to become ethical, moral, creative, and entrepreneurial so that they can adapt and make a better future for all. Students do not inherent the future. They shape it and make it.

In conclusion, CCR is an idea that cannot be realized for all students. It is also an idea that misguides students. Much effort and money have been devoted to the idea and many students have been subject to CCR curriculum. But duck and cover, it can't deliver on all the promises. What we need to do now is to stop what we are doing, stop in our tracks, and move away from the obsessive minutiae that drives these curricula into irrelevance. There are better educational approaches than CCR. But until CCR is removed from education, schools will continue to be guided by this fantasy instead of pursuing other, more desirable options.

RECONSIDER, REMOVE, REPLACE

We recognize that the CCR craze is well meaning, hoping to prepare America's students for a successful and fruitful college and career future. But the inability for standards to guarantee any of the outcomes promised is serious. We've identified multiple reasons why these specific, rather linear standards, built on notions of predictability that doesn't exist, won't succeed. Certainly, students need basic skills and an understanding of how to apply them to life situations. We offer that including academic and non-cognitive skills in a curriculum focused on personalized needs, creativity, with a bent toward innovation and entrepreneurship, is better suited for the unknown future ahead. While many of the skills included in CCR programs are relevant, it is the packaging, the tying teaching to the untested, the cleansing the creativity out of the process, that needs be addressed. To that end, we suggest:

- Move away from the focus on CCR standards that have little real meaning and built-in predictability that doesn't currently exist.
- Build a curriculum with the idea that the specific needs of the future are unknown, so creative problem solving and individual initiative are key drivers.
- If some version of CCR has to be kept alive, and replaced instead of removed, it should be renamed and built on skills that might really help students as they emerge from high school and college—core academic skills, skills and experiences needed if heading into a profession or trade, education that is personalized and fosters creativity and adaptability for the future.
- The Deweyian notion for good education still has value: Focus on problem solving and real-life experiences and activities to engage students in their learning.

CHAPTER 3

Reading Proficiency by 3rd Grade

Everyone wants kids to read, and read well. Indeed, there have been out-and-out "reading wars" in the education profession as experts, policy-makers, pundits, parents, and others duke it out over the best way to assure that all students are proficient readers. Every time a truce in the war seems to be emerging, new waves of criticism pop up. Certainly, it is hard to argue with the main premise regarding reading's primacy, though with the growth of video, blogs, and other formats for sharing information, it may come to a point in the future that reading as we know it will be transformed, too. For any who find this impossible, consider this—writing in cursive is a relic of a bygone era—kids who still write with cursive these days are looked at like they are writing in a foreign language. Also consider that reading for everyone did not happen before the printing press invented by Johannes Gutenberg made books widely available in Europe.

But the emphasis on reading and its importance for students is rarely questioned. According to the National Conference of State Legislatures (NCSL [National Conference of State Legislatures], 2019 #5690), as of April 2019, 17 states and the District of Columbia passed laws that require retention for students not reading at proficiency by the end of 3rd grade. That is, these students cannot be moved to 4th grade because they cannot achieve proficiency on state tests. More states have laws that recommend but do not require retention. Other states are working on enacting similar laws.

The idea behind these legislative efforts is very simple: to make sure that all children can read at some identified proficiency level by the end of 3rd grade. The NCSL website states:

> In 2015, roughly 2 out of 3 fourth graders failed to score proficient in reading. The percentages of non-proficient readers are even higher when looking at specific racial/ethnic groups: 82 percent of African-American fourth-graders were reading below proficiency, along with 79 and 78 percent of Latino and American-Indian students respectively.

But once again, mandating reading proficiency by 3rd grade is yet another duck-and-cover policy. It sounds great—address the issue of children not being able to read by 3rd grade, with the implicit promise that if children can read at the end of 3rd grade, they will do better later in life. Few would argue against the idea that reading skills are important for students. Indeed, experts have been fighting the aforementioned "reading wars" for decades regarding the best approaches for getting students to read—emphasize phonics, some mixed approaches, etc. But the end game, reading well, is a bipartisan policy that nobody challenges. Could you possibly imagine, for example, a U.S. politician running for office on a platform that that we need to weaken reading performance? Not going to happen.

But this is a misguided obsession with reading by 3rd grade. This obsession is largely based on the data-driven assumption that 3rd grade reading proficiency determines the quality of a child's future education and life successes. The assumption goes like this: If you cannot read by third grade, your chance of success in life is severely diminished. You are very likely to fail and drop out of school. It has been concluded that American students who can't read proficiently by 3rd grade are four times more likely to drop out of school (Hernandez, 2012). You are more likely to end up in jail or other unpleasant places. We even understand that if you read the fine print, other side effects might include children losing their hair, possibly growing a tail, or even never having Amazon packages delivered to their house! Serious possible consequences for not being on board.

The Anne E. Casey Foundation is a major promoter of this assumption. In 2010 and 2013, the Foundation produced two reports with correlational data to support this belief (The Annie E. Casey Foundation, 2010, 2013). Basically, the data show that students who can read at grade 3 do better in future grades, have better education attainment, and achieve more in life. Those who cannot read at 3rd grade have a higher probability of failing school or going to jail.

As a result, the foundation has worked with various organizations and schools to promote reading by 3rd grade across the country. The Foundation reported tremendous impact of its call and widespread adoption of the idea to make sure that low-income children can read by 3rd grade (The Annie E. Casey Foundation, 2013). Communities and schools have taken actions to improve children's reading as early as possible. State governments have also developed policies to retain students if they cannot read by 3rd grade (National Conference of State Legislatures, 2019). Schools tend to provide more reading instruction, reading remediation, or grade retention to those students unable to pass the reading tests by 3rd grade.

The basic hypothesis of the foundation is: (1) If adults work hard enough, low-income students will read proficiently by 3rd grade; (2) if low-income students can read by 3rd grade, they will be more likely to succeed academically and graduate from high school; and (3) if they graduate from high school, they are more likely to succeed in life (The Annie E. Casey Foundation, 2013).

This hypothesis seems to be backed up by data. The data used to support the hypothesis are correlational analyses. There is no empirical experimental data that directly connects reading abilities at 3rd grade to future success in school and life. Correlation does not mean causation. While the correlation exists, there could be many reasons behind the correlation. One of the most likely reasons is poverty. Poor children have poor reading scores, which is a symptom of the poor education and life opportunities they have. In other words, it is not reading that stopped these children from graduating and going to college. Rather, it is their poverty that affected their poor reading ability and their dropping out of school; this can lead to disastrous results for children from low-income families.

The Casey Foundation's report, using the National Assessment of Educational Progress (NAEP) data in 2009 and 2011, says: "Nearly three-quarters (74%) of fourth-graders who scored at the low end of the NAEP scale (below the 25th percentile) on the most recent test were from low-income families, while only 23% of children from low-income families scored at the high end (above the 75th percentile)" (The Annie E. Casey Foundation, 2013, p. 3). There was a 29-point gap between higher- and lower-income students (free lunch) and the gap was 17 points between higher-income students and less poor (eligible for reduced-price meals).

It is apparent that students from low-income families are far less likely to be able to read at proficiency or higher levels than their wealthier peers. In other words, the majority of the students who cannot read by 3rd grade are from low-income families. These poor students often lack the necessary resources and support to have the opportunities for a decent education experience and outcomes, including reading abilities. They are more likely to drop out of school, less likely to graduate from high school, and do not attend college at the rates of their wealthier peers. Family income has been a persistent factor in student achievement, including reading (Konstantopoulos & Borman, 2011; Lindo, 2014).

Not being able to read is just a symptom of the problem. Fixing their reading at 3rd grade is not easy without fixing the problem of poverty. Despite the efforts to make sure children can read at 3rd grade, the reading proficiency of children in the country has not improved since 2010. An analysis by the Brown Center on Education Policy at Brookings found that the score gap in NAEP reading remains about the same between 1996 and 2017, despite all policies and practices to improve reading (Hansen et al., 2018).

Moreover, forcing poor children to read at 3rd grade can have significant problems. A large proportion of the students who typically fall behind in reading from kindergarten to third grade are from monetarily disadvantaged families. When these students are placed in remediation or retained for a grade, their educational opportunities shrink. They are exposed to possibly boring reading remediation programs but are deprived of other educational experiences such as arts, music, and even sports. Elkind's (2007) ideas about the power of play are obscured when test score performance dominates policy. These children's families may not be able to buy such programs or provide opportunities that may trigger their children's interests. The result is broadened opportunity gaps (Tienken & Zhao, 2013).

Retention also has significant negative impact on all children. Megan Andrew, a sociologist at the University of Notre Dame, analyzed two large data sets and found that retained children are 60% less likely to graduate from high school than those not retained (Andrew, 2014). Pagani et al. (2001) found that grade retention affected children's developmental outcomes, "regardless of the characteristics they brought into their situation and the developmental trajectory predicted by such characteristics" (p. 309). A recent review of prior studies (Valbuena et al., 2020) concluded that grade retention is not an efficient policy as the costs associated with it easily outweigh any potential benefits. In their words, "the policy is clearly associated to relevant costs in terms of academic outcomes, career choice, delayed labor-market participation, forgone income, formation of undesirable traits as well as the necessity of using a vast amount of public resources to implement it" (p. 427).

Furthermore, these children may be placed in remediation programs or grade retention that they are not capable of learning. These programs, which aim to improve student reading, can teach children that they are not good at anything. The students can be depressed and suppressed. In the end they develop a sense of learned helplessness. Additionally, children who are not good at reading in the beginning may have talents in nonreading areas. If provided the opportunity, they could become extremely capable in other areas of learning. When they are allowed to work on nonreading areas, the students can see their potential and capacity. They can become more engaged with schools, which could lead to better reading in the long run.

It is also possible that our schools do not know how to help children who cannot read by 3rd grade. Perhaps it is because schools begin to rely on more reading for education purposes starting in the 4th grade. If so, can we change that? If schools do not demand students to be able to read by 4th grade and accommodate each student's need, we may not see children who don't read by 3rd grade fail.

Reading is important, but is it that important? We are NOT against children learning to read. In fact, we encourage it. What we do question are the rather absurd mandates and hyperbole attached to reading measures thrust upon schools, especially focused on lower-income students. While perhaps well intended, they're foolish and misleading.

Part of the rhetoric is that if students are not reading up to some high standard by 3rd grade, their lives are essentially over. No good outcomes are possible. The great irony, of course, is that not only are these arguments wrong, they fly in the face of reality.

Think of it this way. Did you ever buy your child a Lego set? You sit on the floor together, empty the box of the hundreds of pieces, and search for the directions. When you find them, guess what? No words, just pictures. Legos are a reading-free zone. Adults our age are lost, thinking, "Where are the directions?" All you get are pictures. But kids love them. They figure it out. Ever tried playing video games with your children? Same thing! Ask your kids for the directions and they'll laugh at you. You learn by doing. You learn by trial and error. In essence, you use how science works to learn. Frankly, our own products are increasingly much the same. Buy anything lately from IKEA? When the flat boxes arrive, the directions are essentially wordless. Imagine the anxiety this produces for so many who were actually reading proficient by 3rd grade! Once again, pictures prevail. Having problems building your beautiful IKEA desk or dresser, no problem, just go watch the instructional videos. No reading required. That may be the future, and it is already here.

Get the trend? While about three quarters of American adults report having read a book in the last year, the share of those listening to audiobooks is up to about 30% (Faverio & Perrin, 2022). Digital audiobooks are the fastest-growing segment in the publishing industry (Kozlowski, 2020). Grand View Research (2022) projects that the audiobook industry market value was $4.2 billion in 2021 and is expected to expand at a compound growth rate of 26.4% from 2022 to 2030. Listening, not reading, is the growing trend.

In higher education, university after university is dropping the requirement for SAT or ACT scores for admissions or even merit-based scholarships. Memorizing all those esoteric words that nobody ever uses is out, unless, of course, you have a burning desire to win a Spelling Bee or become a contestant on the game show *Jeopardy!*. And in the K–12 space, students are pushed by teachers to take advantage of resources like Kahn Academy. Want to learn your math lessons? Go watch the video. Reading isn't a huge requirement.

Even in the home, so many people rely on YouTube videos for instruction, rather than books or articles. Want to learn how to rid the shower of mold, bake a cake, fix your car? Go to YouTube. Interestingly, research examining successful adults with learning disabilities (Reiff et al., 1997) found dentists, lawyers, scientists, business people, and a wide array of individuals in multiple occupations unable to read who succeeded at incredibly high levels. They adapted, found supports, tied their tasks to their strengths.

None of this means that reading isn't important. But it does suggest that the hyperbole and scare tactics being fed to students and parents are overblown. And the entire argument misdirects attention away from the structural underlying problems in our culture holding back certain students.

We also find it ironic that with the emphasis in schools on strengthening students' socio-emotional skills, schools are at the same time pushing strategies for academic performance based on scary projections that likely heighten students' socio-emotional needs. Nearly half a century ago psychologist David Elkind (1988) warned about the stress high school students were put under in his landmark work, *The Hurried Child*. In later years, he cautioned about the focus on academics for young students and the concomitant lack of attention to play (Elkind, 2007). The point is, duck and cover, there is more to a child's health, growth, and success than her or his 3rd-grade reading proficiency scores.

RECONSIDER, REMOVE, REPLACE

Assessing for reading proficiency in third grade is a duck-and-cover policy. It should be removed. There is nothing wrong with administering assessments to see how kids are doing, hopefully informing teachers how to fashion lessons to address students' personal needs. Sadly, that doesn't happen. Sometimes, kids who don't meet the grade are held back, a policy that has been shown time and time again to be useless and potentially harmful.

We aren't arguing against the idea of teaching reading, though educators do need to come to grips with the reality and understanding that there is a growing trend towards looking and listening, rather than just reading. How these can be co-involved in future education practices and teaching is worthy of consideration. But it is the obsession with tests and assessments, and the misinformation they provide, the lack of useful data that flows from it, and the policies that spring from poor performance that make the idea of 3rd-grade reading proficiency senseless. As with other policies reviewed in this text, much of what the assessments show is tied to socio-economic status and other variables that schools alone can't do anything about. Certainly not in the short term.

So what do we offer as a remedy? Take the pressure off children in third grade and only use assessments sparingly; use those that realistically help to personalize their education. Students and teachers need feedback for success—develop means for providing that. Remove the high stakes and punitive results often attached to these assessments that are just indicators of factors outside of educational practice.

Moreover, don't ignore what is in front of us all. Reading and learning approaches and habits for acquiring information are changing. Embrace the changes, work with other educators, students, parents, and experts to develop better ways for students to gather information in a technologically evolving world. Several hundred years ago, when novels first hit the scene, they were eschewed by aristocrats and other critics as evil and the symbolic of the potential downfall of culture as it was known. Today, novels are ubiquitous, a part of many high school and college courses. We study them, there are whole classes taught using them. Think about that when trying to conceive of ways to take advantage of the growing interest in audiobooks and videos as the vehicle for learning and gaining new information. And focus on understanding and comprehension, something the assessments often struggle to capture.

The next time you help a child or grandchild build with Legos, or play a modern video game, think about how bad you feel that you can't figure out what to do. Remember, with our 3rd-grade proficiency assessments, duck and cover, we do that same thing to a portion of the student population in every school, dealing with issues that they struggle with due largely to circumstances beyond their control. How do we do that to them? With the pernicious assessments we expose them to and the punishments that follow. Time to figure out ways to do better.

CHAPTER 4

The Achievement Gap

Years ago, we were on a panel with some legislators who were bemoaning spending extra money and providing extra services for certain students and not others. "Kids are kids," they exclaimed, then took a swipe at we academics by asserting that those of us in higher education treat people unequally by demanding extra support for certain students, while legislators like them treat everyone the same. When we suggested that some students might need extra supports, due to background, disability, etc., they scoffed at us. "You higher-ed types. . . ." But we had done our homework and inquired about the how high school football teams in the rural communities they represented were doing. In that particular state, schools were classified for athletics based on size. Their districts were small. So small schools played small schools, bigger ones each other. After commenting about how well their teams were doing, we asked why they didn't play the bigger schools from the cities and suburbs in the playoffs? They responded that wouldn't be fair, those schools were bigger, had all sorts of advantages in terms of number of potential players, facilities, equipment, coaching, etc. When we commented back, "Kids are kids, the scoreboard starts at zero for both teams, why do you non-higher-ed types treat kids so differently?" they were speechless. Is it really okay to ignore differences in the classroom, but build systems based on them for athletics? Our legislative friends were dumbfounded.

Educational equality has been a dream for a long time. In 1964, President Lyndon B. Johnson declared the War on Poverty, which included training programs for youth in poor communities and Head Start, an early education program for disadvantaged children. Over the past few decades, the war on poverty and efforts to improve education for disadvantaged children continued. In 2002, President George W. Bush signed into law the No Child Left Behind Act (No Child Left Behind Act of 2001, 2002), which made it a national goal to close the achievement gap between advantaged and disadvantaged students, racial and ethnic minorities, with the more advantaged and White majority. In 2015, the new education law passed under the Obama administration, the Every Student Succeeds Act (Every Student Succeeds Act, 2015), continued the same pursuit: Close the achievement gap.

Indeed, historians and scholars have lamented the legacy of inequities in American education since the nation's forming (Tyack, 2004; Anderson, 1989). For Black Americans, Native Americans, and other racial and ethnic groups, there are historical roots of disparity that predate the situation that plagues the nation today. Ladsen-Billings (2006) suggests that the idea of the achievement gap is so pervasively accepted in our culture that "it has made its way into common parlance and everyday use. The term is invoked by people on both sides of the political spectrum and few argue over its meaning and import" (p. 3). Kozol (1991) applied the term "savage inequalities" to underscore how the educational system gives advantages to some groups over others based on race and class.

While American education has been pursuing strategies and practices to close the achievement gap for a long time, so have other countries. For example, Australia and the United Kingdom have been working hard to narrow the gaps of achievement among students from different home backgrounds (Cobbold, 2010; Ford, 2013). International assessments such as PISA (Programme for International Student Assessment) have also highlighted the achievement gaps among students with different backgrounds and praised countries where smaller gaps exist (OECD, 2016).

Governments have invested heavily to close the achievement gap. In the United States, for example, a primary goal of the No Child Left Behind Act in 2001 (No Child Left Behind Act of 2001, 2002) was to close the achievement gap through increased standardized testing, higher requirements for teacher training and performance, adoption of evidence-based reading and math teaching strategies, and serious accountability measures for schools. The new law passed under the Obama administration, the Every Student Succeeds Act (Every Student Succeeds Act, 2015), followed the same approach, although with less mandate for assessment. Rick Hess, an education scholar at the American Enterprise Institute, called the widespread movement to close the achievement gap a mania (Hess, 2011). Finnish educator Pasi Sahlberg (Sahlberg, 2012) referred to global efforts to close the achievement gap as the Global Education Reform Movement, or GERM, with a focus around greater standardization, emphasis on core subjects, prescribed curriculum, copying models from corporate cultures, and high-stakes accountability.

While these laws and other factors plunged the entire U.S. education system into an "achievement-gap mania" (Hess, 2011), the gap has not narrowed over the past three decades. The achievement gap remains large among students of different racial and ethnic backgrounds. Black and Hispanic students, students with disabilities, and students from immigrant families still score worse in math and reading than their White peers (Zhao, 2016; Hansen et al., 2018; Hanushek et al., 2019). Recent data from the long-term assessment of the National Assessment of Educational Progress or NAEP, which is often referred to as the nation's report card, shows the gap has not changed significantly ever since such data were first collected in the 1970s (National Assessment of Educational Progress, 2021).

Closing the achievement gap is yet another duck-and-cover idea in education. It sounds great. Who can logically be against closing gaps in education? Everyone wants an equal education for all students. Horace Mann, the great early architect of education in the 1800s in the United States argued that education is one of the best ways for the wealthy to protect their wealth because it uplifts the poor (Mann, 1848). But the problem is that, for various reasons (Zhao, 2016), disadvantaged children have significantly more challenges than their advantaged counterparts. Simply put, the disadvantaged get a worse education. Thus, while investing in closing the achievement gap seems to make great sense, realistically, the gap can't be closed as easily or completely as the pundits suggest. In fact, billions of dollars have been spent to institute large system-wide comprehensive strategies to ameliorate the problem, but like a bad cough, the gap persists.

The question is: Why? Why has the gap lingered for so long with no seeming end in sight? Educational experts, presidents, governors, and leaders from across the political divide have weighed in, strategy after strategy has been tested and failed, sometimes after great effort and billions of dollars of investment. We pose several answers to this question which underscores the duck-and-cover nature of the policies and practices.

First, the gap is the reflection of historical debt for Black students, anti-immigrant mindset against Hispanic students, social inequity against the poor and disadvantaged, and racism against non-White students (Gamoran, 2007; Ladson-Billings, 2006). In other words, the gap is a symptom of a bigger disease in our society. The disease is historical and derived from systematic racism and social inequalities. Racism and associated social inequity have created very different homes, communities, and opportunities, which give children very different access to resources from birth to school age. Contrary to the political critics who today are moving to whitewash curriculum of the historical truths about disparities and the country's hand in creating them, effectively treating the problem requires a more systematic approach. Unless and until this disease is cured, the symptoms will exist. Not only does directing schools to solve societal problems fail, it actually misdirects what schools can do to alleviate the symptoms. As Perkinson (1977) has persuasively argued in *The Imperfect Panacea*, schools are ill-equipped to correct societal ills. Or, as any physician might put it, to cure a serious disease, you need treat both the symptoms (e.g., the achievement gap in test scores) and the underlying conditions (the issues and circumstances that lead to the test score differentials). Renowned Harvard sociologist William Julius Wilson (2009) highlighted that growing up in neighborhoods of concentrated poverty and deprivation has long-term effects on educational attainment. Just focusing on "fixing" schools won't eradicate the problem.

To underscore the point, a devastating reality is that economic inequality in the United States is a core part of the dilemma causing the achievement gap. In terms of income inequality, for example, the United States is among the most unequal countries in the world. The Pew Research Center (Schaeffer, 2020) found that income inequality in the United States was the highest of all the G7 nations. The median Black–White income gap has persisted over time in their analysis of 1970 to 2018. The wealth gap between America's richest and poorest families more than doubled from 1989 to 2016. The achievement gap is about more than just what is happening in schools.

Second, as it is defined now, the achievement gap is largely the gap in test scores and educational attainment. Test scores are largely math and reading scores on standardized tests and educational attainment is the completion of high school and college attendance. This definition fits the current education system, which is in fact designed and enforced to create the gap because it promotes ranking and competition. In other words, when some students score high, others will have to score low. The system does not allow all students to succeed in the same domains. As the system favors those who have better educational resources that supports the development of reading and math abilities or test-taking abilities in math and reading, it is natural that those who don't have equal resources are on the other side of the gap. It is also to be expected that those who come to school with better math and reading abilities would not wait for others to catch up to them. So other than just allowing everyone to graduate or finding assessments that result in higher scores for larger numbers of students no matter their actual knowledge, the gaps will persist until significant broad changes are undertaken. This was clearly exposed during the second Bush presidency, when Rod Paige was appointed as U.S. Secretary of Education, based largely on what became known as the "Texas Miracle" of high tests scores for all groups of students on the Texas state assessments he engineered. The sad truth, however, was that when other more valid tests were examined, such as NAEP, the miracle proved to be a mirage (Haney, 2000). Give easy tests, everyone passes, and voila! Decrease the achievement gap.

Third, when schools are misdirected to solve the problem of achievement gaps or gaps in test scores, they are forced to deprive children from disadvantaged backgrounds of opportunities to be engaged in productive educational activities. To improve the test scores of disadvantaged children, many schools place children in remedial courses or after-school programs in reading and math. When the time is spent on reading and math, children have no time to spend on other activities that might engage them. Moreover, in order to provide more time in reading and math, schools must cut off investment in teachers and time for other subjects and activities that may trigger students' interests and strengths. Thus, quite often, efforts to close achievement gaps in reading and math actually broaden the opportunity gap for children (Emler et al., 2019; Tienken & Zhao, 2013).

Fourth, while academic gaps arising from socioeconomic strata should not be accepted, gaps on most assessments are quite natural because children are born with different intelligences and have different experiences when they come to school. Thus, when they are in school, children naturally vary in terms of competencies and interests in different subjects, activities, and skills. A great musician may stink at English, a talented actor or athlete underperform in math. But since their strengths and skills aren't tested, they heighten the gap when the only measure is a standardized test in designated subjects. Tests, incidentally, are predicative of very little of consequence (Heckman & Kautz, 2012).

If allowed, children can become uniquely great in their own ways. That is, children can further develop their strengths and passions. An overemphasis or exaggerated stress on what children cannot do, or their low performances in reading and math, can force them to experience failure and anxiety all the time. It creates a snowball effect regarding poor performance and failure. More important, given the school's limited focus on certain subjects, and the time and emphasis on addressing these, it makes students neglect their strengths and passions.

Fifth, the gap in math and reading at early grades may not last long at all if children are engaged in schools. Basic reading and math can be mastered by children but the mastery may take time, and needs different approaches rather than forced testing. What schools need to do is to ensure that children are happily engaged with the school experience—to focus on their strengths and passions, and ensure that they are confident and curious.

Closing the achievement gap sounds politically appealing but is impossible to achieve through school practices and pressures alone. Children will never achieve identical results in reading and math; gaps in test scores will likely appear in perpetuity. More important, the wealthier children born into families with advantages are not going to wait for their disadvantaged peers to catch up. Making up for the lost time and limited school resources of disadvantaged children takes time and strategy. But no matter what, disadvantaged children start from a worse place than their counterparts when it comes to performing on standardized tests.

So what needs to be done is to stop obsessively focusing on test score numbers to close the achievement gap. Much as our rural colleagues tell us about farmers wanting to have hefty cattle to bring to market, simply weighing the cow or pig doesn't make it any fatter. Instead, we should focus on helping disadvantaged children develop their strengths and passions. Education is not about running a race against each other. It is about developing individual talents. And regarding addressing income gaps, schooling could be about creating financial supports for financially poor families (as other countries do), so that all children have adequate nourishment, healthcare, and exposure to a great variety of pursuits.

RECONSIDER, REMOVE, REPLACE

We aren't arguing against the best education for all students or attempts to ameliorate inequities or equalize what kids get in school. Those are lofty goals. We are flabbergasted at the belief system characterized by our interaction with state legislators highlighted at the start of this chapter. Some kids need different sorts of supports than others. We agree that gaps appearing between students are horrifying. But we recognize that the strategies to minimize the differences are wrong-minded in their approach. Schools have never been able to fix what ails society. The United States tried for decades to desegregate schools in a society that wasn't ready, learning that the Supreme Court's 1955 *Brown vs. Board of Education* remedy to address segregation in schools "with all deliberate speed" could be defined rather loosely. The change wasn't deliberate, characterized by speed at all. The old 1966 Phil Ochs folk song, "Love Me I'm a Liberal," captured the dilemma in a line that emphasized that hard issues require difficult, often unpopular solutions: "And I love Puerto Ricans and Negros, as long as they don't move next door, So love me, love me, love me, I'm a liberal." Of course, that was a long time ago, but as Ochs captured for his time over 50 years ago, inconsistencies in words and actions even among those ostensibly sensitive to the issues at hand, the liberals, made changes really hard. They weren't thrilled with integrating their own cherished spaces and eradicating the entrenched problems.

For schools, the history is well documented. You can't fix what the larger society won't seriously tackle. Addressing gaps will require ameliorating the huge gaps in wealth, access, and supports that characterize our culture. That is a systemic issue for the country to address. We recognize that schools won't and shouldn't sit idly by, waiting for what the nation as a whole struggles to correct. But focus on strengths and talents and individualized attention, and not assessments that capture finite and focused types of information that likely adds to the students' disdain for what they experience.

Regarding the achievement gap, we see it as a duck-and-cover policy that requires being replaced and revised. What we do in schools will need to be complementary to society seriously taking on the larger issues. The achievement gap initiative is well meaning and highlights issues that need to be addressed. But perhaps dropping the anal-retentive obsession with test scores, and instead moving to a more comprehensive consideration of knowledge, skills, and outcomes, including a much more nuanced assessment of broader outcomes, would help find ways to address the gaps that exist. It is clear after decades of attempts, closing test score differences among groups is hard and likely impossible. But what if other outcomes were considered, perhaps including longer time frames to assess what is happening of consequence to students. The "outcomes gap" would allow analyses of a myriad of talents, perhaps including some kind of assessments in all subjects deemed important enough to teach in schools. Other skills, knowledge, and expertise might also be included.

We recognize that a lot of good people are working really hard on resolving the achievement gap. But thinking about all the years, efforts, and funding that has gone for naught reminds us of the quote attributed to Albert Einstein: "Insanity is doing the same thing over and over and expecting different results." The obsession with the achievement gap on standardized test scores in math and English has become insane. No doubt different things have been tried, yet none have really worked in the long term. Time to move on, and build a more systemic plan to deal with the root and causes and not just the symptoms.

CHAPTER 5

Social and Emotional Learning

Kansas appointed a Blue-Ribbon Task Force a few years ago to consider issues related to bullying in schools. One of us served as a co-chair. Upon announcement of the Task Force, companies around the country with anti-bullying programs came out of the woodwork asking if their programs could be included in any recommended solutions when the report was completed. While recommending any specific remedy wasn't part of the charge for the work, it made some sense that we might compile a list of resources for schools and districts to consider. We considered these companies and programs well meaning, so we asked for any evidence these groups had that their programs actually worked. That eliminated most of them immediately, though a few sent us literature-review types of studies on socio-emotional learning (SEL). There is some evidence that SEL addresses some of the behaviors that are associated with bullying, but we responded back that this wasn't evidence that *their* specific program actually worked. One place assured us they had the evidence, but that turned out to be a simplistic "case study" that assessed knowledge of SEL components prior to the training, then reassessed with the same instrument after it was complete. Like magic, the scores improved, to their way of thinking, clear evidence that the program worked. After explaining to them that this had no relationship to evidence about the impact of their program, and that we expected every program on the planet teaching SEL concepts would get the same improvement in knowledge of concepts on a post test, they walked away in anger.

What does this have to do with SEL? It displays the constant pressure school leaders no doubt face from experts and researchers, do-gooders, and sometimes snake-oil salespersons shopping their wares to fix everything about teaching, likely everything from poverty to world hunger to the cure for cancer! Moreover, it displays how ubiquitous SEL has become as the panacea for a whole array of ills that penetrate our schools.

We understand this impetus for remedies and the attractiveness of SEL. When children are socially sound and emotionally healthy, they learn better. Put it more simply, when children are happy in schools, they seem to do more positive things and their learning outcomes improve. Moreover, according proponents of SEL, "[W]hen SEL skills are intentionally, systematically implemented and reinforced in school settings, students are better equipped not only to be successful in school but also to become informed and engaged citizens" (Schwartz et al., 2022, p. 1).

SEL is so powerful. How can schools refuse to have SEL? Well, they cannot. In the 2021–2022 school year, 76% of principals reported that their schools used SEL programs or curriculum nationwide (Schwartz et al., 2022). In 2019, the Collaborative for Academic, Social, and Emotional Learning (CASEL), the leading SEL proponent, reported that participation in its SEL collaboratives has grown "from eight states to more than 30 states and one U.S. territory, collectively representing more than 11,850 school districts, 67,000 schools, 2 million teachers and 35 million students, preschool to high school" since 2016 (CASEL, 2019). All 50 states have SEL standards and competencies for preschool and 18 states have standards for K–12 as of 2020 (Zhao, 2020). There has also been significant increase in the use of SEL in schools. While 52% of elementary school principals and 37% secondary school principals reported inclusion of SEL in the 2017–2018 school year, the numbers jumped to 81% and 70% in the school year of 2021–2022 (Schwartz et al., 2022). As early as 2003, CASEL reported (Hoffman, 2009) there were more than 200 types of classroom-based SEL programs used in U.S. schools.

Schonert-Reichl (2019) concluded, "Clearly, SEL is a worldwide phenomenon and not just a passing fad, with SEL approaches and programs being implemented in countries around the world" (p. 223).

We also recognize for certain student populations, specific preparation in SEL-related concepts is offered by professionals with training in areas of need, such as psychologists, special educators, speech language pathologists, and others. In no way are we suggesting that services should be withheld from students with identified needs.

But as SEL spreads across schools in the country and world, we need to be cautious because it is just another duck-and-cover kind of policy. Like duck and cover, it makes people feel good and certainly is well meaning. Who does not want their children or students to be socially and emotionally sound? There are no parents or teachers who want behaviorally troublesome, socially awkward, and emotionally disturbing children. We all want our children to be socially appropriate, to know how to manage their emotions, and to behave properly. We want them to do well in school and to thrive as individuals. Thus, if SEL promises to make our children the good kids everyone wants, why not?

However, do SEL programs or curricula truly produce such overwhelmingly positive results? What data are there to support the claims? SEL proponents have often cited evidence to support the positive SEL outcomes. For example, the Rand report developed on behalf of CASEL says, "Over the past two decades, a growing body of research has shown the importance of social and emotional development in a student's short- and long-term academic success, emotional well-being, positive behaviors, and life outcomes"

(Schwartz et al., 2022, p. 1). The evidence behind this statement is the same two meta-analytical studies as other similar statements have drawn from. The two studies, one done by Taylor and colleagues (Taylor et al., 2017) and the other done by Durlak and associates (Durlak et al., 2011), were both published in the journal *Child Development*. The Rand report also cites a number of other studies that appear to show some positive outcomes.

Previously, SEL proponents relied on similar research. "Research reviews consistently show that SEL programs have positive effects," wrote a group of scholars, some of whom are closely associated with CASEL, in a 2017 article in the journal of *The Future of Children* (Greenberg et al., 2017, p. 17). "The sum total of the existing evidence, we found, strongly suggests that SEL programs do, in fact, have significant benefits for participating students," repeated three CASEL employees in another article in the *Kappan* (Mahoney et al., 2018). Another recent meta-analysis (Cochoran et al., 2018), only found 40 studies out of over 600 they identified that met their criteria for high quality, but did find small positive impacts for SEL on academic achievement, though they cautioned, "some of the SEL approaches most widely used in schools, tested via large randomized experiments, do not present strong evidence of effectiveness" (p. 69). They cautioned this may be due to wide variation in SEL interventions.

An additional meta-analysis was also positive but cautious. Boncu, Costea, and Minulescu (2017) confirmed many of the prior meta-analysis findings, eliciting effect sizes that were statistically significant but small. Moreover, they found that while the effect sizes for externalizing problems were reduced by SEL programs, internalizing problems yielded an insignificant effect size. In their words, "Internalizing problems can prove to be more difficult to change because of its internal behaviors that can be missed by others" (p. 39). They concluded that SEL programs have an impact on children, but the effect is small.

The empirical evidence SEL advocates generally use to support the value of SEL have been criticized as being oversold by some critics. The Pioneer Institute whitepaper calls SEL a pseudoscience and seriously questions its claim that "socio-emotional learning can fill the gap in the lives of America's children" (Ryan, 2019, p. 4). Finn predicts that "social-emotional learning will almost surely turn out to have no real scientific foundation—just a lot of much-hyped 'qualitative' and 'anecdotal' studies that nobody could replicate via gold-standard research" (Finn Jr., 2017).

The Pioneer Institute whitepaper did a fairly thorough review of the research literature SEL proponents have used to show the efficacy of SEL and concludes: "As this discussion shows, the certitude with which proponents, especially CASEL and the Commission, express their faith in the efficacy of SEL may be based less on science and rigorous research than on their own hopes about what 'ought to' work (and perhaps their own financial interests in the outcome)" (Effrem & Robbins, 2019, p. 22).

It may be difficult, if not impossible, to settle the dispute over whether advocates have overstated the effects of SEL. One of the reasons is there is no clear definition of what SEL is and is not, and advocates have been accused of being unable or unwilling to come up with one. Hess (2017), for example, complains that "[T]rying to pin SEL advocates down on precisely what's on the table can feel like I'm questioning a wily, reluctant suspect" as "I'll hear that it's about motivating students and anti-bullying and 'inclusion' and a recipe for higher graduation rates and 'restorative justice' . . . with the 'it' sometimes morphing in the course of a single sentence" (no page number). Hoffman (2009) reported similar concerns this way:

> Part of the difficulty of doing any kind of research in this area concerns the basic question: What is SEL? There is a fair degree of ambiguity and conceptual confusion, as the term is often used as an umbrella for many kinds of programs, including school-based prevention programs drawing from public health, mental health, and juvenile justice perspectives, as well as programs in conflict resolution and moral character education. (p. 535)

The lack of a commonly accepted definition may have worked in favor of SEL advocates because they can make it as broad and general as possible to appeal to a broad range of audiences. SEL has often been presented as a catchall phrase that captures skills, competencies, and abilities that are non-academic but are very important for success in school and life. "SEL goes by many other names. Common terms for this set of skills include character education, personality, 21st-century skills, soft skills, and noncognitive skills, just to name a few" (S. M. Jones & Doolittle, 2017, p. 3). Kamenetz (2017) quoted Martin West from Harvard in explaining that grit, mindset, the 4Cs (creativity, critical thinking, communication, and collaboration), habits of mind, resilience, and whatever that is "not directly measured by standardized tests," is part of how some define it (no page number).

With such a broad and unspecific definition, SEL can be anything that is missing and desired from today's schools. As such, it is thus difficult to say SEL has been oversold. But at the same time, the particular SEL state mandates that schools adopt, students experience, and researchers study is very specific. Out of the numerous constructs, concepts, programs, and instructional approaches, Harvard's EASEL lists nearly 40 different frameworks on its website (EASEL, 2020), one can only choose a limited number for adoption. For example, the CASEL SEL framework, which organizes social and emotional learning competencies around five clusters—self-awareness, self-management, social awareness, relationship skills, and responsible decision making (Greenberg et al., 2017)—dominates most of the state-level socioemotional learning standards/competencies. Many schools adopt a specific program such as Stanford University psychologist professor's growth mindset (Dweck, 2008) or any of the other numerous SEL programs on the market (S. Jones et al., 2017).

As a result, what students learn is limited to one unique experience rather than the broadly defined social and emotional learning. The empirical evidence provided in the meta-analysis studies (Mahoney et al., 2018) is limited to a much smaller set of outcomes than the broad definition that SEL claims to encompass, notwithstanding their methodological issues and potentially exaggerated findings. For example, it does not say anything about creativity, entrepreneurial thinking, or other so-called 21st-century skills. Thus, it is disingenuous for any SEL program or framework to claim that it teaches all the nonacademic skills or develops the nonacademic capacities for success. This is as absurd as claiming that teaching math is teaching all academic subjects just because math is one of the many academic subjects. In this sense, it is hard not to agree that SEL has been oversold.

Even many of those supportive of SEL and its potential for students recognize the questions that remain regarding the topic. The journal *Educational Psychologist* devoted an entire issue to SEL in 2019, drawing from many of those who research and promote the concept. But cautions emerged among them as well. For example, Immordino-Yang et al. (2019), highlighted key issues yet to be understood:

- "How do SEL skills develop, including potential sensitive and high-leverage developmental periods, and what supports are needed at different ages and stages?
- In an era of unprecedented immigration, inequality, and exposure to trauma, how can we ensure that SEL practices are reliable, culturally responsive, appropriate for individuals' needs, and equitable applied?
- How are SEL skills, academic emotions, and learning related, and how can SEL skills be most meaningfully integrated into educational experiences?
- How should SEL skills be measured, or for which set of skills can schools be reasonably held accountable?" (p. 186)

Others in the special issue raised issues about challenges with assessment (McKown, 2019), having ample expertise to do it well (Elias, 2019), considering teacher well-being because of stress contagion in classrooms and the needs related to preparing teachers to teach this content (Schonert-Reichl, 2019). Hoffman's (2009) analysis of SEL trends went in a different direction, that if SEL is conceptualized as an individual competency, it implies a set of political, ethical, and social consequences when it is approached through a lens of deficiency and remediation. As she explained, "when the focus is on what is 'wrong' with the individual child and what can be done to change the child, attention is directed away from the equally if not more critical aspects of what can be done to change social contexts and cultural systems in which the child is a participant" (p. 547).

Determining whether SEL has been oversold or not is not our intention nor is it important. No matter how broad or specific advocates of particular SEL approaches may be, criticisms of SEL are an excellent reminder of the danger of panacea thinking in education. Panacea thinking is a common phenomenon in education, accompanying almost all new big ideas that catch on. In other words, whenever a new idea is promoted, it is often promoted as a wonder drug, a powerful solution without any adverse side effects (Zhao, 2018b).

Panacea thinking is not only fantasy but also dangerous on multiple fronts. It is first and foremost harmful to students because it gives educators a false sense of accomplishment. In the case of SEL, adopting a program, no matter its outcomes, could lead schools to believe they have taken care of the social and emotional needs of all children and all the skills they need to succeed in the future. But we know for a fact that a specific SEL program is not the same as educating the whole child, neither is it the same as cultivating all the nonacademic skills (Zhao et al., 2019) or personal qualities (Duckworth & Yeager, 2015) that matter for the future. We also know that the same program cannot possibly have the same positive effect on all children in all conditions, a fact borne out by the empirical studies SEL advocates cite as supporting evidence (Durlak et al., 2011; Mahoney et al., 2018; Sklad et al., 2012; Taylor et al., 2017; Wigelsworth et al., 2016).

Second, panacea-thinking powers the perpetual wars and pendulum swing in education. Quite often, when an existing idea loses appeal because it is found to be not as potent as intended, or having adverse side effects, often a new idea is enthusiastically embraced as another panacea. However, the new idea will inevitably repeat the fate of its predecessor as it shows signs of side effects and broken promises. It will be displaced by another idea—most likely a reincarnation of its predecessor.

The enthusiasm about SEL can be seen as a rejection of policies and practices aimed at improving academic outcomes that include test-driven accountability and centralized and standardized curriculum and assessment. These policies and practices were once embraced enthusiastically as a panacea to improve the quality of education (Zhao, 2009, 2012) but have shown signs of ineffectiveness and adverse side effects (Nichols & Berliner, 2007; Nichols & Berliner, 2008; Zhao, 2018b). SEL could face the same rejection in a few years if it is promoted as another panacea. Thus, it is important for SEL advocates to not oversell it, and be honest about its limitations, challenges, and side effects.

Another major issue about SEL that should raise some caution is whether it is ideologically driven and racist. Advocates say no. "In fact, the basis of this approach is not ideological at all," maintains the National Commission on Social, Emotional and Academic Development in its report (National Commission on Social, 2019, p. 6). The commission argues that the social and emotional learning movement is freed from ideological bias for two reasons. First, the SEL movement is based on science, instead of ideology: "It is rooted in the experience of teachers, parents, and students supported by the best educational research of the past few decades" and "[T]he research is compelling" (National Commission on Social, 2019, p. 6). Indeed, scholars associated with CASEL and some other associates (Jagers et al., 2019) have been promoting what they call "transformative SEL," directly intended to promote equity and excellence.

Second, the SEL approach to education is locally owned. It is not a top-down federal mandate as the NCSEAD argues:

> This approach didn't take shape at the federal level. It is based on the emerging consensus of successful communities, convinced that this is the missing piece in American education. It will only expand to scale on the strength of local owner-ship, promoting these efforts school by school, district by district, and state by state. (National Commission on Social, 2019, p. 8)

In fact, the commission believes that the SEL approach to education is an exception to the toxic divisive political debates in the United States. The Commission claims: "This movement of local leadership and civic re-sponsibility is a welcome contrast and a refuge from ideological bitterness" (National Commission on Social, 2019, p. 8).

But critics have a drastically different view. Much of the criticism comes from those wanting more traditional and/or market-driven approaches. To many of them, SEL is nothing but ideological. The SEL movement is considered a significant and substantive ideological victory of progressive education. For example, Kevin Ryan, an emeritus professor of education at Boston University and founder of the Center for Character and Social Responsibility, argues: "The current popularity of social-emotional learning (SEL) represents progressive education's greatest victory in its 100-plus-year campaign to transform our public schools, and, thus, the nature of America itself" (Ryan, 2019, p. 4). He explains:

> SEL advocates see teaching students their five "competencies" of self-awareness, self-management, social awareness, relationship skills, and responsible decision-making as the effective replacement for schools' former moral education and character formation. Committed as they are to development of "the whole child," progressive educators are promoting these skills as a secular replacement for what parents used to instill in children according to their faith, and to cultural and fam-ily beliefs and values. (Ryan, 2019, p. 4)

Critics do not accept SEL competencies as necessary skills for success in school, careers, and life. Rather, "SEL teaches the young the flattering message that they themselves are ready to guide their lives by inner feelings and to reject the thought that they 'have a lot to learn'" because "[a]t its core, the skills of social-emotional learning aim to shift the center of moral decision-making from traditional wisdom and an awareness that we are children of God to the newly enlightened self" (Ryan, 2019, p. 4).

Greene (2019) maintains that SEL is deeply rooted in religious and moral education. Different from Ryan, Greene thinks SEL skills correspond to the values of Christian theology. "The cardinal virtues, first described by Socrates in *The Republic* and later incorporated into Christian theology, consist of prudence, courage, temperance, and justice," writes Greene. "There is nearly a one-to-one correspondence between the cardinal virtues and the core SEL competencies as identified by the Collaborative for Academic, Social, and Emotional Learning (CASEL)" (Greene, 2019, p. 2). Nonetheless, Greene is in agreement with Ryan that SEL is not free from ideology.

The Pioneer Institute commissioned whitepaper takes on the two reasons undergirding the National Commission's claim that SEL is not ideological. First, the authors attack the claim of SEL is based on science by challenging SEL advocates' empirical evidence and bringing on evidence to show the insignificance of SEL's effects on learning. Second, the authors make an attempt to show the SEL movement is not locally owned or initiated by local communities. For instance, they believe "SEL and Common Core are closely and intentionally intertwined" (Effrem & Robbins, 2019, p. 14).

We are basically agnostic about the arguments regarding whether or not SEL is ideologically driven. The dispute tends to pit those from differing ideological sides against one another, and really doesn't speak to SEL's merits or shortcomings. Frankly, to our way of thinking, the dispute over whether SEL is ideological is both divisive but pointless because all education is ideological or value-based (Biesta, 2010). A scientific foundation or empirical evidence does not make education free from ideology or values. Scientifically collected evidence can help determine the degree to which a method or intervention can effectively lead to certain educational outcomes, but it cannot say anything about the value of the specific outcomes, which are determined within certain ideological frameworks (Zhao, 2018b). In the case of SEL, for example, scientific research can indicate whether a program improves the SEL competencies or academic outcomes in students but cannot tell how much the SEL competencies and academic outcomes are valued in certain communities.

It is thus meaningless and unnecessary to hide the ideological bias behind empirical evidence. It is equally meaningless and unnecessary to reject SEL just because of its ideological basis. SEL is ideological, as are all aspects of education. Academic outcomes, for example, are not value free. There have been plenty of ideological disputes over what to include in academic subjects such as biology, history, literature, and of course, civics. The battle over sex education is deeply ideological and has played out in many school districts. Even math, reading, art, and PE can be ideological. Issues such as what books should children read and whether math instruction should be about concepts or computational skills have divided people into different ideological camps. Gifted and special education have long been battlefields of different educational ideologies.

Another way the National Commission tries to avoid being labeled ideological is to claim SEL as a local decision instead of a federal government mandate. While this may be a genuine intent, the reality is that the growth of SEL has certainly benefited from federal policies such as the ESSA. More important, state governments, not necessarily local, have been defining the value of SEL in public education through creating SEL standards for all children. Many states have adopted the CASEL model of SEL, which in essence has become the definition of SEL universally and uniformly applied to all students.

There is much danger in applying a uniform set of SEL standards to all children, the same kind of danger in applying a uniform set of academic standards to all children. Whether determined by local schools, state, or federal governments, or global powers such as the Organisation for Economic Cooperation and Development (OECD)'s PISA, a uniform set of SEL standards, especially when implemented through curriculum and assessment, can do exactly the same kind of damage as uniform academic standards—homogenizing diversity, penalizing individual and cultural differences, artificially manufacturing achievement gaps, alienating students and parents, and suppressing creativity and individuality. And ironically, it will lead to more stress, anxiety, and other social emotional issues that SEL claims to address (Zhao, 2012; 2018a; 2018b).

RECONSIDER, REMOVE, REPLACE

The purpose of SEL is definitely laudable. Just like duck and cover in protecting kids from bombs, the idea that all children need to be socially and emotionally strong and prepared sounds great. Truth be told, we want that for our kids. How can we question such a wonderful idea?

To us, the real issue is whether formal SEL programs can realistically do all that is promised, if they are a good approach, or whether there may be other ways to get there. Schools should make people socially and emotionally sound because learning should be interesting, engaging, and happy. Schools are also places where children should learn to socialize, to make friends, and to be socially appropriate. We need to get better at these things. Some programs can help with that, likely without new standards, teachers being retrained, experts coming in sharing their wares, and all the controversy that seems to attend SEL's ideals.

We worry about adding new curriculum or standards called SEL in schools. In fact, the SEL curriculum or standards can do much harm by adding more load on teachers and students, by imposing a new homogenous view of behaviors on students from different backgrounds, and by assessing students with the same definition of social and emotional readiness. No doubt, different kids will need an array of different things. Teachers aren't trained psychologists, so all sorts of new training would likely be necessary for schools and classrooms to do what the varying standards imply in any meaningful way. This can't be done quickly. So, years more training would likely be needed.

What do we suggest? First, states and schools need to take a step back and think about what they want and what is realistically possible. Consider the implications that adding a whole new set of expectations will have on classrooms and teachers who largely aren't trained or prepared to do what is being asked of them. What SEL promises is a series of deep changes in students, changes that require a lot of expertise to address. We aren't against training to help kids cope, become more resilient, happy, successful, social, etc. But these are not simple concepts or things to teach and include in schools. So even if inclined to make this happen, if this is going to be done right, time and money will be huge concerns and we expect what is realistically needed will be lacking.

Second, think about what is being offered up. CASEL, for example, offers nine potential outcomes for an SEL program—improved positive social behavior, reduced problem behavior, reduced emotional stress, improved development/agency, improved school connectedness, improved school climate, improved academic performance, improved SEL skills and attitudes, improved teaching practices. Holy cow, that is incredible! All, no doubt, worthwhile goals and outcomes, and in CASEL's defense, they do caution that districts need identify their specific priorities and offers advice on the various components of implementing a program well. So, what to include and what to leave out? Does doing only part of the full package really work? Frankly, we are a bit taken aback by all that are held up as possibilities. It is easy to be skeptical, and fits what we've described as panacea thinking.

Third, we definitely aren't against teachers and others in schools providing supports for kids along many of the dimensions highlighted in the SEL programs. But the research base for SEL, while mildly positive related to academic outcomes for some, doesn't show huge impacts on all the many proposed outcomes and the major meta-analyses all call for more sophisticated studies on what actually works. There is great variation in the definition and what is presented. At the same time, evidence is clear that students' belief that teachers like them is a powerful start (that is, teachers who are caring, respectful, praising; Hallanan, 2008), as is evidence from work on our campus that the most memorable and impactful teachers to students are those who were encouraging, supportive, and helpful to kids across their academic careers—essentially doing much of what the SEL proponents call for. None of that required a whole new set of standards or curricula. We clearly understand the desire here and hope for finding ways to reach more kids and serve them well. Our mantra is: Be cautious.

Fourth, this stuff is highly controversial. We are no strangers to controversy ourselves (just read this book!), but potential benefits of any curricular change, even the well-meaning ones, can be completely undermined by ideological debates. As we suggested, the ideological schism here is basically just silly. Of course, SEL is ideological in nature, as are all other components of education. But to us, we wonder if other ways to get to the goals set out for SEL would be more advantageous before whole programs and training and high-profile ventures are put on a silver platter for critics to demean. To the critics now, SEL is akin to devil worship. Our solution is to hold back and wait for the science to be more convincing about tangible benefits and thoughtful ways to help kids. Evidence-based practice is needed.

Finally, as long as standardized tests dominate as the main component of evaluation systems, anything like SEL is likely doomed anyway. The point is that there are systematic issues to be dealt with. Building curriculum and training teachers for all that SEL implies is likely at odds with what is realistic, especially if tests continue to be the element that rules. Schools remain competitive places, kids continue to bully, COVID-19 has brought greater stress to students and teachers than likely ever before. We aren't aware that much of that has changed even with the onslaught of SEL. Also, we question whether teachers need to be fully regarded as having a high level of SEL personal competence in order to realistically teach it to children. Schonert-Reichl (2019) raised the issue of the importance of teacher well-being in relation to teaching SEL. These are complex matters, but if teachers need to be developed in this area, are we going to change the standards and expectations for becoming a teacher? Simple professional development offered in schools likely wouldn't come close to providing what current teachers need. We don't know what teachers might require, but you sure should be competent in mathematics before teaching that to kids. Our point is that we think about this systematically and worry about adding whole new facets to what teachers must do, without removing whole portions of other parts of the curriculum and expectations for teacher work, and without dramatically altering the key assessment schemes focusing on tested subjects currently used in schools. Without this kind of systematic approach, promoting what might happen related to SEL is a fool's errand.

Moreover, making schools engaging for students would probably serve many of the same needs that the SEL advocates want to train into kids. Much can be done in this realm, perhaps including key components of what the SEL advocates desire. Caution needs be paid to the potential deleterious effects on kids from disadvantaged backgrounds. Nothing wrong with the goals SEL sets out, but duck and cover, they likely won't have broad effects.

Foreign-Language Instruction

We have both spent time in multiple different countries. Years ago, on a visit to South Africa, one of us visited many of the townships and schools populated by the South African Black and "Coloured" (mixed race) populations. Our mission there was to help elevate education in the schools, townships, and communities still controlled by apartheid. Here we were, the supposed American experts coming in to breathe some modernity and state-of-the-art technique to uplift the locals' education, yet they had a leg up on us in multiple ways. What struck us was that maybe this needed to be more of a two-way street. Maybe we had things to learn from our South African colleagues. For these apartheid-ravaged people, with underfunded and under-staffed schools, nasty systemic restrictions on their lives, many times with 50 or more students in classes devoid of modern technology or sophistication, all had teachers and students that spoke multiple languages. They easily conversed with us in English and could speak Afrikaans (a German–Dutch language of the oppressors); most spoke multiple native languages depending on the region of the country. We spoke English, with a silly-sounding American accent, not the British one they all employed. Truth be told, we felt pretty unhinged by our inability to communicate as well as those we were supposedly there to uplift. Whose schools was it that needed help?

We realize this experience in South Africa with the sense of language insecurity might be replicated in most other foreign countries. Americans have never put much emphasis on learning foreign languages. In fact, if anything, America, as a country, intends to kill foreign languages and successfully does so. As a country of immigrants, the United States always has a new input of foreign languages coming with new immigrants. But because schools do not teach foreign languages until secondary school, and given the apparent value of English anointed in our education system, the majority of the children of these immigrants lose their native languages during school years while successfully learning English.

Historian Peter Stearns (2009) indicated that Americans have a legendary reluctance to learning languages other than English. This reluctance plays out in schools. Foreign language is not part of the core subjects emphasized in schools across the United States. Historically, while some educators and curriculum experts called for foreign-language instruction, duck and cover, even when it is a part of American schooling, it is arguably fashioned in the worst way possible. Rather than teaching foreign languages early in students' school years when the likelihood of developing competence is greatest (recent research suggests it is best to start prior to age 10, Hartshorne et al., 2018; see also DeKeyser, 2018; Lichtman, 2016; Singleton & Ryan, 2004), the common model is to delay teaching any foreign language until the secondary level. Thus, foreign languages are typically taught to American students at ages when it is more difficult to learn. The implications are either that Americans just don't really care about foreign-language competence for our culture, or, duck and cover, we are too thick-headed to realize that our approach is upside down.

The outcomes are predictable. According to the American Academy of Arts and Sciences (2017), 66% of all Europeans have some knowledge of more than one language. The share of U.S. adults with similar abilities is closer to 20%. And within that 20%, the majority possess those foreign language abilities not due to their U.S. schooling, but because they were new immigrants to the country (Zeigler & Camarota, 2019). Simply put, our schools don't teach foreign languages as much as other countries do, and when we do it, we have probably adopted the worst model imaginable. Predictable as well, most immigrants to the United States lose their foreign-language abilities by the third generation in this country (Santiestevan, 1991). As a result, Americans as a whole are basically monolingual, which is shocking given the number of immigrants who come to the United States every year speaking non-English languages.

It doesn't have to be this way, but sadly, in schools anyway, history tends to be a precursor for the future. As schools were developing across the American landscape, foreign language was typically a part of the dedicated curriculum, albeit in most cases with a focus on secondary schools. But with millions of immigrants coming to our shores in the late 19th and early 20th centuries, and the country moving from its agrarian roots to a more industrialized economy, many organizations had to reform to accommodate the changing demographics and emerging new societal needs, schools among them. Key reports compiled by teams of experts organized by the National Education Association in the 1890s and the second decade of the 1900s led this effort (National Education Association, 1893, 1895, 1918), and the basic curriculum we still follow today was conceived. These created a more comprehensive curriculum focusing on multiple subjects, including foreign languages at the high-school level. Mirel (2006) argued that the later report in 1918 backed away from the earlier reports suggesting that all students learn the same curriculum, instead promoting a more differentiated model, given the common assumption by many scholars that not all students were capable or intelligent enough for college and the stronger curriculum. In terms of foreign language, the 1918 report promoted the idea that elementary schools needed to focus on what we might call "the basics" today. Thus, our duck-and-cover approach to foreign language instruction was born.

So educational leaders 100 years ago had broad concerns driving their curriculum decisions, and foreign language, especially at the elementary level, wasn't primary in their thoughts. Interestingly, there have always been periods where the lack of foreign-language ability was considered deplorable, but this has never translated into an educational approach that might realistically address the concern. Strengthening foreign-language instruction and proficiency has been an elementary education–free zone. If done at all, the focus for more foreign-language proficiency has been at the secondary or post-secondary levels.

The concern about America's foreign-language inadequacies became quite salient in the second half of the 20th century, notably in response to fears about Russian military dominance. President Eisenhower even argued that strengthening foreign-language deficiencies was tied to national security (Diekhoff, 1965). Specifically for educators, James Conant's (1959) *The American High School Today,* helped bring the importance of foreign-language instruction back to prominence. Reports by the National Association of Secondary School Principals and the Bureau of Secondary Curriculum Development in the late 1950s and early 1960s reinforced this new emphasis (Vocolo, 1974). Indeed, a New York Bureau of Secondary Curriculum Development report in 1960 highlighted key values for foreign-language study (quoted from Vocolo, 1974, p. 295):

- Stimulus for growth in language arts through the study of another language.
- Enrichment of the pupils' knowledge of the world they live in . . .
- Increase in the knowledge and appreciation of the American heritage by an awareness of the contributions of different peoples to national growth and development
- Promotion of international understanding
- A recognition of the human experience
- A sympathetic comprehension of the foreign people through insights into their values and behavior patterns

But despite these efforts, this chameleon never changed its colors. Some kind of sensible approach and consensus for increasing the country's multiple-language proficiency never emerged. The focus was always on the secondary level. And sadly, as these midcentury developments and resulting efforts emphasizing the importance of foreign-language instruction popped up, not much changed. Educators seemed entrenched in keeping foreign-language instruction where it was, ducking under their desks by using a model that was less likely to produce foreign-language speakers. Ironically, none of the calls for math or science improvements ever suggested the foreign language model of withholding those subjects from the earlier grades. Important subjects need to start in vitro. Arguing that early foreign-language instruction really made sense, too, would have been considered educational heresy. Instead, reformers demanded more and more rigorous instruction in those obviously more important subjects at all levels. But foreign-language instruction remained stuck right where it always had been, when kids were older and the process for fluency harder.

Later initiatives to promote foreign-language instruction again underscored why learning a foreign language was so important for individuals and the country's future, and even employed fear tactics to spurn on change. For example, President Carter in 1978 established the President's Commission on Foreign Language Instruction and International Studies, issuing a report a year later that included the ominous assessment that American incompetence in foreign languages was scandalous (Report to the President From the President's Commission on Foreign Language and International Studies, 1979). The report highlighted that instruction in foreign languages and culture in elementary schools had "virtually disappeared" (p. 1).

Years later, in 1991, the federal government again passed legislation that advanced funding for scholarships and fellowships for American students to study abroad, and also created the National Security Education Program, including the Language Flagship Program focusing on strengthening curriculum in higher-education programs (McGinn, 2015). Other initiatives emerged for strengthening foreign-language instruction, mostly tied to military-related needs, especially for filling the shortages of proficient speakers of the tongues of countries that might threaten American security. But, duck and cover, promoting foreign-language instruction for elementary students was never mentioned.

More recently, an American Academy of Arts and Sciences report (2017) highlighted key needs related to foreign-language instruction and learning, suggesting that language education needs to be valued as a national need as much as mathematics or English. The report findings suggested a multipronged rationale beyond the military argument fashioned in earlier decades:

- The ability to understand, speak, read, and write in world languages, in addition to English, is critical to success in business, research, and international relations in the 21st century.
- The United States needs more people to speak languages other than English in order to provide social and legal services for a changing population.
- The study of a second language has been linked to improved learning outcomes in other subjects, enhanced cognitive ability, and the development of empathy and effective interpretive skills. . . . (also) linked to a delay in certain manifestations of aging.

- The United States lags behind most nations of the world, including European nations and China, in the percentage of its citizens who have some knowledge of a second language.
- One of the biggest obstacles to improved language learning is a national shortage of qualified teachers.
- Technological innovations will play an ever more significant role in language learning. . . .

Even the Council on Foreign Relations (Wiley et al., 2012) weighed in on promoting foreign-language instruction as a national priority. They highlighted that the global economy is shifting away from the English-speaking world, suggesting, "In a competitive global export market, there will be a premium on foreign-language skills and international competency. It is an old adage that you can buy in any language, but you must sell in the language of your customer" (p. 2).

But even with these multi-decade pleas for more foreign-language instruction, tied to all kinds of powerful needs, it remained that most of the coursework and programming that occurred before college was at the secondary, not elementary level. Note that in 2018–2019, there were 67,606 public elementary schools in the United States (Statistica, 2021). A report by the Language Flagship (2017) collected data from elementary schools in 35 states and Washington, DC (these included 12 of the 15 largest states in the nation, including the six largest), and found a total of 291 elementary schools were offering foreign languages in grades K–8. While their data don't encompass 100% of the elementary schools in the country, the results emphasize the paltry percentage of programs that exist. This is even less than what Pufahl and Roades (2011) reported, who found about 15% of public elementary schools offer any program for languages other than English, and the numbers are trending down. Sadly, according to Pufahl and Roades (2011), even at the high school–level, foreign-language offerings are declining down to 79%, with the number for middle schools at only 58%.

A sane person should ask, "Why?" Why the declines, why the lack of urgency to do this the right way and start foreign languages in the elementary years? Perhaps part of the answer comes from Pufahl and Roades's (2011) survey, which asked those elementary schools not planning to change why they weren't. Reasons cited included lack of funding, decisions at the district level, foreign languages not being considered core for an elementary curriculum, lack of feasibility, teacher shortages, and after-school or extracurricular options. In other words, best practice aside, the planets just aren't in alignment when it comes to offering foreign languages when they should be taught at the elementary level.

Reasons for changing this curious set of practices are powerful. Recent research in cognitive science (Hartshorne et al., 2018) found that grammar-learning ability is preserved throughout childhood and declines rapidly in late adolescence. They also found that ultimate attainment is fairly consistent for learners who begin prior to ages 10 to 12. Educational researchers tend to agree, as Lichtman (2016) reported, "when it comes to long-term attainment in second-language learning, children have the advantage over adults" (p. 707). In other words, the younger children are when they begin studying a second language, the greater the likelihood for success in learning it (Singleton & Ryan, 2004).

To add to the rationale for questioning what is happening in schools today, research suggests that there are an array of secondary cognitive benefits that language learners get from foreign language instruction, including stronger working memory, attention, problem-solving abilities, even stronger primary-language comprehension (Morales et al., 2013; Utah State Office of Education, 2013). Others found stronger executive functioning and more effective communication by strengthening empathy through better perspective taking (Bialystok, 2009; Fan et al., 2015). Uslu (2020) even found that for early childhood education programs in foreign language, foreign-language acquisition has a positive effect on preschool children's self-regulation and social skills.

To change years of accepted practice is hard. And we recognize that multiple factors are associated with the success of any foreign-language program, whether for younger or older students—quality of instruction, learning strategies applied, amount of contact time, immersion versus other methods, coming from a multi-language home—these and other variables all impact foreign-language acquisition (Chamot, 2004; Renandya, 2013; Sun, 2019). The type of instruction employed needs to differ depending on age (DeKeyser, 2018; Lichtman, 2016), so the country has a steep learning curve to get this right. Length of exposure to foreign language is likely another important ingredient for success (Nikolov & Djigunovic, 2006).

But from our perspective, this is a classic example of the kind of duck-and-cover mindset that perpetuates practices continually be done with little thought of the rationality for doing so. Either all the leaders and organizations lamenting the country's foreign-language deficiencies are wrong and we should just shut up, or the idea of improving foreign-language proficiency in the United States needs a new approach. While it is clear that learning a foreign language at any age has value, the preponderance of evidence suggests that starting early, certainly well before high school, improves the likelihood for speaking fluently and ultimately learning the language. Regrettably, American educators have closed their eyes to this reality for generations. In our country, the basis for waiting until secondary school to offer foreign-language programs isn't well specified, it isn't well reasoned, and it makes little sense. Few probably ever even think about it.

Focusing foreign-language instruction at the secondary level of schooling is upside down. It is the American way. While foreign-language instruction at all levels has declined, how the United States got to the place of de-emphasizing foreign-language acquisition is concerning. If there was a rank-ordered list of subjects to be taught and skills to be outcomes of elementary and secondary schooling in America, foreign-language instruction and proficiency would fall near the bottom. This is curious nowadays as speaking multiple languages likely would give graduates at any level of schooling a leg up in the job market. But making the starting point the secondary-education level is a major problem, a mindless duck-and-cover policy that needs correction. Clearly, our comparative foreign-language outcomes are poor, likely weakening individuals' workplace opportunities and competitiveness. According to many prognosticators, it may be damaging for the country as a whole.

RECONSIDER, REMOVE, REPLACE

The obvious suggestion is to call for a major reconsideration of what we do with more foreign-language programs in elementary schools. This will require a mindset shift and likely a need to deflect an onslaught of challenges evolving around how this de-emphasizes core subjects. What we maintain is that foreign language should be a core subject. Moreover, there is the very real issue of having sufficient teachers available to teach multiple or any foreign languages at any grade level. Teaching younger children well requires different approaches than for secondary students or adults. We suggest multiple approaches to this, all starting with and requiring that policymakers recognize foreign languages to be as essential as math and reading, despite the advancement in artificial intelligence (AI) supported translation technology. Learning a foreign language is about much more than simple communication with foreigners. We must also recognize that the current approach is wrong, that learning a second language is not only important but should start earlier in school at lower grade levels. Specifically, our reconsideration calls for:

- Altering elementary curriculum mandates and standards to require foreign-language instruction for all children as a basic part of their education. It should start in the elementary years.
- Recognizing that as with most things in education, there is a good deal of nuance in getting the teaching and learning of foreign language right. We have focused on one factor, the issue of age of foreign-language instruction commencement, as a key policy driver. Conversely, we argue that that the current model is a thoughtless approach. But other variables will need be considered to alter the current approach and move to increase foreign-language instruction beginning in the early grades. Students at different ages need different sorts of instructional approaches, the amount of daily and

weekly time dedicated to foreign languages needs be appropriate for learning a new language. Instruction needs to be continued over time. Student motivation, teacher efficacy, the learning environment and strategy, and grammar and vocabulary are just some of the many issues that need be considered (see, for example, Chamot, 2004; DeKeyser, 2004; Lichtman, 2006; Nikolov & Djigunovic, 2006; Renandya, 2013; and Sun, 2019).

- Working with government offices to support the development of more programs for preparing foreign-language teachers, with a particular focus on providing elementary-education language instructors.

- Implementing programs that take advantage of new software and online programming that can be used with younger children to learn foreign languages in appropriate age-related approaches. Technology and software that can make learning a foreign language fun for students already exist. We suggest that software be available for elementary-aged students to begin foreign-language instruction that is incorporated into the required general elementary curriculum. It is also quite easy to organize online learning programs with teachers and students from other countries. Moreover, approaching elementary foreign-language instruction this way will limit some of the fiscal and personnel pressure attached to having enough qualified teachers and funding for this new initiative. Figure out what can be removed from the current curriculum mandates to make sure this isn't too taxing on teachers and students.

- When possible, use immigrant children and parents as teachers to introduce foreign languages in elementary schools. This approach makes immigrant children feel proud of their native languages and cultures, and helps them develop a strong sense of belonging and contribution in their schools and local communities.

- We leave it to school professionals and local leaders to determine what specific foreign languages should be offered, recognizing that learning any foreign language has multiple benefits for students.

CHAPTER 7

Educational Technology

We go out to eat a lot. Something curious strikes us every time we do. Look around the restaurant the next time you go out. What do you see? People engaged in vigorous conversation? Couples holding hands, gazing into one another's eyes with loving stares? Parents talking with their kids about the day's events? Perhaps a little of all of this, but mostly what you see are people glaring down at their phones, ignoring everyone at the table, often playing a game or reading a recently posted headline, or tapping on their phones writing out a text or tweet or snap or whatever to someone not physically present.

The truth is, technology, like phones, is everywhere and all encompassing. Nearly everyone in the United States has a cell phone. According to Pew Research (2021), as of early 2021, 97% of Americans had cell phones, with 85% of the total being smartphones (more than double the percentage of 35% in 2011). The ownership of other forms of technology like tablets and computers is also ubiquitous across our culture. Social media has become a primary source for getting news, streaming videos, following sports, playing games, shopping, and connecting with other people.

But before Google, before Facebook, before Amazon, before Instagram, before Twitter, before YouTube, and before TikTok, there was a big dream for education and technology. In the early 1990s, Bill Clinton and Al Gore pushed the idea of an information superhighway in their presidential campaign and later their administration. Part of the message, at least as promoted and interpreted by enthusiastic proponents, was that the information superhighway would revolutionize education by connecting students and teachers around the world, by allowing students to have virtual tours of museums and science labs, and by enabling students to access information anywhere. Learning would be possible anywhere and anytime. Some even predicted that schools would not be necessary anymore because students can learn on their own online (Perelman, 1992). This message pushed schools to wire their classrooms and purchase computers. Some 30 years later, billions of dollars have been spent and nearly all schools are wired and all classrooms have computers, laptops, or smart devices. And COVID-19 further expanded student access to devices and connectivity from home. That is, today's children live with devices connected to the information superhighway, which has become the Internet. In fact, students spend as much as, if not more time, with digital devices than going to school (Rideout & Robb, 2019; Zhao, 2020).

But education has not been revolutionized. Google, Facebook, Amazon, Instagram, Twitter, YouTube, TikTok and many other technological changes have revolutionized our lives. They changed how we access news, how we read, how we play, how we socialize, how we shop, and how we work. Technological changes have also revolutionized the economy, industries, societies, and wars. Schools, however, remain pretty much the same. They teach the same content in the same way as in the 1900s, if not pretty much the same way as in the 1800s. Schools are still the primary organization and place where students gather. Despite the fact that the COVID-19 pandemic forced millions of schools to temporarily suspend classroom instruction and technology was used to support remote learning during that time, schools have rushed back to pre-pandemic operation. Even during remote learning, instruction was organized in the same way as in-person learning: a group of students taught by a teacher from the same school.

So just as predicted, kids can get on the superhighway and visit museums, gather any kind of information imaginable, connect with others, do amazing things. But so what? The processes in education have been incredibly resistant to significant change. Duck and cover, all the hype about technology and education has been more of a whimper than a smash. Great ideas, incredible intentions, little to show for it. And interestingly, to further temper the enthusiasm that some might have for the new technologies, scholarship has emerged lamenting the harm technologies like the iPhone have had on children (Twente, 2018).

This is of course not the first time that technology failed to revolutionize education. In the 1920s, Thomas Edison predicted that films, then a new invention, would replace teachers and books (Associated Press, 1923). Radios and TVs were also predicted to revolutionize education (Cuban, 1986). Every time significant new technologies developed, schools or education systems were seduced to invest in them. Today, we are experiencing another wave of new technologies—particularly artificial intelligence (AI), virtual reality (VR), and augmented reality (AR)—which again promise to transform education.

Investment in technology in education is not a bad idea. Can anyone really imagine a classroom not connected to the Internet and without computers or devices today, despite the reality that they do not seem to have a transformative effect on education? No school today can afford to claim that they have no new technology, though many schools still rely on printed books and pencils. Certainly, technology in schools and classrooms offers advantages, like allowing students to search the Internet for projects or connect to helpful software. We want our schools, teachers, and students to have modern technology, despite some schools actually prohibiting students from operating their own well-connected smartphones, tablets, or computers during the school day—ostensibly because of the potential for disruption or inability to control what kids might be doing. Sadly, as Cuban (1986) pointed out decades ago, technology historically rarely touches the core of teaching and schooling, but instead lingers around the periphery, supporting but not changing the core of what happens in classrooms.

Investing in technology in schools is another duck-and-cover idea. There is no question that technology is certainly powerful, with the ability to dramatically transform society and human living. It also has the potential to transform education, but the transformation of education cannot be realized until and unless education transforms itself. Today's technology could make education look and operate differently but it has failed to do so, not because technology does not have the power, but because schools, for various reasons, duck and cover, have chosen not to change. While technology offers the potential to support a different kind of education, it cannot turn education into something new unless systems are willing to reconsider what they do and how they do it, and make significant change. Thus, no matter how powerful technology is and how much of an investment we make, education will likely be the same as it was 30 or 50 years ago for a number of reasons.

First, schools are in an education system or multiple systems that have multiple stakeholders. In the United States, a school technically belongs to a local community-based district, which is run by a school board that hires the superintendent and makes all sorts of policies. But the district is not truly independent. Financially, the district may be able to raise its own funds from local taxes in some states, but in other states, the money comes from the state based on complex formulas, which collects and redistributes taxes. The federal government also affects school finances through grants, awards, and money for special education and other targeted populations. Legally speaking, schools have to implement curriculum or curriculum standards created by the state, hire teachers licensed by the state, administer state exams to students, and follow various other laws passed at the state level. At the same time, schools have to be sensitive to college and university admissions requirements because K–12 is supposedly preparing students for colleges—at least for the majority of their students, as college attendance is considered the ultimate endgame by many students and parents. In addition, schools have to respond to the local community, which has its own culture and expectations. Moreover, schools exist to serve many functions for the community beyond teaching. For example, they provide food for some students and are the primary source for mental health services for many.

Schools support numerous business organizations with vested financial interests. Textbook publishers rely on schools, so do test-making companies. Technology hardware companies sell computers and other devices to schools, which also buy software and connectivity. Schools buy furniture, and plenty of supplies. Schools also hire consultants of all sorts to give them advice on a variety of things. Besides businesses, schools hire teachers prepared by colleges or schools of education, which also provide professional training and advanced degree programs for teachers and administrators who wish to go beyond a bachelor's degree. The majority of colleges or schools of education exist solely because of schools, primarily preparing future employees, much as educational researchers rely on the existence of schools as the focus for their research. In many ways it is a very incestuous system, with powerful disincentives built in for making drastic changes.

Schools directly affect the life of millions. There are over 50 million K–12 students and more than 3 million teachers in American public schools. There are also thousands of school leaders: superintendents, deputy superintendents, building principals and deputy principals, curriculum directors, staff development directors, and many other different titles such as technology director, director of budget, and human resources specialist. For these individuals, dramatic changes that might affect their work have serious consequences and certainly heightens resistance.

All the people directly or indirectly connected to schools have a default image of what schools should be, due to their own experience with schools. All parents, for example, are armchair quarterbacks when it comes to schooling since they all experienced schools first-hand. They also rely on schools for cheap childcare during the workday. Even students, after a very short period of time in school at a very young age, quickly adopt an image tied to continuity. So all people expect schools to be certain way. The most typical model of schooling is that students are split into groups or classes according to their age, each class has one teacher teaching in a didactic relationship with the students they manage, each class is in a classroom, and all students in the same class learn, or are taught, pretty much the same thing. A school day, most notably at the middle and secondary levels, is split into a certain number of periods, each about 40 to 50 minutes long. School curriculum is based on a number of subjects according to their state prescription or standards. Educational historians David Tyack and Larry Cuban call the typical school image the grammar of schooling in their book *Tinkering Toward Utopia: A Century of Public School Reform* (Tyack & Cuban, 1995). The grammar of schooling was first discussed in 1994 by Tyack and Tobin in their article "The 'Grammar' of Schooling: Why Has It Been So Hard to Change?" which powerfully explains how this common grammar makes schools so difficult to change (Tyack & Tobin, 1994).

There is much benefit to have schools conform to the default image of schools. Teachers, who likely entered the field because they liked what they experienced in their school days, have gone through schools and are taught in colleges about schools, have the comfort of going into familiar conditions, basically the same schools with the same arrangement. Parents know what to expect when they send their children to school. Government officials and the public feel good when schools operate like their schools or the schools in mind and in experience. As Ginsberg (1995) suggested, changing what happens in classrooms and schools is akin to a religious conversion for the teachers and others who work there. Any major transformation of the grammar of schooling is a significant departure from the norms and understanding they carry, and much like religious conversion, a radical change few ever choose to undertake.

Besides psychological benefit, there are also ensured financial benefits for the ones involved in school business. Education is among the largest industries in the United States. In 2022, there were about 51 million elementary and secondary school students in the United States and the average per-pupil spending was $14,891. That's a lot of money! Staff salaries take a huge chunk of this money, and other businesses—from textbook publishers to hardware and software manufacturers, from educational consultants to insurance companies, and from furniture makers to test makers—all make money from schools. But their way of making the money is largely tied to the default model of schooling because their products were created based on that model.

Thus, if school practices change dramatically or if schools become something different, the majority of people involved with schools will become uncomfortable, disoriented, and have to make changes in themselves, which is challenging. Those who make money from schools will also have to make new products based on the need of the changed school. This can be more than simple inconvenience, but revolutionary. This is why schools are so difficult to change!

Second, schools are also hard to change because our society values credentials. Almost every institution or business requires, often as the first item on the job announcement, a degree, which is granted by schools. A high-school diploma is necessary for many jobs, and colleges are, among other things, credentialing mills, providing the piece of paper necessary for entry to many positions and fields. Some professions require advanced schooling beyond four years of college. So going through school often begets going to more school. When a person has more competencies and experiences than what is required by a job, that can create obstacles. But without the right credentials, it is very unlikely that he or she is offered the job.

Consequently, there are specific systematic pressures to keep schools the way they are. They have to have grades that fit into different levels—kindergarten, elementary, middle or junior high, high school, college, and post-graduate school, based on the age of pupils. Although there is no scientific evidence that supports such divisions, students are all organized following the same model. There is also no scientific evidence that schools must be arranged into 12 grades plus kindergarten, and indeed the system varies by a year or so in different countries. Sahlberg (2018), for example, the

Finnish scholar, suggests that the best age to start formal schooling is seven, a full two years after most American kids jump in. If governments wanted, the length of K–12 education could become 14 or 10 years, not the current 12. Of course, major changes like that would face the need for changing state constitutions or legislation, as well as the wrath of multiple groups, including the accrediting agencies that govern both pre-K-12 and higher education. But except for a very small number, the majority of students go through different levels around the same age in order to get the proper credential, which gives them the ticket and opportunity to find a job.

Third, technology is purchased and deployed to support schools, not to transform schools. One of the most popular software applications used in schools, for example, is PowerPoint, which basically allows teachers to present their content like they would on a traditional blackboard. Teachers may use Google or YouTube to look for content related to their courses, but again the use is closely connected to what they want to teach. Software to manage students' attendance, grades, and disciplinary behaviors is also popular. In many cases, schools allow parents to access the software to check on their students. Technology is also used for financial purposes and human resource reasons. Students and teachers may communicate with each other using technology such as email and social media. But by and large, technology is not used in any way that shows its transformative power.

A great example is Kahn Academy, in many ways an impressive warehouse of videos and offerings across a multitude of subjects and grades broken down into small bites or lessons by topic and grade. But the videos include pictures, or in some lessons an image of a hand writing on a board with voice layover, presenting the lessons using arguably the weakest pedagogy imaginable. Would your kids sit still if their teachers spent entire lessons with their backs to the class talking to their hands while facing the wall? Or showing pictures and just talking nonstop for minutes at a time? For sure, Kahn Academy is an impressive array of subjects and lessons. But it isn't transformative of what is happening in schools in any sense—perhaps it is a great supplement for what teachers are already doing or provides clarity or practice for students who need support, yet it's nothing radically different in pedagogy or approach, cultivating or harnessing the immense potential for technology to do so.

When technology enters schools, very few teachers, school leaders, and policymakers think that it is to transform education, despite the potential power of technology. They all are typically thinking about different ways to enhance what is already happening in schools. This is logical and, given how we have described the environment, quite predictable. Even today, the so-called powerful artificial intelligence (AI) is often used to control students, for instance to monitor if they are paying attention to the teacher. AR and VR technology is also used to better teach students the curriculum in the classroom, but again, in traditional ways with some fancy techie stuff infused.

Fourth, however, some innovations do happen, though these typically haven't been technology-based. There have been numerous people who are unhappy about schools as they are. Many have proposed and even tried to run schools differently but inevitably they fail to spread or survive for long. Montessori education has existed for more than 100 years, but it remains on the periphery of options for kids. The Summer Hill school has also been in existence for nearly a century and has inspired many democratic schools, but it is far from being popular. We have also had the Dalton Plan and Dalton schools that run schools differently—an approach that has failed to enter the mainstream in education. Many lesser-known innovations have been piloted. An example is the Bridge Academy in Los Angeles, which is devoted to twice-exceptional children and adopts a strength-based educational approach. It also runs a graduate school of cognitive diversity in education. But again, it is a small operation that is unlikely to enter public education.

Ironically, the innovative schools look for recognition from the traditional schools and the overarching traditional systems. They want to be accredited by traditional accreditation agencies. They want to show that their students can get good grades and high test scores and be admitted to prestigious colleges. In essence, no matter what the innovation, students and parents still have to comply with societal demands—going to college or proving that their alternative is as good as or better than the students in public schools.

It is unbelievable that the powerful technology has not released its power in education. Seymour Papert, former MIT professor and author of influential books such as *Mindstorms* (Papert, 1993b) and *The Children's Machine* (Papert, 1993a), once commented on the relationship between technology and schools. His analogy is that schools are like a horse wagon and technology is a jet engine. When you connect the jet engine to a horse wagon, you either have to stop the engine or crash the horse wagon (Papert, 1999). Basically, the power of technology cannot be truly realized in the current or traditional schools. Given the power of schools and teachers, which typically make technology do what they already do, as former Stanford professor Larry Cuban observed, there is really no use of technology in schools (Cuban, 1986, 1993).

Given this powerful set of forces and reality driving what Lortie (1975) referred to in his landmark study of teachers as the conservative proclivities built into aspects of education, technology as it has been employed are duck-and-cover policies and practices. Great intentions, widespread, in many cases helpful, in all cases incredibly expensive, in some ways rather useless. Its use needs to change, or the investments dramatically curtailed.

RECONSIDER, REMOVE, REPLACE

So what can we do? We have to think about investing so much in technology because it does not really change the traditional school that much. This is not saying that technology has no use because it certainly has facilitated access to information and materials, made presentations more interesting and colorful, and improved management of students' data. In many schools, it has opened up student performance and classroom activity to parents. However, the impact of technology has been very small in terms of both traditional educational outcomes such as test scores and the larger potential for actually changing schools. Or if we want to invest more in technology, we need to undertake transformative ways to change schools so that technology can realize its power.

During the universal experiment with remote learning throughout the COVID-19 pandemic, schools and teachers showed tremendous courage. Without training or much preparation, they taught online. This shows that schools can change. While the change did not necessarily make for better education, although the vehicle for delivery of instruction was altered, the fundamentals of schooling didn't change much. That really is regrettable. However, as schools return to in-person education, many schools are ignoring remote learning. Instead of learning from the various innovations and possible benefits of remote learning, schools are eager to return to normal (Zhao, 2021a). There is much we can learn from the remote learning during the pandemic to change schooling. Here are some brief points for consideration:

First, does learning have to be organized in the traditional way? Can students organize their own learning? Today, technology definitely has the power to bring learning resources and experts/teachers from all over the world to students. The pandemic has shown that students do not need to be with their peers and teachers in order for learning to happen. Thus, why not allow students to be the center of learning and organize their own learning? If students can organize their own learning and if we allow them to organize their own learning, at least partly, schools do not then have to be the same as before. They can remove the idea of classes, for example. Instead, schools can organize students based on their individual interests and assign them advisors. Schools do not then have to have grades. Instead, students follow their passion and abilities and develop their learning pathways (Zhao, 2021b).

Second, do teachers have to teach all the time? If students can access resources and experts online globally, the teacher no longer needs to be the only source of learning and perhaps does not need to teach as much (Zhao, 2018). Instead, the teacher becomes an advisor, a mentor, a coach, and a resource curator for each individual student. The local teacher provides social and emotional support and encouragement to students.

Third, does school have to be in one physical building? If learning is global and teachers play different roles, do students have to be in one physical building all the time? Can they formulate online and global learning communities? Can they participate in global peer-tutoring and peer-supporting (Aragon et al., 2019; Elmore, 2011)?

A final point needs be highlighted as well. While the pandemic certainly offered a brief snapshot of the potential for change and the incredible ability for teachers, school leaders, and students to adjust, it also exacerbated some of the inequities already present in schools. Some kids got lost, many didn't have Wi-Fi or other kinds of access, not everyone had the right equipment. All solvable dilemmas, but part of the reality in moving to a technology-driven space.

We offer these ideas of ways for reconceptualizing what we do in the name of better education. There may be other more inspiring and trans-formative ways to go about using technology for change. There may be better approaches to have technology alter the standard cognitive processes employed in the student–teacher learning paradigm. But our point is simple. Having this tremendous technology used in such uninspiring and non-innovative ways is a tragic waste of potential. So school leaders, teachers, students, and community members should either stop wasting huge sums of money on minimalistic technology uses that are typically just structural add-ons or figure out ways to truly transform the work.

Part II

OPERATIONAL BUGABOOS

CHAPTER 8

Professional Development

A few years ago, one of us was appointed to a term on the Continuing Legal Education Council (CLE) in Kansas, responsible for approving professional development for lawyers that is required annually for license renewal. Most states have a CLE, in Kansas the board reviews providers and programs, the number of hours to be awarded for training, and so on. The board is made up of attorneys, law school faculty, a judge or justice, and one non-attorney, all appointed by the state supreme court. At the first meeting of the CLE board that was attended, after thoroughly reviewing all the guidelines, standards, and so on, the one of us there asked a simple social scientific assessment kind of question: Does the continuing legal education make a difference? When asked by one of the attorneys what that means, the response was easy: "Does the required professional development make the lawyers better lawyers?" A room full of highly legally trained professionals sat there with glazed, deer-in-headlights expressions on their faces for what seemed like several minutes, until one finally said, "Well, no. We don't know. That is why we need someone like you on the board!"

So there you have it. It is frankly unknown if the professional development required by nearly every state for lawyers to annually renew their licenses has any impact. The amount of hours they must take is specified by law and clearly documented. Sometimes topics are specified. A quick review of legal literature suggests that despite the requirements for continuing legal education, there is little research on the topic, and no research-based consensus on its value. No doubt the legal profession is chock full of duck-and-cover policies and practices, too!

Professional development, ongoing training for any professional, is intuitively logical. Keeping up with the field, getting training to maintain and advance skills, all makes sense. Especially in those fields where technologies can rapidly change—for example, in some medical specialties—the need for ongoing training is obvious. No computer programmer would last very long if all they knew was Cobol, or BASIC, or Fortran, and not C, or Java, or Python. The implementation of new programs, processes, or approaches in any field naturally demand some kind of professional development and training.

In our world of education, most districts and schools provide teachers with professional development throughout the school year. Annual school calendars often have days set aside for this. Sadly, teachers, probably like all professionals, complain about a lot about the professional development they receive—easy to confirm, just ask them! Torff & Sessions (2009) simply observed that professional development doesn't have "a lofty reputation" (p. 67). As Richardson (2003) explained: "Most of the staff development that is conducted for K–12 teachers derives from the short-term transmission model; pays no attention to what is already going on in a particular classroom, school, or school district; offers little opportunity for participants to become involved in the conversation; and provides no follow-up" (p. 401). Guskey (2000) went further, criticizing much of the professional development offered as lacking any scientific base and being faddish in nature.

While professional development for teachers should be beneficial if done right—implemented well, with necessary support and follow-up, and respect for the teachers being "developed"—it appears that what is typically done is meaningless. Duck and cover, another school practice with great intentions that needs to be thoughtfully altered or dropped off at the local junk yard as a waste of precious time, money, and energy. In fact, The New Teacher Project (TNTP, 2015) found that the districts they studied spent, on average, $18,000 per teacher per year on what they called teacher support spending—salary incentives for improved performance, the costs of instructional leadership development, and select data strategy expenditures. The largest share of those costs, according to their report, "is in the salaries and other costs related to teachers and the hundreds of people who provide instructional support at all levels of the district" (p. 10). It isn't clear exactly the dollar amount per teacher spent on direct professional development. But it is significant. Indeed, they estimated that this means that the 50 largest school districts in the country spend at least $8 billion a year on professional development–related activity, with teachers devoting nearly 10% of a typical year on these activities. This number certainly inflates the actual dollars spent on typical professional development activities in schools. But the dollars and time spent even on regular teacher PD are clearly significant. But sadly, despite the huge sum of dollars TNTP project calculated, the research found that while some individual teachers improved, there was no evidence that any particular format or amount of professional development consistently helps teachers to improve.

What is professional development? Judith Warren Little (1987) defined it as, "any activity that is intended partly or primarily to prepare paid staff members for improved performance in present or future roles in school districts" (p. 491). This, of course, allows for a wide array of activities to be considered professional development. Scholars have identified an array of things that fall under the umbrella of what is called professional development— for example, workshops, conferences, classes, interactions with colleagues, study groups, learning communities, etc. (Birman et al., 2000; Desimone, 2009; Garet et al., 2001; Guskey & Yoon, 2009). Some approaches, like the work in the United States developed for the National Board for Professional

Teacher Standards (NBPTS), has shown promise for teachers (a form of national, rather than state licensure, recognition). While the NBPTS process is time consuming and expensive, many teachers report that the practice it entails, the use of video tapes to analyze instructional practice, and other aspects of the program are a great form of professional development (Ginsberg & Herrmann-Ginsberg, 2005; Lustick & Sykes, 2006).

The irony is that researchers have studied professional development for years. Guskey & Yoon (2009) described the work performed by the American Institutes for Research (AIR) which analyzed findings from over 1,300 studies to address the effect of professional development on student learning outcomes. This was a study funded by the U.S. Department of Education (Yoon et al., 2007). One discouraging finding was that only nine, yes nine, of the original 1,343 studies they reviewed met the standards of credible evidence established by the U.S. Department of Education's "What Works Clearinghouse." Guskey and Yoon (2009) concluded, "Obviously, these findings paint a dismal picture of our knowledge about the relationship between professional development and improvements in student learning" (p. 497). Similarly, Heather Hill (2009), from Harvard, put it this way, "The professional development 'system' for teachers is, by all accounts, broken" (p. 470).

That said, over the years, a consensus of what actually does work has emerged. Desimone (2009), confirmed by a number of other analyses (e.g., Birman et al., 2000; Desimone et al., 2002; Garet et al., 2001; Thomas, 2013), has drawn from an array of studies to identify five components of successful professional development:

- Focusing on content—both subject matter and how students learn—what some refer to as content pedagogy.
- Promoting active learning—observing, providing feedback and correctives, include both discussion and reflection. Indeed, Hattie (2012) has argued that feedback, when presented correctly, is the most powerful element for increasing student learning. It likely follows that similar forms of appropriate feedback are necessary for professional development of teachers to be effective.
- Assuring professional development is both coherent and aligned with teacher work and needs, their knowledge and beliefs, as well as local district and state needs.
- Allowing for sufficient time (duration of professional development) spread over a sensible period of time (e.g., 20+ days are suggested as a minimum).
- Having participation be collective—for example having teachers from schools, departments, etc., work in collaboration.

Similarly, Timperley (2005) argued for a focus on student learning (rather than, say, working conditions) and identified several elements for successful professional learning: working to create shared values and expectations about students, focusing on student learning, strong faculty collaboration, deisolating teaching practice, and allowing for reflection among teachers and professionals.

Some of the current trends that have evolved over the years have become part of the professional development landscape. Coaching and peer coaching have been in active use for decades. Trained instructional coaches work with teachers to set and reach goals around student and classroom improvement (Cornett et al., 2009; Heineke, 2013; Knight, 2007). Coaches can serve a variety of roles in schools, with Killion and Harrison (2006) identifying ten primary ones. The importance of an effective coaching program and cycle is emphasized (Knight et al., 2015). The use of video recording of classes is highlighted by Knight (2014) as key for monitoring how well teachers are implementing various teaching strategies. Kraft et al. (2018) reviewed the literature on teacher coaching and affirmed its potential as a development tool, though they cautioned that scaling up the practice effectively faces challenges such as having enough high-quality coaches attached to teachers' individual needs, along with challenges of getting teacher buy-in.

Many schools deliver professional development to teachers through professional learning communities or PLCs (DuFour, 2004). Derived from business, these communities focus on the capacity for organizational learning to occur. Bolam et al. (2005) defined a PLC as a community "with the capacity to promote and sustain the learning of all professionals in the school community with the collective purpose of enhancing student learning" (p. 145). A comprehensive review of the research on PLCs (Vescio et al., 2007) argued that well-designed PLCs have a positive impact on both teaching practice and student achievement. Certainly, there is a wide spectrum of effectiveness of PLCs across schools and districts, as they typically function differently and focus on varying issues from place to place. As DuFour (2004) explained it, the term professional learning community has been used to describe "every imaginable combination of individuals with an interest in education" (p. 6).

Clearly, examples can be drawn of instances where professional development was effective. But what remains so frustrating is that effective professional development appears so spotty that its continued use has to be questioned. We posit several reasons for the paradox that we know what works regarding professional development, but just can't seem to do it right on a consistent basis anyway.

First, teachers are busy, overworked, underpaid, and criticized all the time. Having time to learn something new and use it effectively is challenging and very time-consuming. Oftentimes, new leaders come along and push their favorite ideas. When this happens, the implication to teachers is like going to the doctor when one is ill—in this case, the message to teachers is: "You don't know what you are doing, so take this pill and get better." Teacher buy-in is a necessary ingredient for any new practice to work, and as Kraft et al. (2018) highlighted, especially for a mandatory practice, it is always hard to get. We recently met with some teachers who felt patronized by their recent professional development experience, as there were ongoing spot checks making sure people were paying attention. As one put it, "they treat us like elementary students, not professionals." This is not a good formula for getting buy-in.

Second, as Guskey (2000) underscored, so much professional development comes on the heels of the new reform du jour spreading across the land like a wildfire. How well tested or research-based any reform might be is often unknown. Anyone working in schools knows that teachers often figure that if they are patient enough, they can wait out any new reform, then ultimately get back to what they find works best. The new practice and the professional development associated with it can't be seen as frivolous and be ineffective.

Third, as is true of any reform implementation, monitoring professional development effectiveness is hard once teachers are back in the classroom ostensibly carrying out what they learned. Teaching is typically an isolated activity, where once in the classroom behind closed doors, it is difficult to judge what the teachers are actually doing. So fidelity of implementation is always a concern. If something is new and different, coaching and mentoring in the classroom are needed, and this can't be just minimal spot checks.

Finally, effective professional development, as Desimone (2009) highlighted, needs multiple factors to be in sync in order to be effective. It needs be done over time, not a quick, hear-the-expert kind of approach. It requires collaboration, buy-in, being imbedded in practice, and an array of variables that all too often are ignored. Even within tried-and-true approaches like peer coaching and PLCs, there is a wide continuum of effectiveness.

Professional development has become a big business. Many professionals make a career of giving advice. Oftentimes, outside experts are brought in to wax eloquent on the latest and greatest new approach. School and district curriculum may be changed. New technology or software brought aboard. Even new kinds of furniture and classroom space patterns developed. All require buy-in, training, mentoring, and ongoing support. Truth be told, duck and cover, it doesn't happen very often.

RECONSIDER, REMOVE, REPLACE

School districts and schools spend a lot of money on professional development. Entire journals are dedicated to the practice; many experts—some real, others self-proclaimed—make enormous sums of money traveling the circuit and sharing their pearls of wisdom. It makes sense. Education is important, and we want teachers and leaders to improve and students to have the best outcomes possible.

We aren't calling for an end to professional development. Instead, we are suggesting an end to nonsense, practices that aren't tested or evaluated, and spending money and time on things that have no known likelihood for impact. Good professional development takes time and needs to be done well. School leaders need to be respectful of the teachers in the schools and not throw untested, unsubstantiated time-consuming work at the professionals they work with. Even the very critical TNTP (2015) report suggested inventorying current professional development practices, evaluating effectiveness of what is done, considering alternative approaches, and reallocating funds based on what actually works.

Professional development as currently employed is a quintessential duck-and-cover policy. Done for the best of reasons, done with the right goals in tow, and done really badly in the majority of instances. It screams out for change. Wasting time and money in education the way we have should be considered the equivalent of a crime. Something has to give. We suggest school leaders and school districts do the following:

- Reconsider what you do in the name of professional development. Sometimes teachers' time may be better spent on their own work rather than on useless or unelated professional development activities that they are forced to attend.
- Determine exactly how much is being spent on teacher professional development per year. Unlikely it is anything near the $18,000 per teacher figure set out by the TNPT (2015) estimates, but it likely is pretty significant. Given the lack of impact of professional development so widely reported (understanding if done well this might change), we suggest pulling out a chunk of the money and just raising teachers' salaries with it. Lord knows they don't earn enough for the work they do. The added funds might actually help with recruitment planning.
- Be certain that any professional development offered has a sound basis behind it. Real research, not advocacy reports or proclamations in the guise of research from the presenter or creator. Home remedies are often just nonsense based on folklore. So is much of what we do in the name of professional development is well-intended junk. Do your homework. Make sure what is being asked of teachers or those being trained has value. There is so much isomorphism in education where districts just copy what their colleague districts have done. It often comes right after someone attends a professional meeting. Good to be exposed to new things. But check them out. Make sure something works first, and it fits your circumstances.

- Understand the components of what works in professional development. There is a lot to it. Develop your professional development plan based on the best-known science in the field, recognizing that what fits each circumstance may differ.
- Early-career teachers need a lot of mentoring and support. Figure out what kinds of professional development would be most effective for them. Here is a way to do that—ask them. They generally know the areas where they feel the most challenged and at risk. Some kind of standard surveying of early-career teachers in terms of their professional development needs might help. And understand that whatever is offered follows the tenets of the identified best approaches.
- In some instances, enable teachers to design their own professional development. Teachers understand better what they are interested in and what they need. Schools or districts can distribute professional development funds to individual teachers and/or teacher organizations such as teacher unions to support their pursuit of professional development.
- Assess, assess, assess, and provide feedback and assistance.

CHAPTER 9

Class Size

When the colonists came to America and forged the path to a new country, education in the initial settlements was derived from the medieval past, with few formal institutions, as the family was the primary instrument for transferring culture (Bailyn, 1972). Education came from many fronts, even as more formal schools evolved across the colonies. For example, both apprenticeships and tutoring were part of the landscape for ways to learn and be schooled.

Perhaps it is from these roots that the intuitive belief in having smaller classes, with more individualized attention, emerged. Today, smaller class sizes are desired by almost everyone. Parents want their children to have more attention in smaller classes. Teachers want to teach smaller classes so they can give more attention to individual students and provide more in-depth feedback in assessing smaller numbers of assignments and papers. There is generalized agreement that kids will learn better in smaller classes. Think about how small, liberal arts colleges market and promote their supposed advantage of smaller classes and greater individualized attention. It is intuitively attractive and makes sense. But intervening variables pop up and make this more complex than might meet the eye. One obvious reason is that smaller classes are more expensive because of the costs of teachers, classrooms, and equipment. At a time of challenged school budgets in many places across the country, the likelihood of small classes, especially classes with significant declines in classroom enrollment, is pretty unrealistic. Simply put, not all schools can have very small classes.

Class sizes vary a great deal from country to country. A typical class in the United States and some developed countries has about 20 to 25 students (published American class-size numbers are often misleading in terms of the actual numbers of students in each class due to reporting vagaries), while a typical class in some other countries has 40 to 70 students. Ironically, countries with larger classes often do better in international assessments. The oft-stated truism about the benefits of smaller class size obviously isn't necessarily true at all. Multiple variables need be considered. Even then, who knows what the true impact is or if it differs by student, subject, grade level, and so on? For example, classes in China are much larger, twice or three times the size of classes in the United States, but Chinese students have performed much better than American students on international test comparisons. But are Chinese students better prepared for all the aspects of life an education might offer? Duck and cover, the whole subject of class size is laden with confusion.

The question of the effects of class size has become a point of contention for policymakers, researchers, schools, and teachers. Does class size matter? This seemingly simple question has been argued among numerous educational researchers, policymakers, and teachers for a long time (Shen & Konstantopoulos, 2021). Abundant research has been conducted. Numerous meetings have been held. Professional groups and pundits have written reports and waxed eloquent on their idiosyncratic findings from one study to the next. Many policies have been developed in relation to how many students can and should be in a class. Class-size changes have been implemented by schools, districts, and states. It is no exaggeration to say that class size has become one of the most important issues in educational research, policy, and practice.

One interesting tidbit in the class-size movement is that specifically how the size of classes is determined really matters and isn't consistent. Some studies consider the ratio of students to teachers, others use a mathematical approach dividing the number of teachers and/or other part-time teaching workers or professionally licensed staff into the total number of students as part of the calculation. What results is a mixed bag of reality, with some approaches dramatically driving down the averages of class sizes that result. As one New Zealand newspaper reported after examining the OECD Study of Education at a Glance (PPTA, 2022), teachers wondered how the average of 14 was determined, when their classes were typically larger by 12 to 16 students. So inconsistencies exist in how class size is determined, whether a mathematical average or pupils per teacher is a consideration, and when averages are calculated, who is being counted as professional staff impacts the number derived. In many cases, when class sizes are calculated, the different techniques result in two numbers being derived for class size, and often the numbers aren't very similar. Moreover, as is the case whenever averages are used, they are prone to inaccuracy given that outliers can skew the results. Likely reporting medians would correct this, but that isn't common. As an example of just one complicating consideration, one key study concluded that it is more important to have fewer students in a class, rather than more students with a teaching assistant, even though adding the teaching assistant drives down the average number of students (Finn & Achilles, 1990). That said, few special-education teachers would give up their paraprofessionals (additional adults who work with sometimes challenging students). The point is, class size isn't as simple as the concept may appear.

Nonetheless, the whole question of the impact of class size seems to be very important for policymakers and practitioners in education, mostly as they strive to find that silver bullet to move us down the path to educational nirvana. If class size matters, it appears that educational policies should find ways to reduce class sizes so that teachers can have a better impact on students. If it does not, class sizes can be large and educational funding can be spent elsewhere; teachers can teach fewer classes, albeit large ones. To find the answer, educational researchers must then study the effects of class sizes.

But, duck and cover, questions about class size don't have simple answers, and the research has been all over the place. The concept assuredly sounds like an interesting idea that can have significant policy and practical consequences. But the complexity of education makes it impossible to have a definite answer that is true in all educational contexts. As a result, it is no surprise that decades of research on class size have not yielded consistent findings. Research has reported the benefits of small classes, which can boost students' academic achievement both in the short term and long term (Biddle & Berliner, 2002; Fredriksson et al., 2013). Research has also provided evidence that the short-term and long-term effects do not exist for smaller classes (Hanushek, 1999). Other studies suggest that the effects of size may vary in different educational systems (Shen & Konstantopoulos, 2021; Woessmann & West, 2006). In other words, decades of research cannot provide any certainty in answering the question regarding size.

As suggested, the reason for the lack of certain answers is simple. Education is a complex phenomenon. There are many factors that affect student learning, which can also be measured in different ways. Different curricula may require varying approaches. The impact of a multitude of other factors may be much larger than class size alone. How learning is measured also plays a significant role. Several considerations obviate why class size falls into the duck-and-cover zone.

First, many class-size research studies use student test scores and/or grades as the measure of learning. If test scores and grades are primarily based on students' memorization of information, class size may not matter at all because teachers can pass information on for students to memorize no matter how large the class is. There are education systems with fairly large classes in which teachers often use a microphone to teach large numbers of students who perform well on standardized tests nonetheless. However, if the measurement is deep understanding, creative problem solving, and/ or critical thinking, smaller classes likely would do better because students need individual attention from the teacher. They also need the flexibility of time and space to work on problems independently or in collaboration with others with the personalized guidance and support from teachers. This is why education systems and education culture matter a lot more than class size as an independent reform. In education systems where the evaluation or assessment focuses mostly on how well students can regurgitate what has been taught to them in class, and listening and remembering what the teachers tell them is paramount, then large classes can work well. But if the system wants students to become independent critical thinkers and creative and entrepreneurial individuals, smaller classes where students can be guided to apply their learning or learn to solve problems, perhaps even collaboratively in teams, may work better.

Second, teachers matter a great deal in student learning. Teacher effectiveness must be recognized (Darling-Hammond, 2009), but we also need to consider that teachers are different and they deliver effectiveness in different ways. There are highly effective teachers and very poor teachers. Perhaps teaching effectiveness may be driven for different individuals by the number of students in a class, but it also makes sense that many poor teachers will flounder delivering or facilitating highly effective learning no matter the size of the class. Of course, think of your own educational history: We're sure you'll recognize that there are some teachers who are much more effective in engaging students and explaining the subject matter content than others. There are also some who are a lot more effective in organizing students. Additionally, some are great at leading students into project-based inquiry learning. Some are excellent storytellers and information presenters, while others may be great at working with individual students. As a result, different teachers may perform differently in different sizes of classes. For instance, teachers who are great information presenters would do better in larger classes than those who are good at working with individual students. At the same time, teachers who are excellent at leading projects may do better in smaller classes. The point is, the concept of class size with smaller being better doesn't fit all teachers or the reality of schools.

Third, students play a significant role as well. They aren't passive players in this enterprise. Students have different personalities, talents, and perspectives of learning (Zhao, 2018b). Depending on the students and the composition of students, different sizes of classes may not matter at all. For instance, a small class of students who are not interested in the content of the class may not work nearly as effective as a large class where all students are deeply engaged with the content and the teacher. Similarly, student age may be an intervening factor. Colleges and universities, for example, have no qualms about filling large lecture halls with hundreds of students for courses in various subjects, but you rarely see 3rd-grade classes with the same structure. This doesn't mean that some younger students might not thrive in larger classes, just that maturity and development are considerations, too.

Fourth, what is being learned or the curriculum matters as well. If the curriculum is engaging and all students love it, a large class may not matter. If it is boring, no matter how small the class size, students may not be learning much. Related to that, there may be some subtle differences depending on the specific subject being taught. Might foreign language, mathematics, writing, any subject require different approaches than other subjects?

Fifth, teaching methods are another important factor. If teaching is simply giving a well-prepared lecture during which all students sit and listen, the size of the class may not matter nearly as much as when students are divided into project groups and conduct exploratory learning when project teams need the teacher's attention all the time. Likewise, project teams that are well developed and know where to get support and resources may not need as much attention from the teacher as new teams. Thus project-based learning does not necessarily need teachers all the time when resources are made available through other means, such as technology.

From a simple research perspective, it is very difficult to establish a causal relationship between class size and student achievement. A critical problem, according to Woessmann & West (2006), is that parents and schools make placement decisions that can affect the causal relationship. Parents may be interested in having their students in bigger classes because of the reputation of the school or class. A school district may sort students into different schools or classrooms based on their performance. Some schools also practice tracking, placing students in different classes according to their academic achievement. As Woessmann & West (2006) explain it:

> As a result, naïve estimates of education production functions may be biased both by endogeneity of class size with respect to student performance and by omitted variables. Estimating "true" class-size effects, i.e., the causal effect of class size on student performance, thus requires an identification strategy that restricts the analysis to exogenous variations in class size, thereby allowing for the causal class-size effect to be disentangled from the effects of sorting. (p. 695)

Such ideal conditions for research are almost impossible to have in education. More important, class size may be an issue that does not need data or debates to settle. We come to that conclusion for multiple reasons.

First, class size of course matters in certain circumstances. A class of 5 students is definitely better than a class of 50 or 500 students in many situations. It is possible that a class of 10 is perhaps better than a class of 20. But there are multiple issues to be considered—for example, issues around teacher availability and competency—to be able to teach in multiple arrangements.

Second, class size, of course, does not matter in other circumstances. A class of 30 is perhaps no different from a class of 50 or 500 because 30 individuals might be the limit a teacher can pay attention to in a class. Above some threshold, size likely becomes more and more irrelevant. Once the number of students reaches 30 or whatever the threshold is, size may not matter at all. For example, we've both given talks to audiences of thousands. We assume that some learning went on among the participants listening to our brilliant lectures, though no sense of what class/audience size makes for the greatest impact.

Third, the size of classes is driven by many variables, research not often being the primary or determining factor. Instead, issues like class size are mostly driven by funding and related resource issues such as teacher availability. Some private schools can afford to have small classes of about 10, but given typical funding patterns, public schools have to have classes of more than 20 in the United States. In developing countries, class sizes can go up to 60 or 70. In subjects facing teacher shortages, or regions across the country struggling to find qualified teachers, hiring enough staff to offer small class sizes is a luxury many can't afford. A noteworthy review of research produced by the Brookings Foundation (Chingos & Whitehurst, 2011) concluded that very few studies are of high enough quality to properly drive policy considerations. So, if they are to be believed, the research itself isn't very good. Moreover, they found that the research implied when class size mattered, large class-size reductions have to be made, roughly 7–10 fewer students. If true, duck and cover, the fiscal repercussions of making such significant reductions is no doubt beyond the financial ability of most school districts to consider.

RECONSIDER, REMOVE, REPLACE

Class-size reduction is an attractive-sounding remedy for what troubles many schools in terms of student performance, promulgated by well-meaning intentions. But when examined with a careful eye, it is revealed as a reform with so much nuance it just isn't practical in the majority of schools and districts. Another duck-and-cover policy, well intended, but lacking the substantial consideration of all it implies for both policy and practice. Perhaps it is better to simply drop the quibbling the research generates and the ongoing debate about class size prevalent in policy circles. Instead, we suggest other considerations for reconsidering the class size issue.

First, technology has changed so much that teachers are no longer the only source of information for students. The interest in the effect of class size is at least partly based on the idea of a class where an adult individual, the teacher, holds the knowledge and must be the only one to pass that knowledge to all students. Thus the smaller the class, the easier a teacher can manage the class and ensure all students listen and learn. But with broad access to technology and its expanding sources of learning, the role of the teacher can be changed from instructing to supporting students' growth (Zhao, 2018a; McDiarmid & Zhao, 2022). When students learn from technology-enabled resources, the role of the teacher becomes more a facilitator than an instructor. Instead, the teacher becomes a personal coach and can develop a plan to work with individual students. Helping teachers adjust to these realities, with training and support, is likely a more appropriate undertaking than just focusing on large-scale class-size reductions.

Second, classes do not need to be the only way to organize students. With all the advances in technology and cognitive science, schools have historically organized students into classes and that is still the typical arrangement even today. Walking into a classroom in 2022 wouldn't likely look and feel all that different than in 1922. A teacher is assigned to teach a class for a certain period of time, usually 40 to 50 minutes, perhaps longer depending on grade level or scheduling approach (e.g., more modern block scheduling). But this does not have to be the only way. There are schools that organize students into project groups co-taught by a group of teachers. The historic approach of individual teachers in a didactic relationship with often passive students has evolved to some degree, but teaching remains what Lortie (1975) described as being characterized by separation and low-task interdependence among teachers. This need not be the norm. When students are not organized into individual classes assigned to one teacher, the effect of class sizes is even more difficult to detect.

Third, policymakers need to understand that teachers matter and the teacher–student ratio matters despite the mixed conclusions the research suggests about impacts on student test score results. That is, if we have more adults per younger students in a school, the learning results should be better, especially if assessed more broadly than is common practice today. Closer relations, greater personal support, mentoring—multiple things need be considered without necessarily focusing on reduced class size for all students as the key issue. What the class-size obsession doesn't capture is the importance of multiple kinds of supports and opportunities for learning that may be outside the formal classroom structure and typical interactions as we know them. Thus, if possible at all, financial challenges aside, we should reduce the adult–student ratio without relying on class-size research, which has provided minimal guidance over a long period of activity.

Fourth, some scholarship shows that class size only matters when there are higher-quality teachers. Simply put, teachers matter. As Woessmann & West (2006) speculated following their review of class-size research in 11 countries, "it may be a better policy to devote the limited resources available for education to employing more capable teachers rather than to reducing class sizes" (p. 727).

Finally, if class sizes are to continue being calculated and shared publicly, a single approach to making these calculations should be widely used to correct for the disparities in approaches that exist. And moreover, report medians and not means, since that will provide a better representation of the true numbers of students teachers are teaching.

Overall, our point is that class size likely matters in some circumstances and not in others, with some students but not all. We really don't know many of the details. Teachers need be prepared for multiple roles and approaches. Offering students varying paths to learning rather than just focusing on the single issue of class size would provide greater payoff. Research might help with what subjects or approaches can allow students opportunities in differing arrangements. But the love affair with class size as the cure-all or significant ingredient for improving schools' needs is a duck-and-cover policy that has passed its expiration date.

CHAPTER 10

Time

Schools are obsessed with time. When to start and end the day, length of lessons and classes, how many days a week, how many months a year, start in August or September, end in May or June? What about the summer? One of our kids struggled mightily years ago because of timed tests. She didn't just need to answer so many addition and subtraction equations correctly, she had to do so within a specified amount of time. It was very anxiety producing. In schools, time matters.

Specifically considering school calendars, they haven't changed much in the United States over the past 100 years. Kids go to school for nine to ten months, typically for about 180 days, and are usually required to be in school for about six hours a day. The structure of time within classrooms has undergone some changes (e.g., not all elementary classrooms are self-contained, some high schools use block scheduling, etc.), but not all that much, and the time-related activity within the school day has steadfastly been rigid. Over the past many decades, astronauts have landed on the moon, cars became ubiquitous, air travel emerged, television became everyone's main vehicle for accessing news and entertainment, nuclear power and energy replaced steam and electricity to warm and cool our homes, antibiotics were developed to treat diseases, personal computers were introduced, social media became a thing . . . but schools follow the same schedule, from about 8:00 or 9:00 A.M. until 3:00 P.M., five days a week, summers off, weekends are sacrosanct. Pretty hard to believe given the advancements in science, technology, and many other fields in our rapidly changing culture that school calendars and schedules have remained so static. Time largely stood still in this regard for schools—ostensibly, duck and cover, because the developers of the school calendars and schedules hit the jackpot the first time they were set.

The big issues in the discussions about time are generally about school calendars, length of day, and the use of time for instruction. In our estimation, the entire issue of time falls into the duck-and-cover portfolio. For reasons hard to fathom, how time is employed in schools has steadfastly remained the same. Little changes sneak in, often not well conceived, but the school day, school year, classroom engagement practices, and related time issues all seem resistant to alteration. Concerns and challenges and fixes periodically pop up, but duck and cover, time literally stands still in schools.

Current school calendars have a long history and were built based on a variety of variables and conditions. While the agrarian nature of our culture in the late 19th and early 20th centuries was certainly part of it, the full story is a bit more nuanced. It is true that many students had to work on family farms during part of the summer, but that was also true during other times of the year. As Gold (2002, 2018) explained, there were fiscal concerns, medical concerns about crowded facilities, heat worries especially in the summer with people stuffed in overcrowded old facilities, even popular public pressure for breaks and vacations driving the schedules that developed. Standardization was important, especially in larger cities with multiple districts. Bottom line, no matter the exact causes, what emerged all those years ago continues today.

In the 19th and 20th centuries, when schools expanded with the flow of people into cities, what Tyack (1974) referred to as the one best system was organized. Efficiency concerns ruled the day, making certain that none of the school building remained idle (Callahan, 1962). Interestingly, as part of this push, some even suggested that schools stay open through the evenings and into the summer. One state superintendent in 1912 actually called for 12-month schooling. The plan largely failed, as Callahan (1962) explained: "the increased cost was the most important reason for this failure but it is possible that the children of America, who would have been the unwilling victims of this scheme, played a role in getting their parents to protest" (p. 128). National Child Labor advocacy groups also challenged the idea, calling for reverence to the importance of leisure for healthy childhoods.

Concerns regarding time in the late 19th and early 20th centuries continued in later decades, with the influential report, *A Nation at Risk*, raising the stakes, warning that "history is not kind to idlers" (National Commission on Excellence in Education, 1983, p. 2). The report argued that students in the United States spend far less time on schoolwork than in other nations, and time spent in the classroom and on homework was often used ineffectively. Time, whether related to school calendars or school-related work, was a matter of public discussion and debate.

As the 21st century was nearing, another national report emerged arguing that learning in America was handcuffed by time (National Education Commission on Time and Learning, 1994). Referring to the constraining ways time is utilized in schools, with the apt title of *Prisoners of Time*, this report suggested that:

> For the past 150 years, American public schools have held time constant and let learning vary. The rule, only rarely voiced, is simple: learn what you can in the time we make available. (p. 5)

A follow-up to this report 10 years later found that little had changed in the intervening decade. In fact, the report lamented that "the length of the school day and school year are virtually the same today as they were throughout the 20th century" (Education Commission of the States, 2005, p. 2). Laying the blame for past reform effort failures affecting student learning on time-related issues, the report pronounced that:

> [D]ecades of school improvement efforts have foundered on a fundamental design flaw, the assumption that learning can be doled out by the clock and defined by the calendar . . . our usage of time virtually assures the failure of many students. (p. 13)

Eight broad recommendations emerged, including the call to keep schools open longer during the day and year.

More recent advocacy groups and research studies continue to challenge the limiting time constraints schools have established. The National Center on Time & Learning released in 2015 its report *Case for Improving and Expanding Time in Schools* (Farbman, 2015). "The great irony," the report argued, "is that our nation's public school system, has by its rigid adherence to the conventional calendar of 180 six and a half hour days for roughly 100 years, essentially disregarded the fundamental connection between time and learning" (p. 1). This paper suggested that expanding time would allow for more engaged time in academic classes, more time for teacher collaboration and embedded professional development, and more time devoted to enrichment classes and activities. A key part of their case is that expanded time plays a role in improving student achievement, citing a review by Patall, Cooper & Allen (2010), that extending time can be effective in supporting student achievement for students most at risk for failure, when considerations are made for how time is actually used.

Clearly, challenges to the current school calendar and the use of time in school are not new. Over the years, some pockets of reform have been successful. For example, the growth of block scheduling in secondary schools— allowing for longer, more concentrated time for certain subjects certain days of the week—danced away from the prior adherence to classes typically lasting about 55 minutes for all classes and all subjects. Early proponents touted likely benefits and saw this innovation as a catalyst for change (Canady & Rettig, 1995). Others challenged the premises and argued for greater nuance by subject, teacher, and student in implementing any such changes (Thomas, 2001). More thorough research (Veal & Schreiber, 1999) and an analysis of 58 studies (Zepeda & Mayers, 2006) were cautionary, suggesting inconsistent findings and a troubling research base. In practice, changing the original conceptions about time met resistance. As Zepeda & Mayers (2006) concluded in their study on block scheduling:

> We did not get a sense that teachers were really changing their practices as a result of the implementation of the block schedule. Nor did we get a sense of how

student learning had changed, if at all . . . we found clues in the research that suggested that the implementation of block scheduling was worth examining." (p. 161)

Ironically, as with other duck-and-cover policies, block scheduling proliferated and is pretty ubiquitous across high schools in the United States today.

Related to this alteration of class time length and weekly class schedules, multiple lines of research focus on how time is used in classrooms. Here, the issue isn't solely the total amount of time available for instruction (the National Commission called for 5.5 hours daily for instruction on core subjects; National Educational Commission, 1994), but rather what is done with the time that is available. Research on time-on-task, student engagement time, and related variables emphasize that it is not just the length of time, but rather what is done with the time teachers have with students. Bloom (1974) differentiated between elapsed time and time-on-task, arguing that, "the amount of time the student spends on task in the classroom may be a powerful variable underlying . . . differences" (p. 687). Anderson (1976) slightly refined this to an understanding of what he called time-to-criterion. The Beginning Teacher Evaluation Study (BTES) developed a measure called Academic Learning Time (ALT), the amount of time a student engages in a task that is performed at a high level of success (Fisher et al., 1981). Stallings (1980) concluded from this work and various follow-up studies that teachers can be trained to use time effectively. Indeed, Berliner (1990) differentiated multiple concepts under what he referred to as the superordinate concept of "instructional time":

- Allocated time—the time allocated to instruction by school, state, etc.
- Engaged time—amount of time students appear to be paying attention
- Time-on-task—engaged time on a particular learning task
- Academic Learning Time (ALT)—that part of time allocated in a subject when students are successfully engaged to the materials exposed
- Transition time—noninstructional time before and after some activity
- Waiting time—time that a student must wait to get help
- Aptitude—amount of time needed to reach some criterion of learning
- Perseverance—amount of time a student is willing to spend on a learning task
- Pace—amount of content covered during some time period

What Berliner's work exposes is the complicated nature of the simple concept of time, and how within school and classroom variables are clearly important along with total time allotted during the day and year. But changes in how time is utilized have been slow to come.

As a duck-and-cover policy, seemingly impervious to significant alteration, time should be reconsidered for several reasons. First, as discussed earlier, time isn't a simple concept when it comes to schools, student learning, and student success. Longer isn't necessarily better, but how time is actually employed is the key. Finland and its success on international measures of student performance is a case in point. Sahlberg (2010) highlights the great paradox of this high-performing system, namely that they teach less but students learn more. Even homework is limited for students. As Sahlberg explains it, "the Finnish experience challenges the typical logic of educational development that tries to fix lower-than-expected student performance by increasing the length of education and duration of teaching" (p. 62). Instead, students are given more time to explore after-school activities or recreational clubs, "offering youth opportunities to participate in activities that support their overall learning and growth" (Sahlberg, 2010, p. 63). For teachers, it expands opportunities for working on school improvement activities, curriculum planning, and personal professional development during the school day. The key point is that time is a significant concept, but the simple notion that "more is better" must be couched in the reality that how time is used is most relevant for improving schools, teaching, and student performance.

Second, specifically regarding the school calendar, the National Association for Year-Round Education (NAYRE) has been promoting various year-round calendar designs for decades. They posit six benefits to a modified calendar—maintains student interest, different students need different configurations, with multiple breaks intercession classes could offer remediation or enrichment, second-language learning is benefited, co-curricular and extracurricular activities can take place throughout the year, and it allows for yearlong faculty development opportunities (Ballinger, n.d.). A 1994 study by the North Carolina Educational Policy Center at UNC Chapel Hill examined 20 years of year-round education (YRE) research, coming up with largely positive benefits regarding student learning, student attitudes, attendance drop-outs, and better attitudes, less absenteeism, and lower burnout for teachers (Worthen & Zsiray, Jr., 1994). Even parent attitudes were not seen as a barrier, and if done right, the report argues YRE could actually save money. More recent research showed slight academic increases in reading and math using a single YRE model (Fitzpatrick & Burns, 2019). Despite these potential benefits, the percentage of schools moving to yearlong calendars has remained low.

Third, research has lamented the problem of learning loss in the summer, what is often referred to as the "summer slide," a phenomenon in which some kids return to school in the fall having lost some of the achievement gains they held in the spring (Alexander et al., 2007). Some are skeptical of this conclusion, suggesting that the measures may not accurately capture what is happening (Hippel & Hamrock, 2019). Of course, the pandemic added another wrinkle to the time-and-learning-loss issues, as students were forced to be away from school during the academic year; the concept of time took on a whole new meaning when so many were remote, hybrid, or simply academically adrift. McKinsey & Company (Dorn et al., 2021) reported losses of five months in mathematics and four months in reading. Another study (Bailey et al., 2021) suggested equity impacts, with achievement gains for advantaged students .3 standard deviations higher in mathematics and .25 standard deviations higher in reading than for disadvantaged students. Demands to address the learning loss and the inequitable impacts created by school closings and online instruction due to the COVID-19 pandemic are powerful today and have risen high on policy agendas for reformers and politicians.

Fourth, with all the technology available today, the concept of time has taken on new meaning. Consider, for example, how many people work at home these days, using software like Zoom, Slack, and Microsoft Teams to connect with colleagues, making time considerations a whole new ball of wax. For adults, anyway, not everyone has to be in the office five days a week, eight hours a day. Do students really have to be engaged in classrooms the same way today as they were in the early 1900s? Technology affords multiple options.

Fifth, different configurations of schools and classrooms may drive new conceptions for time in schools. For example, the current divisions of subjects are old and treat subjects as if they were products on the shelves of grocery stores—math in aisle 6, English 5, Social Studies over by the meats in the freezer (see Ginsberg, 1997). Integrating subjects could be a game changer in how we conceptualize time for subjects in schools. Moreover, cross-subject project-based learning may not need to have class time organized in traditional ways, and students working in groups could change the formula as well.

Finally, there is growing evidence that starting school later in the day may be healthy for students at different developmental stages. The issue of sleep-deprived teenagers is emerging as a concern, with later school start among the remedies (Lewis, 2022). Even the medical community suggests that later start times might help address the issue for adolescents (Hansen et al., 2005). The implication is that the current daily calendar could use a fix.

Concerns about time in school for learning have persisted for over 100 years. While solutions for the time warp matter aren't easy, duck and cover, we've stayed with essentially the same model for over a century simply because we had the same model. The school calendar is sewn into the fabric of American culture. Something needs be done about this. It is a classic school puzzle that nobody seems able to solve, so we just continue to breathe life into what is and always has been. Or, framing this in the vernacular we've been using to describe duck-and-cover policies, we allow a patently ridiculous past-its-prime model to fester because we just do. The need or urgency to move beyond what has always existed can't gain traction. Put another way, how schools use time and allow the school calendar to persist as it has is like taking a horse and buggy to get from New York to L.A. You will get there, but it is going to take time!

RECONSIDER, REMOVE, REPLACE

We recognize that altering the time pattern used for schools and classrooms is fraught with challenges. For example, schools provide cheap day care for young children so parents can go to work. If the time patterns changed dramatically and kids were home, who would watch the kids while parents worked? This was an issue for many parents during the pandemic lockdowns, when children were forced to stay home, and parents had to be there to watch them. It screwed things up!

Summertime is sacred to children and families. Any proposals to change that will meet with resistance from families regarding their summer break and vacations, as well as industries that rely on summer for their livelihood. Kids may not jump for joy as well. We aren't advocating the end to vacations. But there are ways to reconsider the calendar, allow for breaks, and make better use of time. In addition, there likely would be added issues of increased costs if students were expected to be in school more, or buildings were more fully used across the entire year.

But despite these cautions, we firmly believe that the school calendar, school day, and all time-related current expectations need to be reconsidered in a new light. The current calendar has survived for so long, and some of the prior hesitancy to change, due to issues like housing kids in warm buildings during summer months, is no longer an issue with the advent of air-conditioning. Why do we still replicate a model devised centuries ago to fit the needs of those times? It is time to play with time. We suggest a few places to start, including:

- Education should be a year-round enterprise. There can still be breaks, but why have nine months on and three months off? Teachers could be employed in flexible contracts, school schedules could be equally flexible, students could have different amounts of contact time. The potential variety of solutions are endless.
- Make use of technology to engage with students in ways not currently being done. This would allow for all sorts of creative ways to employ time, to engage students, to use teachers, to use facilities. Instructional videos, for example, allow all of us to learn new things without having to go to a school building to

get the new knowledge. Technology opens up many new doors for consideration.

- Think about the Finnish experience. Must all kids be in schools and classrooms, following a strict schedule to learn? Apprenticeship models allowing students to experience and work with business and all kinds of agencies is a wonderful option.
- Build in free time during the day for students and teachers. It is already being done in many schools, and seems to lower stress levels and allow for all sorts of differing interactions.
- Allow students to work in groups on projects, perhaps altering the student–teacher and classroom paradigm.

These are just a few ideas that emerge when considering the possibilities of altering the way time is used. Unlike so many of the prior reform proposals, we aren't necessarily suggesting more time, more hours, or more days. We find that change by accretion of little value across the board. Instead, duck and cover, throw out what has passed its life expectancy and develop new models for using time related to education.

CHAPTER 11

Dress and Grooming Codes

Not all duck-and-cover policies need to be completely eradicated. Sometimes having policies around a topic makes sense, but it is the specifics put into play that are ridiculous. Dress and grooming codes are a case in point. We agree that some policies in this area are practical. Nobody, for example, would want kids coming to school naked. But in the name of dress and grooming, some of the policies promoted by school leaders and school board members are truly absurd. Those need to be altered or tossed away so a level of sanity prevails.

School officials with their school boards have been creating dress and grooming codes for students since the advent of public school systems in this country. Certainly, school officials want students to deport themselves in ways that allow for them to be prepared for the work world and larger society, a form of civic socialization that makes great sense. This, of course, needs to be balanced with the desire for permitting students to express themselves, certainly a major function of education. The legal question is always where students' rights to freedom of expression or liberty end and school official authority prevails.

So while we aren't arguing for the idea of banning all dress codes, we are suggesting a bit more sanity may emerge as these policies are formed. Dress and grooming codes which curtail individual liberty or expression or discriminate against one's gender, race, or background, are highly problematic. At a minimum, any restrictions should have some meaningful relationship to good learning, health and student wellness, and the proper functioning of schools and classrooms. When they don't, duck and cover, they are nothing short of ridiculous.

Why would school officials take this on? One reason is clearly historical. Schools have always had dress and grooming restrictions. Often thoughtless, sometimes well meaning, dress codes have hung around like your favorite aunt. Certainly, school leaders want students to be able to succeed in school; they no doubt worry about distractions, or sending the wrong messages, or not challenging local norms. Whatever the reasoning, policies often emerge that are really hard to fathom.

Some of the early court cases related to dress and grooming codes make the point. In *Bannister v. Paradis* (316 F. Supp, 185 - D.N.H. 1970), a New Hampshire school district banned the blue jean! The opinions of those promoting the policy were pretty remarkable. The principal felt that proper dress is part of a good educational climate, and the relaxed attitude that follows if jeans are worn "detracts from discipline and a proper educational climate." The chairman of the school board agreed, claiming that such clothes don't fit in with the atmosphere of discipline and working. He asserted that California's students had poor academic records and this was due to the sloppy and casual attire they wore to school. Science be damned, the chair certainly didn't let any data get in the way of his laughable opinion.

Another case a few years later dealt with hair length. In *Massie v. Henry* (455 F. 2d 779 - 4th Cir. 1972), from North Carolina, the students wore their hair below their collars, covering their ears. Some even had long sideburns. They were suspended from school. The court ruled with the students, arguing that many of the founding fathers, as well as General Grant and General Lee, wore their hair in a style comparable to the students, as do depictions of Jesus Christ. Presumably, they all would have been kicked out of the schools there as well!

Among the more visible attempts at restricting student garb related to the story of Spuds MacKenzie, the venerable fantasy spokes-dog for Budweiser Beer. Hard to believe, but the challenge to Spuds hit the floor of the U.S. Senate in 1987, when Anheuser-Busch was accused by Senator Strom Thurmond of using Spuds in the form of commercials, stuffed animals, and T-shirts to encourage student drinking. To this day, many school districts disallow T-shirts which might suggest anything related to alcohol, guns and weapons, smoking, etc., implying that the wearing of a shirt leads to negative behaviors. As a local psychologist in Vermont commented after a librarian pushed the banning of T-shirts with Spuds's likeness, "Rather than complaining to kids about what they are wearing on their T-shirts, I think we ought to teach them how to read" (Bredice, 1988). Or as one student we talked to explained, "Geez, it was just a dang toy stuffed dog."

These cases and examples are decades old, but many dress and grooming policies remain in schools with equally shaky regard for evidence and reason. Given that the United States has about 13,000 to 14,000 school districts, the range of dress and grooming policies differs dramatically, aligned with the local political atmosphere, social climate, and other regional factors. For example, allowing shorts to be worn in school might be a less pressing issue in Montana or Alaska than in Florida or Arizona.

Sadly, even today, dress and grooming codes often lead to significant controversy and end up seeking remedy within the legal system. Issues emerge about the legality of requiring uniforms, wearing gang paraphernalia, the ability to permit religious garb, gender-related inequities (restricting female students differently than their male classmates), and even hairstyles reflecting racial and ethnic heritage. Often, the offending garb is related to images appearing on clothing which supposedly promotes behaviors schools restrict. A report prepared about the Washington, DC, school district by the National Women's Law Center found that Black high school girls have more dress code restrictions than other students, forcing them to miss class time solely because their clothes or their hair or makeup offend district dress codes (National Women's Law Center, 2018).

Legally, those challenging dress and grooming regulations often refer to their first amendment speech and expression protections, or their 14th amendment protections for substantive liberty. Perhaps the key case setting the standard for later decisions was *Tinker v. Des Moines Independent Community School District* (393 U.S. 503—1969), determining whether students who wore black arm bands in silent protest of the war in Vietnam violated school policy. They were suspended from school and challenged in court. The U.S. Supreme Court ruled with the students, arguing that students and teachers do not shed their constitutional rights to freedom of speech and expression at the schoolhouse gate, and established a test that such rights could not be restricted unless the behavior "materially and substantially interferes with the requirements of appropriate discipline in the operation of the school."

Such tests established by the courts are rather ambiguous, so the controversies continued well after the *Tinker* decision. Many court cases today focus on the gender-, race-, or ethnicity-specific implications of existing dress codes. For example, are restrictions on tightness of female clothing a form of gender-based discrimination? Does disallowing students, predominantly black students, from wearing their hair in dreadlocks based on a racial stereotype and is it a form of discrimination?

To better understand where we are today, we randomly selected school districts from around the country just to see what is happening with regards to dress codes. As expected, there was a great deal of variety, but we found the language still closely tied to the *Tinker* standard, with words and direction that were typically very broad. Many school districts have outlines with wide latitude that allow schools to shape uniform and/or dress codes and policies on their own, always leaving school officials as the final arbiters of what is appropriate. Some specifically moved to require school uniforms, under the notion that such policies would strengthen student learning, reduce bullying, dissipate differences, or provide some other sort of magical outcome devoid of any rationale other than someone's opinion.

While there were some outliers in terms of their degree of permissiveness (e.g., Los Angeles Unified School District was quite permissive), all districts left final authority to school officials, and typical language focused on dressing appropriately for school, with bold assertions about health, safety, and good learning stemming from proper dress. For most, the key element was making sure that dress should not disrupt or interfere with school—an acknowledgement to the *Tinker* standard established over 50 years ago. Many districts did not permit the wearing of hats, none liked bare skin showing, tight clothing (especially for girls) was a standard restriction, most specifically highlighting that images on clothing should not promote drugs, alcohol, violence, and so on. Apparently, the ghost of Spuds MacKenzie lives on. The vagaries of what many of these policies actually meant in practice was left to imagination. It was clear that school officials, school boards, and even at times school communities, spent a lot of time developing these policies, taking up valuable time better spent on teaching and learning related issues or lessons.

What is so frustrating is that there isn't any evidence that any of these policies impact learning outcomes; rather, the policies typically just restrict students' ability to express themselves. While the *Tinker* standard of "materially and substantially disrupting appropriate school discipline" is as vague today as it was 50 years ago, school officials are put in the role of being the dress and grooming despots of their local fiefdoms.

In the end, we find multiple common questionable aspects of policies that exist in many school districts, given those policies' lack of connection to any research or science about learning or educational outcomes. One would think that such connections would be at the heart of any policies related to student expression. The problems fall into two camps: the breadth, ambiguity, and rigidity of many policies; and the breakdown between the policy intent and the outcomes of the violation. Several examples of recent court decisions highlight these matters.

Sadly, many times even in recent years, school dress and grooming codes land students in hot water for rather stupid reasons. Thus, they end up missing school, certainly subverting the very intent of the policies to promote learning. Friedman (2019) reviewed multiple cases where girls' clothing met with the wrath of ridiculous school dress codes. One was the sorry case of a 17-year-old Florida high school student who had a painful sunburn on her chest. She didn't wear a bra to school since it increased her pain, but she wore an oversized dark shirt that wouldn't attract any attention to her chest. Nonetheless, she broke the "bra required" policy so she was in violation and was disciplined. Another involved an 11-year-old student in Maryland who wore leggings to school and was pulled out of class for violating the dress code. In order to return to her studies, her mother was forced to bring a pair of jeans to school, since the district policy implied that it was a distraction when girls wore leggings and the bottom hems of their shirts failed to reach the length of their fingertips. What is the lesson of such a policy, other than adherence even to the most stupid rules?

In a case from Texas in 2019 (Perry, 2020), a district enforced a hair-length policy that didn't allow male students' hair below the eyebrows or ears. Male students had to keep their hair above their collars. A Black student was informed he would not be able to attend classes, would serve in-school suspension, would not be allowed at prom or graduation due to his violation—his dreadlocks violated the school dress code. It isn't clear to us what the student took from this in terms of the kind of learning the policy ostensibly intended.

While courts have typically and appropriately been reluctant to intrude on school officials' decision-making autonomy (e.g., see *Hazelwood v. Kuhlmeier*, 484 US 260, 1988), a recent study of dress codes (Martin & Brooks, 2020; see also Whitman, 2020) found that, "dress code violations disproportionately disadvantage minoritized students, including students of color, LGBTQ+ students and females" (p. 2). Pavlakis and Roegman (2018) argued that dress codes criminalize males of color and sexualize and blame females of color. The messages sent to these students and their communities likely reinforces their sense of marginalization within American culture. This can't be what school officials intended by creating and enforcing byzantine dress codes.

From our perspective, what continues to possess school officials to develop and apply such absurd duck-and-cover dress and grooming policies is questionable. Dress codes as they are currently written need to be reconsidered. This will require careful thought and introspection to depart from historically driven mandates and something more sensible that is respectful of the times and students' rights to expression and liberty.

RECONSIDER, REMOVE, REPLACE

We understand why school districts have dress and grooming codes. School boards and school leaders carry heavy responsibilities for the students in their care; they want students to behave in ways they consider appropriate. Some guidelines surely are needed. We aren't advocating that kids come to school stark naked, or wear or be styled however they want. But the myriad of policies present in many school districts, with often little leeway in implementation, don't serve the students, educators, or schools particularly well, and sometimes provide lessons that are counter to good education. Duck and cover, it is time for school leaders to think about what they do in the name of dressing and grooming policies. We offer several suggestions:

- Get students involved in developing policies and enforcing adherence to the policies. It is a great way to learn and provides students voice and agency in matters they care about.
- Annually review policies for discriminatory practices and bias. This should be done by a committee of local professionals and community members to assure that the wrong kinds of messages aren't being institutionalized through the policies.
- Have a simple and reasonable due process system in place, involving students, teachers, leaders, and parents, in adjudicating

violations. Allow for leeway in applying standards that may be questioned.

- Make the punishment fit the crime. It is counterintuitive to set policies related to student learning that, when enforced, result in students being put out of school so they can't learn.
- Respect that dress and grooming standards change. Make sure the policies are flexible enough to appreciate this and are annually reviewed.
- Reconsider bans of things school officials or communities don't like that only appear as pictures or images on clothes. Obviously, totally offensive language, obscenity, and discriminatory messaging shouldn't be tolerated. But think of it this way—a T-shirt bearing the image of a bottle of beer doesn't cause students to drink.
- We recognize in some places that gang issues are challenging. Dealing with these matters is difficult and requires expertise well beyond our capabilities. We have no elixir for addressing these challenging situations. If gangs are a problem, perhaps engaging members in dialogue to find ways to allow them to express themselves in ways school officials find appropriate might prove helpful and even get the students more involved.

In the end, dress and grooming codes have a place in schools, but the ways they have been shaped, constructed, and implemented is classic duck-and-cover practice. Why these aren't changed is hard to understand. School officials need to think about what they do in this space, engage students and community members in developing sane policies and practices, and recognize that a part of education is allowing students to find their voice and be able to express that in ways that make sense.

CHAPTER 12

Teacher Evaluation

Michael Scriven, one of the leading thinkers and philosophers support-ing the development of evaluation, coined the term "valuephobia." In his words, it's "a pervasive fear of being evaluated, which I take to be part of the human condition" (Scriven, 1983, p. 230). Think about any aspect of your life in these terms. Do you like being assessed, potentially criticized? When our spouses wear something new and ask how they look, we've learned to never offer any kind of critical review or assessment . . . they look great! We never say anything that might be perceived as negative! Truth is, nobody, including us and our wives, really likes being assessed.

The discomfort of being assessed or evaluated certainly impacts teach-ers, who often cringe at the mere thought of the processes employed. In the education world, principals typically evaluate teachers based on some observational scheme, in which the principal or supervisor visits classes once or even a few times for just a short period of time over the course of an academic year, typically ignoring the voice of the students who actually experience their teachers for thousands of minutes each year. Many times, the specific behaviors that teachers must display are known a priori so les-sons can be planned accordingly. In those cases, teachers sometimes put on a show for the evaluator, changing their teaching to match the evalua-tion mandates, often to the amusement of the poor students bearing witness to the carnage of typical teaching. There is even a term for this kind of behavior, derived from studies on principals—"creative subordination"—essentially doing what you need to do when directives from above are in conflict with perceptions of good practice (Morris et al., 1984).

The good news for most teachers is that while the evaluations may or may not be taken seriously, everyone passes. Perhaps not surprisingly, most every teacher evaluated this way gets fairly strong assessments—what might be considered a Lake Wobegone effect (in the fictional town depicted by au-thor Garrison Keillor, all residents are considered above average). The per-centage of those with strong evaluations is really high. The New Teacher Project (Weisberg et al., 2009) found that 99% of those evaluated using a binary system were rated satisfactory, with 94% of those in a broader rating scheme getting one of the top two ratings, and only 1% rated unsatisfactory. To be more specific, New York City had only 1.8% rated unsatisfactory (Brill,

2009), and in Chicago, 99.7% were evaluated as satisfactory to distinguished (Rich, 2012). In sum, duck and cover, just about everyone gets a high rating.

But not to fear, newer, supposedly better methods were devised to assess classroom performance, oftentimes utilizing mind-numbing sophisticated statistical techniques to capture what the eye can't. The Rand Corporation (Schweig, 2019), found that while 44 states require classroom observations, 33 require measures of student growth, with seven requiring student surveys. The use of standardized test producing growth or value-added measures became popular after the implementation of the No Child Left Behind legislation in 2001, growing in popularity during both the Bush administration and then Obama's Race to the Top educational charge. Many states not requiring the use of test scores for teacher evaluation recommended they be employed. The founder of the value-added design, Bill Sanders, built the model based upon his years as a statistician conducting agricultural assessment. Good intentions, of course. But the sophisticated statistical models never improved teaching, or as any farmer might put it, weighing a pig doesn't make it fatter.

Thus were born a series of highly psychometrically sophisticated and controversial models examining value-added impacts of teachers on standardized test scores. A later version focused on what they called growth models, essentially focusing on the same set of test-score improvement as the basis for the approach. Based on the logic that better teachers should produce higher test results in student performance, their popularity for all sorts of accountability schemes emerged. But as Baker et al. pointed out (2010), multiple conditions of schools and teaching aren't taken into account when relying on standardized test scores, the tests carry all sorts of problems associated with their use, and varying factors impact student learning. More specifically, Darling-Hammond et al. (2012) argued that value-added models are inconsistent, they are affected by the students assigned to teachers, they can't disentangle the many influences on student progress. They concluded such models, "are problematic for making evaluation decisions for individual teachers . . ." (p. 13). Even the American Statistical Association (2014) chimed in, arguing that reliance on one quantitative measure could end up detrimental to understanding quality.

What is worse, none of the approaches to teacher evaluation apparently have any discernible impact on teacher or student performance, and according to some, may indeed cause harm. A recent study found dismal impact of over a decade of heavily funded reform of teacher evaluations systems:

> We find that, on average, teacher evaluation reforms had no detectable effect on student achievement or attainment. We also find that little evidence that the effect of teacher evaluation reforms varied depending on the rigor of the new evaluation systems states implemented or that teacher evaluation improved outcomes for the academically vulnerable groups it was intended to benefit. (Bleiberg et al., 2021, p. 24)

Others point to potential harms of such models. Johnson (2015), for example, suggested that the unintended consequences of the heavily test-based approaches to teacher evaluation include negatively impacting filling high-need teaching positions, discouraging shared teacher responsibility for students, undermining standards-based reform approaches, generating teacher dissatisfaction and turnover. Kraft et al. (2020) found that teacher evaluation reforms decreased teacher job satisfaction and feelings of autonomy. They also placed huge demands on administrator time (Neumerski et al., 2018). Notably, Nobel Laureate economist James Heckman and Tim Kautz (2012) were stark in their criticism of standardized achievement tests, suggesting that, "a more relevant validity criterion is how well these tests predict meaningful outcomes, such as educational attainment, labor market success, crime, and health. No single measure of cognitive ability predicts much of the variance in these outcomes . . ." (p. 452).

Teacher evaluation accountability measures are always well meaning. Teachers have to be evaluated. But as suggested, duck and cover, so much of it is nonsense. Certainly, test performance has its value, and the individual elements of good teaching tied to improved test scores have increasingly been identified. But so much more goes into what makes for good teaching and careful consideration is needed to capture what outcomes really count. Liking school, for example, is important for student academic achievement and reducing disciplinary problems. Hallanan (2008) studied 6th to 10th graders in Chicago and found that students who perceive that their teachers care about them, respect them, and praise them, are more apt to like school. Interestingly, teachers' expectations for students' academic achievement have a minimal effect on whether students like school. We work with a teaching award that our university gives each year to secondary teachers who impacted college seniors' lives, nominated by those seniors in any academic field—ostensibly, what great teaching should be about. In the ten plus years this teaching award has been in place, not one nomination letter by a student or teaching statement by a nominee ever mentioned anything about test scores or the kinds of things most observation scales or test-based evaluation systems might capture. What counted for students was the support, encouragement, inspiration, advice, direction that these great teachers provided, typically over a sustained period of time.

Interestingly, none of the criticism of current teacher-evaluation schemes is new. In a prescient paper written almost forty years ago, "Teacher Evaluation: The Limits of Looking," Stodolsky (1984) argued that effective teaching really isn't characterized by one set of factors that are context free. She lamented the unknowns including how many observations, under what conditions, would be needed for observations to really be valid. At about the same time, Shulman (1988) suggested that multiple data gathering techniques would probably be needed to capture good teaching, with such a combination compensating for the inherent weaknesses that each approach brings. What he referred to as a "union of insufficiencies" characterizes the varying approaches to assessing the complexities of good teaching.

The other great irony is that the outcomes of most current teaching evaluation approaches don't carry much weight for anything. Setting aside the incredibly high level of satisfactory ratings in teacher evaluations being used, the reality is that most approaches to teacher pay aren't dependent on any evaluation. Instead, the typical systems rely on years of experience and some level of academic training to determine yearly pay levels. Even licensure renewal is either based on academic attainment or professional development activity. Nobody has yet calculated the number of hours for teachers, administrators and others associated with the teacher evaluation boondoggle that permeates all school systems, or the associated costs these and other aspects of any evaluation system might entail—for example, creating valid and reliable new tests or observation schemes. But it can be assumed that it required thousands of hours to administer, untold hours of professional development to perfect, multiple millions of dollars, and in the end, not much of value is derived. So the cost benefit of teaching evaluation, other than the symbolic political act of holding up a shiny evaluation display to the public in the name of accountability (what Wise et al., 1984, referred to as the "utility" of a system) is probably not terribly high.

In summing all of this up, we come to a single stark reality. Einstein is credited with saying that doing the same thing over and over again and expecting different outcomes is insane. For us, teacher evaluation as is done in the United States constitutes a clear example of that definition of insanity. We've done the same kinds of things for years in the name of teacher evaluation, certainly more recently with increased sophistication, complexity, and greater precision. But in the end, the evaluation systems don't discern good teaching from bad, everyone performs well and is rated at least satisfactory, they cost an arm and a leg, and there may indeed be harmful effects on teachers, schools, and school systems. Duck and cover, if that isn't insane, then what is?

RECONSIDER, REMOVE, REPLACE

The most logical suggestion based on the reality of teacher evaluation as it plays out in most school districts today is that it should just be dropped. Why do something that is expensive, time consuming, and basically useless in terms of improving teacher performance. That said, we recognize that many individuals have devoted a lot of time and energy to these systems, no doubt with some valuable work being done, all with the best intentions of helping to improve teaching practice. We wholeheartedly believe that teachers, like students, athletes, business-persons, professionals of any kind, need corrective feedback to understand their areas for improvement and find ways to improve. Well trained mentors are also useful to offer guidance. We also believe that student voice is largely absent from the mix in the current evaluation schemes, a shortcoming that is hard to understand. They, after all, are the ones exposed to teaching more than any others. Parent voice can be valuable, too. But teachers need feedback, support, and guidance to improve. Why not create systems to help them?

To that end, we recommend the following regarding teaching evaluation systems currently in place in schools across the country.

- Stop evaluating using the systems currently being used. Unless there are some that have evidence of efficacy in helping teachers, they have little value other than symbolically showing that we educators are on top of things. In reality, they add little value other than checking the box annually that teachers are being evaluated.

- That said, we believe that monitoring and support for new teachers in their first three years on the job is important and should continue. We are not suggesting using the current evaluation systems, but something specifically geared towards identifying strengths and weaknesses for novice teachers and offering guidance for their improvement. At some point decisions need to be made regarding long-term teacher contracts, the responsibility of principals, so this new system should be the basis for that assessment by school leaders.

- Expand the types of data collected to support teacher development. Frist, thoughtful systems for providing ongoing student feedback to teachers and supervisors is important. They are the ones experiencing the teaching. In higher education where student evaluations are often the primary or sole sources for data, some universities use mid-semester and end-of-semester evaluations. Point is simply it need not have to wait until semester or year's end. Second, require teachers to provide an annual self-assessment/reflection regarding their performance. These kinds of data should become part of the basis for periodic discussions about teaching and individual professional development work among teachers and leaders.

- Have principal or supervisor periodic evaluations or assessments of teachers move away from the summative approach now being applied. Gear these toward support and improvement, the formative role for evaluation. Since the current models tend not to differentiate at all, and developing a thoughtful system seems daunting, taking an improvement orientation to teacher evaluation seems prudent. Once the summative nature of teacher evaluation is lessened, it likely will free up teachers to collaborate, self-assess, review, and revise more than the current systems generate.

- Teachers need mentors—they should be other teachers who don't serve in supervisory capacities. Berry et al.'s (2013) conception of teacherpreneurs may be a good vehicle for developing more of these teacher leaders. Current teacher coaches in schools could have their portfolios expanded with appropriate training to serve in this capacity as well. Everyone needs this kind of interaction and feedback for growth. A related idea is to require teachers to observe their colleagues teaching, then to write up reflections about their own personal teaching based on what they observed in others. This kind of forced self-reflection can be shared with the teacher they observed and become the core of developing teacher sharing and interactions about best instructional techniques.
- If evaluations need to be done for remuneration or other kinds of summative purposes, school teams, led by principals, should develop the guidelines and take on those responsibilities.

CHAPTER 13

Gifted and Talented
and Exceptional Education

We had a friend who was describing his early education to us. He explained that in 4th grade he got placed in what today would likely be called a gifted and talented classroom. Back then it was labeled "IGC" for "intellectually gifted children." He did well that year, figured he was performing well into the top half of all the students. The class did a lot of what he said were fun extra things he liked. Yet at year's end, the teacher informed him that the following year he was being placed back in a "regular" class for 5th grade. When he inquired why, he was told that his reading score hadn't come up enough above grade level on the standardized test that year to qualify him for continuing in the IGC-designated program. The teacher said he was close, but that wasn't good enough for the system. He recalled telling her that seemed stupid, since he was doing so well in the class. She wasn't happy about it either, agreeing he was among the better students. He said that he re-called the whole thing confusing him. How could he have been smart enough in 3rd grade being in a regular class to be placed in IGC, then fall short in 4th grade after a year in IGC? Then he had an epiphany, realizing that after being in IGC, he wasn't smart enough anymore and was getting kicked out! He said he told that to the teacher, who sighed, but to his 4th-grade mind, he was better off, since the IGC class apparently made him dumber.

We don't know any of the fine details of what happened to our friend many years ago, or the full impact this had on him. But we do know that since our friend's elementary years, gifted and talented education has been established in schools, as have special-education programs, all across the United States. These two programs are supposedly developed to serve ex-ceptional students. The difference is that gifted and talented programs serve those who are considered by some to be exceptional academically or in some other way, while the special education programs serve those who often struggle academically. The broader school programs serve everyone else—apparently, in school terms, the unexceptional, the average, the ordi-nary, the regular students.

This arrangement is based on the idea that students or human beings can be placed into three different groups typically using one criterion. The thinking seems to be that some students are extremely smart or at least a lot smarter than others. They must be afforded better opportunities to further develop their smartness. Many parents often think that their children belong to this group of smarties, and demand that their children be placed there. Apparently schools do not have enough talented and gifted programs nor the capacity to serve all these students, so a process, which includes tests, is set up to select qualified students to be enrolled in the talented and gifted programs. While different schools may have slightly different criteria, the majority of schools rely on academic performance and IQ tests.

Some students are considered to be, for lack of a better term, deficient. In other words, their situation requires special attention and support beyond the majority student population. Some have serious problems that can prevent them from learning in schools. Their problems include a wide range, from learning disabilities to physical disabilities, from speech disorders to emotional disorders, and from autism to ADHD. These students are determined to need special supports and planning. While the range of needs is wide, the goal is to get them help. As with the gifted and talented students, there are also processes to identify and place students for special education. They are labeled.

The majority of students are the big group in the middle—the average and regular group. Based on test scores or sometimes other criteria, they are not at the top end or bottom end. They don't get a special label, but might just be considered ordinary. They are put into regular schools, sometimes grouped or tracked, taking the regular curriculum, following regular teachers, and going through regular activities.

There is nothing wrong with recognizing exceptionality and taking care of students who need special attention. There is also nothing wrong with customizing schooling so that all students can learn. But we see these dividing processes as well meaning but short sighted—in essence, duck-and-cover policies. Not that all children need be treated the same, rather that all children deserve the kind of personalization that the outlier groups are provided.

Gifted and talented education has a long history in the United States. The National Association of Gifted Children (NAGC) has been supporting the field since 1954. The Marland Report (1972), a document from the U.S. Commissioner of Education to Congress, created a definition of giftedness and set out the unique needs of these students and challenges they face. The federal definition of gifted students, located in the Elementary and Secondary Education Act, is broad in scope:

> Students, children, or youth who give evidence of high achievement capability in areas such as intellectual, creative, artistic, or leadership capacity, or in specific academic fields, and who need services and activities not ordinarily provided by the school in order to fully develop those capabilities. (NAGC, n.d.)

Along with mention of the failure of the country's brightest students to compete well internationally, the landmark report, "A Nation at Risk"

(National Commission on Excellence in Education, 1983), highlighted gifted education. In 1988, the federal government passed the Jacob Javitts Gifted and Talented Act to monitor, serve, and improve programs in the field. It also provided a small amount of funding, though most programs in the United States are funded locally or by states. Two key studies followed this century. "A Nation Deceived: How Schools Hold Back America's Brightest Students" in 2004 (Colangelo et al., 2004) lamented the state of education for top students, how they get held back by the current system, demanding the need for acceleration. About a decade later, "A Nation Empowered: Evidence Trumps the Excuses Holding Back America's Brightest Students" (Assouline et al., 2015), focused on how acceleration works, and the need to re-energize the discussion around academic interventions for gifted students.

A sad reality is that the funding of gifted and talented programs is basically left to school districts and states, permitting a wide array of options for students from locale to locale. But the idea is pretty simple, give these smart kids greater opportunities and options. Certainly makes sense, but what about everyone else? The NAGC suggests that about 6% of the student population is labeled as gifted and talented. That number certainly leaves out many who might meet the federal definition, especially given how districts may differ dramatically in their offerings and identification processes. It also leaves out those students who may be exceptional in ways the tests and assessments don't capture.

In special education, the number of areas included in the multiple categories of disabilities is large. Supported initially by the Education for All Handicapped Children Act (PL94-192) in 1975, multiple components were established for serving these populations, including the requirement for an Individualized Education Program (IEP) for each identified student. The later version of the law, the Individuals with Disabilities Education Act (IDEA), continued the mandate for services for all eligible students ages 3–21. According to the National Center for Education Statistics (2022), the percentage of students receiving services in 2020–2021 was 15% of all public school students. A quick calculation, therefore, suggests that roughly 20% of students are receiving some kind of supports as either being gifted and talented or students with disabilities. The big middle encompasses 80% of the student population.

We are thrilled for the 20% getting some level of supports and appreciate the demands of those constituencies. Much research for both groups highlights the strengths and also laments the quality of services provided, so there is work to be done. But we also worry about the under-supported majority not getting special support. Why leave them out? Do they not need some level of personalization, too? Do they not have needs or talents not captured in the identification and labeling processes? Duck and cover, that is the essence of the problem. Moreover, we believe there are significant problems with using one way to identify students as gifted and talented, regular, and special education. Consider the small population of identified twice-exceptional students:

> Twice-exceptional learners are students who demonstrate the potential for high achievement or creative productivity in one or more domains such as math, science, technology, the social arts, the visual, spatial, or performing arts or other areas of human productivity AND who manifest one or more disabilities as defined by federal or state eligibility criteria. These disabilities include specific learning disabilities; speech and language disorders; emotional/behavioral disorders; physical disabilities; Autism Spectrum Disorders (ASD); or other health impairments, such as Attention Deficit/Hyperactivity Disorder (ADHD). These disabilities and high abilities combine to produce a unique population of students who may fail to demonstrate either high academic performance or specific disabilities. Their gifts may mask their disabilities and their disabilities may mask their gifts. (Reis et al., 2014, p. 222)

Apparently, twice-exceptional, or 2E, students should receive services in both gifted and talented as well as special education programs. On the one hand, they are exceptionally good, fitting the criteria for gifted and talented programs. On the other hand, they are exceptionally challenged and should be served in special education programs. There is increasing evidence from scholars, practitioners, and families that supports this assumption. There is also growing acknowledgement that students with gifts and talents can and do simultaneously have deficits in learning, attention, social awareness, and behaviors (Baum et al., 2004; Foley Nicpon et al., 2011; Trail, 2012). There is also evidence that shows students who are identified with specific learning or attention deficits or social and emotional disabilities can have extraordinary gifts and talents (Reis et al., 2014, p. 217).

The twice-exceptional students can be all students. Every person has a jagged profile of capabilities (Rose, 2016). That is, every individual can be good or exceptionally good in some areas and at the same time bad or exceptionally bad in other areas (Zhao et al., 2022). The jagged profile of capabilities is the result of the interaction between nature and nurture (Ridley, 2003). Human beings are born with different cognitive abilities as indicated by Howard Gardner's theory of multiple intelligences (Gardner, 2006). These natural differences can be suppressed or enhanced by experiences. For example, a musically talented or intelligent person can become a great musician if she happens to be born into a family that loves music or the person may not even know what music is if he is born into a family and community where music does not exist. Some parents and schools may force children to develop skills in areas they have no natural-born talent. Definitely children can learn, but it is unlikely that they all can excel at high levels. True talent comes from natural aptitude and hard learning (Coyle, 2009).

In addition to differences in natural-born intelligences, human beings are also naturally different in personalities (John et al., 2008). Some people, for example, are more open to new experiences while others may be much less. Some may be more impulsive and others may be more calm when running into unexpected situations. Some are very interested in talking with strangers while others are shy. These natural-born personality tendencies are also suppressed or enhanced by experiences and environments. A very talkative person can learn to talk less in an environment where silence is considered golden, for instance.

Human beings also have natural-born tendencies in desires, motives, and interests (Reiss, 2000). Psychologist Steven Reiss made a list of desires that drive our everyday action: power, independence, curiosity, acceptance, order, saving, honor, idealism, social contact, family, status, vengeance, romance, eating, physical exercise, and tranquility. But not everyone is driven by all of the 16 desires. Instead, some people are completely driven more by power, while power or seeking to influence others does not motivate others at all. Curiosity may drive some people, but others may have little interest in probing people's life or natural phenomenon. Again, these desires can be suppressed and enhanced in life. Different life experiences can make them stronger or weaker.

However, schools have followed a set of criteria to make the judgment that favors some talents and passions and neglects or downplays other talents and passions. For example, academic performance in general, the ability to pass math and language tests in particular, is considered as the most important. Thus, those who do extremely well in language and math are more likely to be identified as gifted and talented students, while those who do not do well in math and reading are more likely to be placed in special education. The math and reading students are then given more opportunities so they can be even better, while those who undoubtably have other talents or passions are considered less worthy and are never given the opportunity to develop their talents and passions.

For many reasons, schools favor academic subjects, in particular math and reading. The primary one is that schools have been tasked with the job to make sure children can read and do math, following the traditional belief that reading and math are essential skills. It is also believed that skills in reading and math are necessary for expanding into other subjects. Nothing wrong with that. It is clearly reasonable for schools to value math and reading abilities. But it is wrong for schools to devalue other talents and skills besides math and reading.

And consider this. We have focused on these annually tested subjects for many decades, while at the same time always lamenting how bad our schools are. When "A Nation at Risk" labeled it an act of war for what had become of our schools, that we were falling so far behind Russia, Japan, and Germany technologically, economically, militarily, who did they blame? Those darn schools! Years later, when the Soviet Union fell apart, Japan's economy collapsed, and Germany was in the doldrums, nobody came out to praise the schools for their fine work. Instead, report after report continued to emerge about how bad our education system is. Subsequent legislation like Bush's No Child Left Behind and Obama's Race to the Top continued the onslaught, the criticism, and the focused test-based frenzy. Perhaps the mandates of what the policymakers promoted was really the problem, keying up a few subjects, ignoring student talents beyond the chosen subjects that the policies centralized. Decades of the same fixes, the same kinds of assessment schemes, the same old mantra. Our leaders need to look in the mirror, duck and cover, and realize that is some ways, to quote the old Walt Kelly Pogo cartoon, "We have met the enemy, and he is us!"

We have arrived at a time when all aspects of human diversity of talents have become valuable. The traditional useless talents have become useful (Zhao, 2018d). In human history, for example, today's powerful computer geeks were hardly useful in ancient times when physical labor was of more value. A society 1,000 years ago could not possibly need so many musicians and singers, nor actors and artists. Sports today is a multibillion-dollar-a-year business. The revenue of the National Football League, for example, is nearly 10 billion dollars a season. It is hard to imagine that many people could have made much money throwing balls as a profession 200 years ago! Computer gaming has become a huge industry and a sport. Who could have predicted 100 years ago that one could make a living playing computer games as a profession!

Talent diversity has been valuable in building powerful empires in the past (Chua, 2007) and strong organizations in recent years (Page, 2007). Different talents are necessary to building anything significant today because of the complexity of technology and the finer division of labor. Different talents bring complimentary capabilities and expertise. They also bring different perspectives and approaches. This is why tolerance of differences is viewed as a significant indicator of smart and creative communities (Florida, 2002, 2012).

Our world today is changing rapidly. The little phones we carry around are more powerful computers than those NASA used to place astronauts on the moon. Children are connecting differently than before. The jobs of the future certainly aren't clear. All students bring multiple strengths and weaknesses to the schoolhouse gate. The policies related to gifted and talented education and special education are well intended and supports for those students should continue. But all students need personalized attention. Duck and cover, even well-meaning policies, and practices have unintended consequences that hold students back—in this case, the large majority of students not identified at the ends of the spectrum being provided with the supports they need.

RECONSIDER, REMOVE, REPLACE

If we accept that everyone can become great AND weak in their own ways because of their natural-born tendencies and interests and life experiences, we should rethink how we currently operate gifted and talented and special education. First, we can treat students in special education as gifted and talented, which of course requires us to look for the talent of these students. We know, for example, students with autism can be greatly creative. In this case, can we focus on them as creatively gifted and talented students? Instead of excessively focusing on fixing their autism or whatever challenges they face, we should provide more opportunities for them to improve their creativity.

Second, we should treat all gifted and talented students as students who need special education. The talented and gifted students also have deficiencies in domains where they are not talented and gifted. They also need help with those deficiencies.

Third, and perhaps most important, we should treat all students as twice exceptional—being both gifted and talented as well as needing special education kinds of support. In Finland (Sahlberg, 2011), for example, more than half the students have been in special education by the time they complete their compulsory education. So many get support, it isn't a big deal with any sort of negative connotation. To quote Sahlberg, "it is nothing special anymore for students" (p. 47). We should borrow individualized learning approaches from special education and enriching and challenging learning approaches from gifted and talented education in mainstream education. We want every student to have an individualized education plan that is based on and further develops their talent and passion. We want all students to have an enriching and challenging but personalized learning set of experiences.

But how to accomplish this, especially with the country's financial challenges related to schooling? The rethinking is not easy because of traditions and laws but it is necessary and possible. The necessity does not need to be stressed much more as it is generally accepted that all students need personalized learning because of their diversity in talents, passions, and needs. The possibility of making education personalizable exists (Zhao, 2018b; 2018c), and exists in a number of ways. First, students are self-determined learners. As natural-born learners (Beard, 2018; Ekoko & Ricci, 2014), students want to learn, so they do not need external motivation if they are pursuing their own interests. When students are genuinely engaged in learning, they do not need discipline or management either. What the adults or teachers should do is to support, guide, and facilitate learning, which can be done individually instead of always having to lecture to an entire group of students or manage a group of students (Zhao, 2018a).

Second, as COVID-19 has shown, learning can be conducted remotely and technology has drastically expanded the availability of learning resources

(Zhao, 2020a; 2020b). Students are able to learn from online resources and participate in online learning communities globally, which reduces the need to have one teacher teaching to a group of students locally.

What we need to do is reconsider education for all students, pulling the best ideas that gifted and talented education and special education, exceptional education, offers their students. Enhanced curricula, focused attention building on strengths, special attention to needs, personalized plans. We actually suspect doing this will bolster students' performance in all subjects. But this requires a different mindset about education and students. It will require differing uses of technology, roles for teachers, altered arrangements in schools.

So it is not that gifted and talented education and special education needs to go away. On the contrary, it is that all education should integrate services and supports for every student in new and meaningful ways. It requires a re-envisioning of what we do. We understand this is basically a revolution in approach, and no easy or short-term task. But it is being done in some ways already for some students. Why not all?

Part III

SYSTEMIC AND ANALYTIC CONUNDRUMS

CHAPTER 14

State Standardized Testing

Americans love ratings and rankings. From the nightly Top Ten list on the old David Letterman talk show, to the yearly sports rankings leading to incessant debate among devotees of college football and basketball, these pseudo-scientific analyses have become a central part of American culture. When Americans express that theirs is "the greatest country on the earth," they are implying some kind of ranking with unknown criteria and standards, where the United States is on top, and every other country is below. This obsession with ratings and rankings pervades school culture, too.

Parents, understandably, want to know how their children are doing in school. They also want to know if their children's schools and teachers are doing a good job. If not, they may be able to find another school or at-home option or request a different teacher. Governments, on behalf of taxpayers, want to make sure that schools and teachers are working hard to make good use of the tax dollars in teaching future generations of citizens. They also want well-educated and competent citizens. School leaders never want their schools or district to appear on the bottom of any list. Businesses and employers want some kind of indication that their future employees are learning and making appropriate progress on skills they desire. The public, we taxpayers, demand to know if our hard-earned tax dollars are being well spent and if the children are getting a good education. Bottom line, there are a lot of interested parties with demands and expectations for our schools.

How to quench the thirst for information and serve these varied needs? Duck and cover, state standardized tests do the trick for every state in the country. They provide numbers, they allow for comparisons, they have a "scientific air" about them. What these tests do, and what they can't, creates a real dilemma, but ultimately meeting these demands provides the justification for state standardized testing programs.

Standardized tests have been around a long time. The early intelligence tests gave way to achievement tests in the first half of the 20th century. The initial statewide assessment program was initiated by E. F. Lindquist in 1929, when he helped launch the Iowa Test of Basic Skills (Haertel & Herman, 2005; Lemann, 2000). The original purpose of this test, however, wasn't really about assessing school quality, but identifying students who could benefit from interventions to ultimately expand education to more children (Lemann, 2000). The comprehensive New York State High School Regents Exams started in the late 1940s and now test in multiple subjects every year. The critical report, "A Nation at Risk" (National Commission on Excellence in Education, 1983), warned of America's educational shortcomings, and spurred a number of states to launch aggressive testing programs. Kirst (1990) indicated that 40 states either reinforced or created accountability systems in the 1980s. In South Carolina, for example, with its highly visible Educational Improvement Act in 1984, enhanced testing for students was launched as part of a robust reform package (Ginsberg, 1995).

So while the state tests aren't new, the ongoing demands from interested and affected parties continue to be the justification for standardized tests. More recently, early this century, President George W. Bush's No Child Left Behind (NCLB) (No Child Left Behind Act of 2001, 2002) pushed every state to have tests in math and reading for all students in schools. President Obama's 2015 Every Student Succeeds Act (ESSA) (Every Student Succeeds Act, 2015) made slight changes to law but maintained standardized testing for all students in reading, math, and science, although the law removed NCLB's draconian and absurd Adequate Yearly Progress or AYP (which mandated every student to meet a pre-set standard each year with the goal of 100% proficiency by 2014). ESSA allowed states to introduce differing assessments for accountability.

As a result, standardized test results have been used to inform parents of their children's learning, to let the public and governments know the performance of their schools, to satisfy the concerns of employers regarding future job candidates, to make decisions about funding of the schools, and to make judgments about teachers' effectiveness in teaching. Today, standardized testing has well established itself as a major and long-standing policy and practice in American education. Like the plague, no student, no teacher, and no school can escape from it. The specific tests may vary, from state tests for elementary school students and high school students to college entrance exams such as SAT and ACT. But the mandates for state testing persist.

Interestingly, to make sure that students do well on the summative state assessment exams, many states added other tests to provide indicators of progress along the way prior to the year-end tests. Tests like TeraNova, the Measurement of Academic Progress (MAP) tests, and others are supposedly tied to state standards and alert students and school officials about student progress at varying points in time during the academic year. Often, parents are sent sophisticated explanations about student scores, using language from things like the Rausch model that few students, parents, teachers, or school officials could honestly explain in a clear way. So like rabbits in the wild, state assessments begot other assessments, ostensibly so students, teachers, and school leaders could know how kids are doing academically. Of course, these tests take time away from actual instruction, and in some cases, add days of test preparation so the students are well poised for the exams.

In our estimation, state standardized testing is yet another duck-and-cover policy and practice. It came with great promises and best wishes, but it is not only incapable of delivering its promises but also very powerful in damaging students, education, educators, and educational institutions. It can also create societal disasters and lead the country into unfortunate directions.

A great example of the extreme potential for harm came in 2015, when a group of more than 10 educators from Atlanta Public Schools in Georgia were convicted of racketeering and other crimes. Over 20 teachers and principals were charged and the now-deceased superintendent, Beverly Hall, was indicted by a grand jury in 2013. They were not mobsters and did not conduct crimes such as drug trafficking or bank robbery. Nobody cheated on their taxes or committed a violent crime. What they did was cheat on students' standardized tests so the scores would be higher; they basically changed students' answers to the test questions. The educators wanted better test scores because their superintendent, Dr. Hall, wanted her district to show great progress. It worked. Dr. Hall was named national superintendent of the year and was invited to visit the Obama White House (McCray, 2018; Strauss, 2022; Zhao, 2014).

The case in Atlanta Public Schools is just one instance of educators feeling forced by the NCLB law or its specific incentive structure to cheat or manipulate test scores to avoid punishment for not meeting unrealistic improvement goals. Changing students' answers on tests and other manipulations to improve test scores were widely reported in various schools in the United States in the 2000s (McCray, 2018; Nichols & Berliner, 2007; Strauss, 2022). Cheating also took place at the state level as reported by Nichols and Berliner in their book *Collateral Damage: How High-Stakes Testing Corrupts America's Schools* (Nichols & Berliner, 2007).

The cheating scandals show the corrupting power of standardized testing. It is unbelievable that teachers and education leaders would cheat on behalf of students on such a scale. We have read stories of test takers cheating so as to get high scores, but it is truly shocking to see educators, almost in an organized fashion and at the command of their leaders, changing their students' answers. They are supposed to be moral examples for our students but there seems to be a force that makes them neglect their moral duties and ethical standards. That force has to be very powerful or sufficiently seductive. That force is the reward and punishment structure associated with standardized testing. The reward was made very high and the punishment severe in Atlanta Public Schools. The superintendent at the time, for example, would highlight and praise the educators who raised test scores and invite them to sit at the front of district-wide gatherings (Zhao, 2014).

The problem of standardized testing in schools of course extends beyond corrupting educators to behave in nefarious ways and lowering their morale. Standardized testing has created other damage. First, it narrowed the focus of teaching and learning to test preparation (Zhao, 2018). Testing, especially high-stakes testing like the state standardized testing in the United States, drives practices in schools and classrooms. The tested subjects become the most important subjects and thus command the most attention. Since No Child Left Behind, American schools have taken much time and attention away from non-tested subjects, thus reducing time in science, arts, music, and even recess time. The number of teachers in reading and math have increased while teacher numbers for other subjects have declined. Likewise, teachers, even those in the tested subjects, pay more attention to what is tested than the whole subject in order for their students to perform well on the tests. Teaching to the tests has indeed become a common phenomenon in American schools (Emler et al., 2019; Koretz, 2017). Our psychometric colleagues refer to what is known as Campbell's law (Campbell, 1976), that sets out the problem this way: "The more any quantitative social indicator is used for social decision making, the more subject it will be to corruption pressures and the more apt it will be to distort and corrupt the social processes it is intended to monitor" (p. 49).

We all would agree that education should consist of much more than teaching children to take standardized tests. It should be about the healthy growth of children. It should be about children learning to make friends and socialize. It should be about learning to be responsible citizens who can defend a democracy. It should be about learning the skills needed for thriving in the future world. If education is reduced to taking tests, it is corrupted. Such a corruption in the long run produces students who may be able to take the tests but are unable to become productive citizens. As a scientist friend of ours described to us, scientists do science in labs or in the field, they don't take tests, and the relationship between performing on the tests and being a good scientist is probably pretty iffy.

Second, standardized testing has narrowed the opportunity gap for disadvantaged children. While one of the reasons for universal standardized testing was to help bridge the achievement gap between advantaged and disadvantaged children so that all children could receive quality education as indicated by test scores, the reality is that disadvantaged children have lost more possible opportunities for them to learn and grow because of the tests. Because of the desire to teach to the tests and resulting curriculum narrowing, schools, particularly schools in disadvantaged communities that have more challenges to raise test scores, have decided to reduce time for non-math and reading activities, including music, art, sports, and non-academic extracurricular activities. Thus disadvantaged students have lost these opportunities, which might have provided disadvantaged children the opportunity to engage with schools, discover their interests and strengths, and develop their talents. We know that children of advantaged families live in advantaged communities that typically have access to more opportunities and a diversity of resources, and their parents can purchase opportunities to do art, music, and sports outside school. Disadvantaged poor children typically do not have such opportunities or parents with the purchasing power for the same opportunities. Thus, many disadvantaged children suffer the significant loss of those opportunities when schools do not offer them. This is one of the reasons that efforts to narrow the achievement gap have not worked, because while we focus on the achievement gap, we forget that the real gap is the opportunity gap, which actually causes the achievement gap (Tienken & Zhao, 2013).

Third, standardized testing teaches children to be compliant and good test-takers. Standardized tests are typically large in scale, look for correct answers, and are typically easy to be scored by machines. They do not necessarily test students' curiosity, creativity, agentic critical thinking, or ability to apply knowledge to solve ill-defined problems. For students to score high on standardized tests requires them to be familiar with the format of the tests and have great memories of the tested content. As a result, high-stakes standardized testing has taught American students to become compliant with the demands of tests in order to become good test-takers. However, good test-takers are not what our society needs. The tests don't predict very much (Heckman & Kautz, 2012). This is why numerous studies have shown that countries with students performing high in international assessments do not necessarily perform better in economics and creativity and countries with lower-performing students actually do better in economics (Baker, 2007; Tienken, 2008; Zhao, 2012, 2014, 2018, 2020).

Interestingly, a recent study asked high school students their reflections about the state standardized assessments they took (Woolever, 2019). Students were concerned about the length of time tests took, the lack of any meaningful feedback, a sense of irrelevance of the test content, and the reality that the tests caused great stress and anxiety. And this was in a low-stakes testing state with no test-related graduation requirements. Moreover, the significance these tests are accorded in schools with their simple correct vs. incorrect response possibilities teaches students that failure is to be avoided at all costs. This flies in the face of what science and learning is about, where through trial and error, failure, and success, scientists make discoveries and students learn (Ramirez, 2013). As Ramirez put it, "science has taught me the power of persistence and patience, and also has shown me that failure is a friend" (p. 7). So much emphasis on test scores, with no option on these assessments for feedback or continued learning, takes a significant component of the trial-and-error approach to learning out of the mix.

Fourth, standardized testing drives schools to deprive disadvantaged children of a real education. In addition to reduced time for non-tested subjects and content, schools have also developed other strategies to improve their performance on tests. For example, in El Paso, Texas, Superintendent Lorenzo Garcia had a plan to improve test scores in his district. Students deemed not to be able to do well on the tests were not tested, changing failing grades to passing grades, transferring students to schools that didn't test, making sure low performers were kept home on testing days, and forcing struggling students to drop out of school altogether (Fernandez, 2012; Sanchez, 2013). In essence, these students were forced out of a proper education because of the state standardized tests. Garcia was nominated twice for superintendent of year in Texas and was cleared of wrongdoing by Texas Education Agency. Eventually, he was put in federal prison after an FBI investigation (Sanchez, 2013). El Paso was not the only district that enacted such plans. Nichols and Berliner (2007) documented many more classes, schools, and districts that had similar practices to find ways to disallow students from taking the tests. In addition, teachers have been found to largely focus on students who are considered to have the chance to improve sufficiently to do well on tests and ignore those who may not improve enough to pass the tests.

However, and here is the real rub, standardized testing has not improved education. Test-based accountability did not work to make education better for all children or close the achievement gap (Hout & Elliott, 2011). NAEP data show that while test scores improved following the 1990s, they flattened in reading and math since 2010 and have been stagnant for years. On the other hand, the obsession with test results certainly has brought enough damages to American education: distorting education into test preparation, demoralized teachers and teaching, reduced opportunities for disadvantaged children, and deprived children of a real education.

But the biggest problem of standardized testing or the obsession with standardized testing is that it sends education backward while neglecting the future. Standardized testing does not test what many scholars and even government agencies have proposed to be significant skills needed in the future such as creativity, critical thinking, communication, and collaboration or other skills that have been put under the umbrella of 21st Century Skills (Adams & Hamm, 2013; Duckworth & Yeager, 2015; Trilling & Fadel, 2009; Wagner, 2012; Zhao, 2012; Zhao et al., 2019). Instead, it tests the basics in reading, math, and possibly science. It drives educators and students to waste their time on the so-called basics without enabling them to look into the future. Are the basic subjects important? Sure. Are they by themselves the essence of a good education that all students need? Of course not. And for schools to improve test scores, they are stuck in the quagmire of tests without the freedom to innovate and move forward.

The result is that since NCLB started we have wasted at least the last two decades, two decades of incredibly fast and significant changes in the world, two decades of unbelievable technological advances, and two decades of unimaginable geopolitical changes, climate changes, and changes in human values. If education were not stuck with standardized tests and related craziness, duck and cover, we might have seen schools to be more innovative, to be teaching students about the future, and to better address the issues related to equity.

RECONSIDER, REMOVE, REPLACE

The immediate solution we have to what we consider the problem, the duck-and-cover policy and practice of standardized testing, is simply to get rid of it. What would happen to schools if the state assessments were discontinued? Teaching wouldn't stop, indeed there likely would be more days for actual instruction on things other than preparing for the test or on the untested subjects and skills. Schools would rely more on teachers for understanding student performance. Why not? The evidence is pretty clear that all the testing and the problems it has promulgated haven't improved anything very much. Achievement gaps remain and are growing for some groups, test scores are flat, some subjects get short shrift, teachers and students are on edge about the results. Reform after reform is thrown at raising the test scores to no avail. Think about it this way. If your doctor offered you a prescription for some unspoken ailment, ostensibly to let you know how you are doing, explaining that it isn't clear if it will do anything, it will cause you stress, it will take up a good amount of your time, it is expensive, it will take you away from other pursuits, and in the end the evidence is pretty clear that it won't help you at all, would you take those pills?

Moreover, as an increasing number, about half of colleges and universities in the United States have decided to go test optional. That is, they are not requiring students to submit their scores on standardized college entrance exams such as the SAT and ACT, though many states are still requiring students to take them as part of high school. Why? Those tests aren't related to state or district curriculum, and once again, don't predict very much? Although COVID-19 forced many states to stop requiring standardized tests, they are back in operation in many places. There does not seem to be much intention to stop the tests. But the tests as we know them really must be stopped in order to create freedom for teachers, students, and school leaders to think about the future. Tests as we know them must be stopped in order for schools to consider new teaching possibilities such as global and online learning. Tests as we know them must be stopped in order for parents, governments, and the public to expect different forms of assessment of students.

All that said, we aren't naive enough to believe that the thirst the larger culture and school systems have generated for ongoing high-profile assessments, and the ingrained systems for conducting assessments that are firmly in place, will easily dissipate. So we offer a compromise. There are growing kinds of alternative assessments that might provide the feedback some demand, while getting away from the most pernicious aspects of the current testing models. In this sense, if dumping the tests is impossible, we are considering state standardized testing a remove-and-replace option.

A great example of the kinds of possibilities we have in mind are the dynamic leaning maps alternative assessments for students with significant cognitive abilities. These assessments are built into the teacher's instructional practice throughout the school year, just as teachers give their own assessments. They allow for learning to be part of the assessment. They provide teachers and students, and ostensibly their leaders, information on how students are doing, and do so in a timely way so adjustments can be made. They allow for personalized learning to take place. These tests reinforce the primacy of instruction and offer status and growth data that is readily actionable (Kingston et al., 2016). If such alternative assessments and ways to consider student progress are possible for a subset of students with cognitive disabilities, why not a set of potential assessments for everyone that get away from the nonsense we have been doing for so long?

So short of just dumping the state standardized tests, if there is resistance, the point is that there may be other kinds of assessments that provide information without all the harmful effects the current testing systems create. As technology and society keep changing, it's time to get away from the standardized testing models that were developed and have dominated schools for over a century.

We close with a quick story. Years ago we were working with some Dutch educators, who came to the United States and met with groups of teachers. In one instance, teachers asked the Dutch scholars about student testing in their country. They explained that students were being tested three times for about three days. The American teachers indicated that while that was somewhat less than was happening in their schools each year, it was similar. But the Dutchmen immediately pushed back, explaining that the students got standardized tested three times during their entire school career, not every year. The American teachers were shocked. "How do you know how kids are doing" was a question several posed?" One of the Dutch scholars, with a twinkle in his eye, looked at the teachers and explained, "In Holland, that is why we hire teachers!"

CHAPTER 15

Governance by School Board

A friend of ours came to us for advice since the person had decided to run for the local school board. We asked: Why? The response was, "Well, I have kids in those schools and I want to do what I can to assure that every child gets a high-quality education." Fair enough, we reasoned, good reasons for doing so. We avoided asking what was meant by "a high-quality education," but since the person asked for advice, we posed some questions. We wondered how this might affect the person's job as it is a very time-intensive position. We also asked what credentials or background the person had to sit on the school board, make hard budget decisions, guide curriculum, if the person was ready to deal with demands for controversial things like banning books, closing schools, or changing school boundaries, pulling out or adding controversial topics so prominent today, thoughts on assessing superintendents or candidates for the position, just simple stuff we thought the person should consider. We also wondered who was going to financially support the campaign, how the person was going to show how the diverse elements in the community would feel represented by this person serving on the board. Much to our chagrin, looking dazed, the person responded to us and said, "You're right, a really bad idea!" We immediately said we never indicated it was a bad idea, just offered some things to think about in taking on what is a very difficult, important, and labor-intensive role.

Public schools in the United States have been governed by local school boards for well over 150 years. As Americans began migrating to large urban areas with the industrialization of the country in the late 19th and early 20th centuries, elected school boards took hold as the dominant form of governance for the country's expanding public schools. In many ways the governance model has a gut satisfying appeal to it, with local people interested in the running of their schools, much like our friend, able to seek office through election and be part of the leadership structure. For many, school boards represent "the quintessential example of representative democracy" (Cai, 2020). Put another way, local elected school boards are as American as apple pie!

Sadly, that pie may not taste so good after baking. Despite the theoretically attractive idea behind the school board model of governance, the combination of a faulty idea mixed in with a problematic baking process raises legitimate questions about its value. While the intent may be sound, governance by school boards made up of local citizens as currently enacted is another duck-and-cover policy that needs be exposed and reconsidered. Many aspects of the process don't approach the ideals it supposedly represents. That is, the idea of a locally elected group of lay citizens representing the community, serving in the most important policymaking and governance role at the top of the system, making the most serious decisions for our schools.

We aren't suggesting that those populating school boards across the nation are anything but sincere in their approach to the role. Of course, anything relegated to a political process opens the possibility of political maneuvering which may not serve schools well. But state school board associations and the National School Boards Association provide invaluable support for these entities. Being a school board member is an important position, typically for no pay, that requires hours and hours of work to be done well. School board members have multiple responsibilities serving as the chief policymakers for school districts. Likely their most significant function is hiring the superintendent—sometimes firing the superintendent. They deliberate and vote on key policies, whether curricular, personnel, financial, etc., that all drive the school district's work. Some rely a great deal on the superintendent and her or his staff—others less so. For some, being an elected position, serving as a school board member may be the launching pad for a political career. Ironically, the model of elections were often established to try to get politics out of the running of schools, an especially silly idea given how the process is structured and how elections actually work. But the process was established to allow local citizens to control their schools.

The history of governance by school board in the United States dates back over 200 years to the colonies where educational governance was separated from local governing structures. Education isn't mentioned in the U.S. Constitution, so states, and their local educational authorities, became responsible for governing schools. Land (2002) indicated that Massachusetts was the first to organize elected school boards in the 1700s. As people moved from small villages to growing urban areas, school boards based on bureaucratized models of governance began dominating across the country. What Tyack (1974) described as the "One Best System" included school boards promoted by elite reformers. Tyack (1974) explained, "there was tension in the swollen villages between the older forms of governance and the bureaucratic aims of the modernizers. School board politics was one area in which these different interests clashed in the nineteenth century" (p. 79). At first in the quickly growing urban areas, the boards were typically large and elected from local wards, neighborhoods, or other polities, mimicking the larger political system. But during what Callahan (1962) described as the period of the "cult of efficiency" in the early 20th century, smaller elected boards emerged, separated from political parties and local politics in order to get politics out of the schools. Boards would be responsible for policymaking, and hire professionals, the CEO-like superintendent, to run the operation. Educational administration became saturated with business language and terminology in this drive for greater efficiency and performance. Callahan (1962) quotes a school board member writing in the American School Board Journal from 1911, who put it this way: "a board of education is only a board of directors; the taxpayers the stockholders. The superintendent is a sales manager; the teachers the salesmen" (p. 151).

Who should serve on these newly emerging boards? Ellwood Cubberley, a prominent Stanford educator, felt that the best board members should come from large businesses due to their ability to act rapidly, be progressive, spend money wisely, rely on experts, and operate efficiently. Those ill-equipped for such boards included, "inexperienced young men, unsuccessful men, old men who have retired from business, politicians, saloon-keepers, uneducated or relatively ignorant men, men in minor business positions, and women . . ." (Cubberley, 1929, pp. 124–125). Thankfully, Cubberley's rather pompous and sexist characteristics for who should serve on boards were never codified, but this model of smaller elected boards, ostensibly separated from the larger political processes, with overall policymaking authority while relying on expert professionals for day-to-day operation, is the structure that emerged and continues today.

So how is it that this grand bastion of American democracy at its best gets tagged as a duck-and cover policy? Don't we like mom and apple pie? Scrutiny of how school boards are constructed and operate exposes some of the problems with this approach. Interestingly, the key requirements for becoming a school board member typically include interest, residence, and sometimes age. There are no professional requirements, no training, no education expectations attached to taking on the role. There are no special talents needed like those required for many professionals like athletes, entertainers, actors, and actresses. Other than paying taxes, board members have no financial stake in the organization. How many business boards, where board members typically have an ownership stake in the company—ironically the actual model upon which the current school board structure was devised—operate this way? Stated another way, the main requirement for obtaining a school board position is getting enough votes.

In essence, the job is a voluntary, lay position, with little or no pay. It is a part-time job. This resembles some other political offices, though those usually entail some level of financial remuneration beyond what school board members make, and often are full-time positions. But other than politicians, how many fields put people in arguably the most important roles for the functioning of the organization, with no requirement for skills, education, training, and so on. What kind of signal does this send to the students in schools, who are constantly hammered with messages about finishing their education? We tell students we want them in school, to graduate with a

degree in order to become educated to prepare for getting a good job or for
moving on to post-secondary education. But if you want to be in charge of
our school district, no education is required, just wanting the job and being
popular is enough. We honestly understand that lay control by local citizens
has value, and no evidence that requiring some kind of training or education
would help school board members. But it is rather curious in a system built
on the premise that more education is better.

Indeed, while we appreciate that there is something almost un-American
to suggest that other forms of leadership and control should supplant this
long-standing model, we acknowledge that arguments can be made to continue as is. Tyack and Cuban (1995), for example, argued that the success
of any reform is derived from its fidelity to the original design, longevity,
and effectiveness in meeting preset outcomes. In many respects, applying
these criteria, it could be argued that school boards have been a rousing
success. They are still around after well over a century, in much the form
that was created all those years ago. While the specific measurable and original outcomes for school boards are unclear and would be hard to identify,
probably other than reflecting the governance structure from businesses and
other industries, and later moving to nonpartisan elections to get politics
out of the mix, it is true that school districts have operated successfully with
this model for a long time. Three cheers for school board governance, it
apparently works almost to perfection.

But upon closer inspection, such an assessment breaks apart. The nation has about 14,000 local school boards. That means that along with a
myriad of state and federal policies, legislation, and court decisions driving
their work, and the ability to fashion their own policies within these con-
textual guidelines, the country is a patchwork of thousands of local governing agencies, guided by hundreds of policies and regulations from an array
of sources, leaving each school district with some similarities and multiple
differences. As Hess and Meeks (2010) put it, "the conditions and nature
of school board governance vary dramatically across the nation's districts"
(p. 35). Other than the confusion this may create and a lack of uniformity
across districts and states, probably nothing wrong with this, though it certainly underscores the importance of where you live regarding the education
you'll get.

The National School Boards Association (2018) publication, "Today's
School Boards and Their Priorities for Tomorrow," exposes some of the significant problems that the governance model entails as it currently operates.
According to their data, 79% of school board members are White, 77% have
a college undergraduate degree or higher (with another 19% having some
postsecondary education or an A.A. or A.S. degree from a community college), household income is above $100,000 for 62%, 40% are retired, only
32% currently have children in schools. Juxtapose this against the fact that
less than half of public school students are White, with the National Center

for Educational Statistics projecting that by 2029, White students will make up only 43.8% of public school enrollment (NCES, 2018). The U.S. Census indicates that average household income in 2020 was $67,521 (US Census, 2021), while about 37.9% of the U.S. population who were aged 25 or above had graduated from college or another higher education institution (Durfin, 2022). So what these data suggest is that school board members are likely more White, wealthier, and more educated than the students (and their families) populating the schools they serve. Moreover, only about one third of members currently have children in schools, and 40% are retired. These last two features may be due to the fact that board membership is voluntary, time consuming, and unpaid. But taken together, these data vividly highlight the reality of the distinct differences between those that serve on school boards and those being served by the schools. The implications this may have for curriculum and other decisions can't be ignored.

Perhaps the most severe concern with this the idealized political model of school board governance as a pure form of representative democracy is that in practice the reality is not representative at all. The voting record in school board elections is pathetic. While no comprehensive analysis of turnout is available, most estimates put turnout to typically be around five to 10% of eligible voters (Cai, 2020). Perhaps that is democracy at work, but it speaks to the vacuousness of the argument that the public, in practice, controls local schools. All too often school board elections are off cycle, meaning they aren't held at the same time as other elections for key political offices. America's voting record for all offices tends to lag well behind that of other developed countries (DeSilver, 2020), but these off-cycle elections typically attract alarmingly small voter participation. It isn't clear if this keeps politics out of school board elections, as is likely the rationalization for nonpartisan elections, but it clearly does keep voters out of school board elections. What it does imply, as Vitteritti (1983) identified in his study of New York City schools, is that school boards likely best serve their constituents, not their clients. In growing numbers of school districts, the students and their families are largely non-White, not wealthy, or have not necessarily earned advanced educational credentials. Without getting into debates about why the voting patterns are the way they are, appreciating that many school board members do work to represent the schools' clients, it does suggest the real possibility that the students' best interests may not be represented by those who serve on their governing boards.

We are certainly not the only ones who have examined school board governance or been critical of how it operates. The Twentieth Century Fund (1992) examined school board governance and saw them as an obstacle to fundamental reform due to their tendency to micromanage and get caught up in daily operations. Land (2002), in an exhaustive literature review of the field, identified what appear to be the key characteristics of best practice for boards drawn from across the literature, though she lamented the lack of research tied to most of the conclusions, and certainly the lack of research tying aspects of their work to student outcomes. Interestingly, she found that school boards tend to not evaluate themselves. We suppose that is done at the ballot box, but certainly an ironic finding given the obsessions most boards have with student test scores.

Honingh et al. (2020) examined a broader field, including international studies, to determine if there was a link between school boards and educational quality. This did limit the countries to be included, as only a few countries other than the United States actually have school boards in control (the Netherlands, England, and Flemish Community of Belgium). Interestingly, they identified 4,939 articles to review, but found only 16 that were empirical and met their standards of quality. That is less than 1% of the studies done on school boards. As might be expected, in the studies they examined, the dependent measure was test scores, suggesting a very limited view of quality. In the end, they found a lack of empirical evidence on relations between school boards and educational quality. Hess (2010) identified advantages and disadvantages of school board control. As advantages he argued that democratic bodies can make hard decisions when competing interests are at hand. School boards also provide transparency and have the capacity to allow people to be heard. And superintendents seem comfortable with the arrangement. In terms of disadvantages, he identified low voter turnout, apathy allowing mobilized constituencies (like teachers' unions) to exert disproportionate control. Third, he discussed the problem with elected boards creating a lack of coherence, discipline, and continuity. Finally, he argued that urban school boards are too distant from city mayors and local government leadership.

Eden (2021), decrying low voter turnout in school board elections, called for moving these elections on-cycle—on election day in November— to boost turn-out. In his words, "the fact that school board members are by and large elected in off-cycle non-partisan elections renders local control largely chimerical" (p. 1). Sell (2005) offered an array of proposals for altering school board practice, concluding that, "the verdict in the case for or against locally elected school boards is really not determined" (p. 95).

So where does that leave us? School boards have governed school districts in America for a long time. It is a model held up for the values it represents. But in practice, that is a false narrative. Their key function should be at the policy level, though for better or worse, they have no particular skills or training in this area. In fact, they have no required skills or training at all. They tend not to be particularly representative of the students in the schools, just about nobody shows up to vote for them, and the research on their effectiveness, especially in terms of impacting student outcomes, is paltry. The notion that this model of running schools is a great example of democracy at its best is ridiculous. Just as Bert the Turtle would duck into his shell when confronted with the unknown, school board governance, despite its longevity, is a head in the sand, duck-and-cover model that cries out for examination and reconsideration.

RECONSIDER, REMOVE, REPLACE

So what to do? We recognize that school boards have been around a long time, the notion of local control is cherished, and even if we were so inclined to suggest they be eliminated, that outcome is very unlikely. Even when alternative types of schools are created in the United States, like charter schools, they are often governed by boards, though very different types of boards than for the nation's traditional public schools. We also appreciate the value of applying non-expert/non-professional common sense to addressing school issues and policy. Though it is true that good sense isn't always common, much as with the American jury system (the O.J. Simpson verdict aside), lay persons can deliberate and come to meaningful decisions. So we agree that community involvement in the governance of local schools is attractive and offers several advantages if done right. At the same time, we are convinced that the voices of the clients, meaning parents, local community members, and students, is important, as is the professional wisdom of teachers, those most directly involved in the education process. They should have a voice in school governance, much as Berry et al. (2013) argued in promoting the idea of greater teacher leadership.

When it comes to governance by school board, we believe a strategy revision is needed. Indeed, we offer as an example a hybrid model of school board governance, making adjustments to address the most serious concerns. If school board membership is to be held at seven, a size that allows for debate but seems workable in terms of efficiency, we propose the following:

- Three members should be elected from the school district boundaries, much as they are now, all done at an at-large basis, and nonpartisan. They should not be able to accept contributions from political parties or their shadow organizations. To increase voter turnout, these elections should take place on election day in November.
- Two teachers should serve. These should be appointed by the superintendent in consultation with varying bodies (principals, teachers' organization, etc.). Drawing on the work from Berry et al. (2013) on teacher leadership, we believe teachers should have a voice at the highest levels about how their schools and classrooms are run.
- One member should be appointed by the local mayor, if none exists, the local county government. This ties school governance directly to

other local governing leaders and bodies and may make for better cooperation on policies that intersect.

- One member should be appointed by local citizens' groups, ostensibly the parent–teacher organization or the equivalent.

In addition, we call for:

- Appointing two current students serving in an ex-officio capacity. Likely they should be at the high school level. Due to their age and situation, full board membership may be problematic. But student voice is important, all too often ignored, and as ex-officio members, they should participate in all discussions and deliberations.
- The superintendent serves in an ex-officio capacity. This is how it currently operates, with the superintendent generally preparing the school board meeting agenda.

Will this approach solve the duck-and-cover aspects of the current school board governance model? We don't know. We certainly call for ongoing research on how well such a model serves schools. The paucity of good research on this ingrained model of running schools is appalling. School boards should be evaluated on an ongoing basis, with the board identifying clear goals for public scrutiny and debate. But the hope is to increase voter participation, bring in more school-related expertise and academic preparation, and hopefully allow for local groups to assure that board membership mirrors the school and community.

CHAPTER 16

How Teachers Are Paid

We talk to teachers all the time. Our school prepares future teachers and supports current teachers. The conversations recently have been pretty alarming. Certainly, COVID-19 has a lot to do with that, as the pandemic made a difficult job even harder in multiple ways. Issues of lack of respect, working conditions, evaluation, and other processes and practices have always been controversial. The criticisms from the media are hurtful. One teacher explained that politicians pass laws that tell them how to teach, what to teach, and she doubts any of them could pass her class—and she teaches elementary school! But especially scary to us are the rising concerns about pay levels. One group of relatively new teachers lamented to us how ridiculous it is that they need to hold down second jobs just to meet their financial needs. One said, "I don't want to have to live with my parents my whole life!" They are bothered that friends getting degrees in other fields start at salaries that they likely won't earn on a yearly basis anytime in their entire career if they stick with teaching. They are angry at all the money they need to put up for supplies and materials; that along with low salary levels, being a great teacher doesn't mean you will earn more. As a recent Economic Policy Institute report concluded about teacher pay (Allegretto, 2022), "teachers are paid less (in weekly wages and total compensation) than their non-teacher college-educated counterparts, and the situation has worsened considerably over time" (p. 1). To put this in perspective, this wage penalty for teachers was on average 23.5% in 2021, a huge jump from 6.1% in 1996. Simply put, the teachers we spoke to knew what they were talking about . . . they live it!

Teachers' salaries stink. Always have. To us, this is a national disgrace. The poor levels of pay send a stark message throughout our culture that teaching isn't particularly important. As an example, a renowned cover page of *Time* magazine (Help! Teacher Can't Teach, 1980) had a stark headline, "Help! Teacher Can't Teach!" Such critiques of teachers have been around for generations, usually tied to a deeply held lack of respect allowing low pay to persist, and a collective sense that teachers probably aren't particularly smart since becoming a teacher is easy. Given this, it isn't surprising that Americans report in the yearly PDK polls that the public schools deserve grades of C or D, though ironically, they typically rate the schools where their kids attend much higher. Schools, and by extension, teachers, apparently aren't so bad when you actually know what they are doing, but the media represented by journals like *Time* magazine have done their harm for generations by creating a sense of incompetence.

So the blame for the ills that pervade schools is typically leveled at the feet of teachers. Perhaps that helps understanding the historic rationalization for paying teachers so poorly. But while the crux of the salary dilemma is low pay that is comparatively getting worse, it is only part of the problem with the salary situation. Conceding the reality that the challenge of getting communities and states to support significant increased investments in teacher pay is pretty slim, what also confounds the teacher pay issue is that teacher performance, no matter how defined, or other teacher contributions to their classrooms or schools, are largely absent as an element determining what teachers earn. Instead, years of experience and academic credentials carry the most sway. We think these are important variables in determining salary. But certainly not everything!

Let's face it, once tenured, staying alive throughout the academic year pretty much guarantees a teacher's salary going up the same amount as all other teachers with similar years of experience and academic credentials. That is, of course, unless years of experience exceed the total allowed on the salary schedule. If so, then unless some kind of across-the-board percentage increase gets approved, the result is teachers get what some refer to as a small longevity bump. But as the *Seinfeld* "soup Nazi" might put it, "No raise for you!" Performance, of course, no matter how conceptualized, is not part of the longevity equation.

Summarizing the situation for teachers regarding salary can be characterized as follows: Overall, you will be poorly paid; working extra hard, investing personal resources, all great things, but don't count for your pay; doing the minimum, not being very engaged or engaging, pretty much fine, too; teaching in a shortage area, bless you, but pay isn't affected; teaching in an overcrowded field with fewer and fewer students, and not even doing that particularly well, pay wise, basically irrelevant. Could you imagine Tom Brady or Lebron James, with all the work they put into their craft, and the high level they perform at week in and week out, justifying or accepting the same pay as the last person sitting on the bench? Sadly, duck and cover, that is the model determining teacher salaries in most schools.

This has to be one of the strangest anomalies of school functioning. In a field that constantly and continually rates its clients' performance, teachers get a pass in terms of any evaluation's impact on their salary level. While research shows that teachers are the single most important factor in student performance (Opper, 2019), none of that really matters when it comes to actual pay. Teachers naturally get a lot of intrinsic reward from the important work they do facilitating and supporting students over the course of a semester or academic year. Our guess is that these intrinsic highs hit teachers throughout their careers. But sadly, teachers are treated more like missionaries than professionals charged with supporting the development of the nation's children. The truth is, what people get paid is important; the thrill that teachers intrinsically experience from their work cannot be used as currency at a grocery store. The pay system is archaic and broken, it is a long-standing duck-and-cover policy.

Many blame the teachers' unions for this situation. We don't, and we actually believe it is the unions who can fix it. Teachers started unionizing in heavy amounts in the decades after the 1950s with the extension of collective bargaining rights to public employees. Originally formed in response to low pay, restrictive and demeaning policies controlling their lives, minimal influence on decisions, and unresponsive school boards and district leadership, unions began to collectively bargain on behalf of teachers in districts across the country. According to historian Wayne Urban (1990), the driving factors behind the growth of teacher unions were to win and maintain salary increases and other benefits, and to maintain seniority as the criterion for salary increments and promotions in schools. The single-salary schedule as the most common form of determining teacher pay first emerged in the early decades of the 1900s, touting multiple advantages—ease of administration, impartiality, encouraging teachers to teach in field that best fits them (since salary doesn't distinguish by subject taught), and including incentives for further training (Elsbree, 1928). While the single-salary schedules were codified in collective bargaining agreements across the country in the 1960s, they have been controversial for decades, usually because they don't differentiate—by field, need, school, performance levels, and so on. According to Hansen and Quintero (2017), nearly 90% of public school districts pay teachers according to salary schedules, as standardized compensation schemes can reduce gender and racial inequalities, and are considered an efficient approach given the complexities of the work. We wonder about the morale issues that fester among high-performing teachers tied to pay scales that focus solely on simple inputs (experience and credentials) and ignore quality, quantity, or substance of the work performed by individuals.

Performance-based pay systems began appearing in earnest following the release of *A Nation at Risk* in 1983, which called for both increased and performance-based salaries as a means, ostensibly, for improving student performance and test scores. These merit-pay systems in recent years commonly were tied to standardized test scores of students in teachers' classes, often referred to as value-added models. Research suggests that such systems have little or minimal actual impact on student performance measures depending on context and type of program, and they generated significant controversy due to psychometric problems inherent in their use (Armein-Beardsley, 2008; Armein-Beardsley & Close, 2021; Eckert & Dabrowski, 2010; Pham et al., 2021). Nonetheless, to this point in time, teacher salary incentive models haven't replaced the single-salary schedule in any meaningful way.

Given the teacher unions' interest in increasing wages, their involvement in changing how teachers are compensated seems key. And the reality is that teacher salaries are pathetically low. According to the Economic Policy Institute (Allegretto & Mishel, 2018; Allegretto, 2022), what they refer to as the wage gap for teachers, as suggested earlier, has widened to over 23% compared to professionals with similar education. In no state is teacher pay equal to or better than that of other college graduates, and the relative wage penalty is over 20% in more than half the states. Inflation-adjusted wages have been relatively flat since 1996. Indeed, relative teacher salaries have been eroding for over half a century. And sadly, prospects for the future aren't particularly promising, as Darling-Hammond et al. (2016) reported that the percentage of college students interested in pursuing a career in education has gone down. With the cost of higher education going up, and the salaries for teachers relatively going down, the outlook for attracting increased numbers of prospective teachers is pretty bleak.

Notably, the COVID-19 pandemic likely made matters worse, when working conditions in schools for teachers, and the attractiveness of the profession, undoubtedly deteriorated. The CDC Foundation (2021) reported that during the pandemic, 27% of teachers reported symptoms associated with clinical depression, 37% experienced symptoms related to general anxiety, 53% were thinking of leaving the profession, and 19% started or increased their alcohol use to deal with the stress. This is all a convoluted way of saying that young people today aren't stupid—they see what teachers have gone through with COVID-19, and before that the minimal authority teachers had over what they do, and many who might have been inclined to enter teaching may be reconsidering. Adding these less than desirable working conditions to low levels of pay (which honestly never go up much over the course of a typical 30-year career), one has to wonder why young people might be interested in pursuing the field? Notably, 55% of teachers themselves in the 2019 PDK poll of teachers reported they wouldn't recommend that their own child go into teaching (PDK, 2019).

So while strengthening working conditions is certainly an important factor for improving the recruitment strategy for teachers, it seems likely that pay levels, and how salaries are determined, are part of the problem, too. Teachers express this themselves, as 60% of teachers in that same PDK poll said they were unfairly paid. Our sense is that policies that continue to exist around how teacher compensation is determined no doubt exacerbate the concerns. About the best that can be said regarding the lingering teacher pay practices is that while mindless, they are easy—no thought goes into considering exactly what any teacher might be doing to deserve an increase, a simple calculation does that. Ease of operation is efficient and has some value to schools and districts. Likely concerns about potential morale problems also exist if differences are made between salaries due to subject taught or shortage situations. This, of course, ignores the concerns some teachers already carry about working harder or being better and getting paid the same as those who don't perform as robustly. In the end, the complex task of thinking about how best to pay teachers for their input and performance is not part of the calculation. It just seems wrong, a clear duck-and-cover practice.

To further emphasize that point, we find it ironic that the one definitive path for increasing pay for teachers in schools is to leave the classroom, stop teaching, and become an administrator. Want to move up? Get out! The National Center for Educational Statistics data reported that the average base salary for all public school teachers in 2017–2018 was $57,900, for those with a bachelor's degree $49,900 (National Center for Educational Statistics, 2021). For principals, the average was $104,250 (National Center for Educational Statistics, 2021a). Simply put, the underlying message to teachers is pretty clear—the only way to earn more money in education is to get the heck out of the classroom.

In some respects, that makes sense. Afterall, leadership is hard, and the responsibility is increased, as principals are in charge of whole schools and not just classrooms. But it is complicated. In sports, for example, the best players make significantly more than their coaches or managers. And the best players get paid more than the weaker ones. Teachers don't give all students the same grades, they assess student work and assign varying evaluation scores. Yet when it comes to teacher pay, none of this is considered. Why not figure out ways to alter how teachers are compensated and not treat teachers as if their performance doesn't matter? It does. Money is certainly not the sole or even key incentive for entering the teaching field. But minimizing its value seems dumb.

What we really wonder is why the salary structure in place has been so impervious to significant change. The longevity of the same old approach is pretty remarkable. So many fields have created new and differentiated roles. Law, medicine, dentistry, accounting, all have varying roles with different responsibilities, training, and pay structures attached to them. Gosh, even higher education has ranks for faculty members with specified expectations to move up the ladder. It is time that the PK–12 education field do the same in terms of examining what it is doing in this area, and most importantly, create vehicles for those still teaching to carry varying responsibilities with greater remuneration options without leaving teaching, what Berry et al. (2013) referred to as developing the idea of "teacherpreneurs." A lot of smart people populate the education space; the time is ripe for them to conceptualize a transformation of the work, roles, remuneration possibilities, and so on.

To be fair, a number of confounding economic and sociological factors work against increased salaries for teachers as things stand, whether on a single salary schedule or not. First, part of the reason is that there are a lot of teachers—federal data suggest over 4 million in the United States (about 87% of these in public schools). Slightly over three quarters of these are female; more than half have a master's degree or higher (National Center for Educational Statistics, 2020). Simplifying the point, size matters, as any change in teacher remunerations is really expensive. Especially so if the salary increases are significant as we believe they need be. So, for example, even an average increase of $5,000+ per teacher just in the public schools—which isn't nearly enough—is almost a rousing $18 billion proposition. Given that so much of the cost is borne by government through taxes, the will for investments of this magnitude aren't clear.

A second consideration related to what teachers get paid is the reality that teaching is predominantly a female occupation. When it comes to work-related matters, women in our culture are never treated as well as men, certainly not financially. While the gender gap overall in terms of pay controlling for variables such as education, job title, etc., has declined, it still is not equal—with women earning a bit less than men in equivalent roles. Interestingly, even in education, in terms of average pay, female teachers earn a bit less than their male counterparts. Given that women make up about three quarters of the teaching workforce, such differences are hard to justify. Note also that in terms of pay for women versus men, without controlling for any other variables, what is referred to as the uncontrolled gender gap, the gap is much larger, with men earning a good bit more than women (Payscale, 2022). Multiple reasons for this, but women typically dominate in occupations and careers that pay less. Fields like teaching.

Third, the truth is that in the world of occupations, status and pay seem to go hand in hand, rendering teaching near the bottom of the pile for those with college degrees. Relative importance to our culture, or an array of other variables seem to get crushed by issues like status and prestige. Etzioni (1969), in his seminal work on the subject of certain professions, even labeled teaching as one of the semi-professions. Interestingly, in a totally unaligned field, the British have a Reliability Index (2021) for cars in the UK, and multiple small and reasonably priced cars manufactured by the likes of Toyota, Mitsubishi, Hyundai, Honda, Nissan, Kia, etc. appear higher on that list than any cars made by Mercedes or Lexus. The scoring, of course, is directly related to what is specifically being measured, in this case, auto reliability. Does auto reliability matter? One would think it would. But what is clear examining this index is that you likely pay more for some cars that are far less reliable. People probably buy these less reliable machines because they have amenities and luxuries, comforts and bells and whistles that matter to them, and no doubt the prestige that comes with owning one of these. Few, of course, argue that money doesn't matter when it comes to cars, with the common-sense argument being that you pay more for a better car. But that isn't true when it comes to their reliability. Clearly, status has a high price tag.

So multiple factors, including the large number of teachers, cost considerations, the dominance of women, and sense of low status and prestige are among factors holding teacher pay down. But whether considering cars, teachers, or anything else, of course money matters. What a ridiculous argument those who suggest otherwise are making. We aren't at all swayed by arguments that money doesn't matter, whether for teacher salaries or other educational purposes. The controversy about the impact of money on schools has been raging for decades. We find some of the commentary humorous, understanding that such analyses are complex and that conclusions and proposals to remedy the situation are often driven by an array of factors, including politics. This is true in any field or endeavor. But how many fields are saddled with both low pay and constant attacks on their professional status? Recent calls to allow military veterans a direct route to teaching, or alternative licensure paths that may involve only a few days or weeks of preparation, might address shortages (though that is questionable), but certainly are anti-professional and demeaning. Add low pay to the mix, and it becomes a toxic environment for the field.

Regarding education spending, researchers in education have debated the value of spending more money for schools for decades, many focusing on the lack of effects of additional funding (Hanushek, 1997), though multiple more recent studies suggest that more money, including for salaries (Baker, 2016), has a positive impact on student performance. Even a renowned critic of increased spending (Burnette II, 2019; Hanushek, 2016) has come to argue that spending more money on salaries for high performers can make a positive difference. So while increased pay is slowly being accepted these days as making a difference, we argue that how that money is spent appears to be the key variable to consider. Investing in the strongest of the school's employees seems a pretty sound use of increased expenditures, though this is complicated by figuring out how determinations should be made regarding who gets what. As suggested, perhaps considering ways for diversification of the teaching and instructional work force might help. But the reality remains, duck and cover, solely paying all teachers the same, based solely on simple measures of years of experience and degree, seems counter to what should be effective practice. Especially so as teacher salaries make up the largest portion of school district budgets.

We aren't arguing for a privatization accountability model that looks to apply principles drawn from business and other fields as the sole means for fixing the pay problem in schools. Sahlberg (2011) notably characterized such policies as germs, or the global education reform movement. His studies of the Finnish educational experience display the problems with over-reliance on accountability through test scores, transfer of business practices to schools, hyper-focus on core subjects in prescribed curricula, all with little sense of the culture and workings of schools or focus on best practices to educate. For recommendations for change to have a shot at success, they need be sensitive to school culture, as Sarason (1990) starkly emphasized years ago in his book, *The Predictable Failure of Educational Reform*. So our consternation isn't about some business consultants coming in and applying the latest market-based twist to improving school operation. Instead, we recognize that many teachers are angry and frustrated, far too many leave the field too soon. Ignoring the valuable input of individuals into their schools—and the effects they have on their students, colleagues, whole school culture, and outside community—duck and cover, renders the pay system a hindrance to strengthening culture and serving students well.

RECONSIDER, REMOVE, REPLACE

The policies and practices related to teacher pay need to be revised. Teachers have a long history of being paid poorly, and unions entered the scene to strengthen pay, working conditions, and an array of teaching-related factors. We envision teacher unions taking the lead in bringing more sense to the pay formulas for teachers. They represent large numbers of teachers and have teachers' best interests as their main focus. We don't doubt that teaching subjects being paid less, or individuals not being compensated at the levels of their peers for whatever reason, has potential for causing problems in schools. But higher education has survived pretty well with the same constraints, as have most professions. And the morale issues that currently exist among teachers who see their efforts going unrewarded is certainly as potent as the other concerns, yet this situation has festered under the surface for generations.

We see the teacher pay issue as a multi-pronged attack. First and foremost, teacher salaries need to be increased overall. Either we pay teachers better salaries, or our leaders need to shut up about the importance of education and the primacy of our children to society. We also hope that any salary considerations are part of broader efforts to strengthen overall teacher working conditions.

Second, we also believe that better teachers should earn more than their lower-performing peers. That in some cases different subjects should receive higher compensation, that in times of shortage, as is true in most every other field, we should never lower expectations for entry to the field, but instead should raise salaries to attract greater numbers.

Finally, it is high time that the teaching and instructional workforce be reconsidered in terms of how it is currently structured in terms of pay, work, responsibility, etc.

We suggest that the teacher unions take the lead in helping school districts devise new models for salary approaches. Specifically, we suggest the following for consideration:

- Our main recommendation is for school districts to seriously consider diversification of the work force. In schools, teachers are typically treated as a homogenous workforce working on the assembly line. Although there are teacher assistants and aides, the general arrangement is that a teacher teaches a class. As a result, there is little differentiation or diversification of teachers, little opportunity to move to a higher-level teaching role. For instance, a teacher who has taught for 30 years teaches a class that is the same as another teacher who just has one year of experience. A teacher who is paid $20,000 more teaches the same class as her junior colleague. The lack of work diversification makes teacher payment based on experience and credential acceptable. Can schools learn from the medical profession and hospitals to change the arrangement? When we go visit a medical doctor, we are first greeted by the receptionist, then we meet the nurse, then we meet the doctor, only for a short while. Sometimes we engage with a physician's assistant, or even a nurse practitioner—many of whom offer medical services these days at pharmacies. In a hospital, the arrangement is even more complex. Can schools have teacher aides, teacher cadets, teachers, master teachers, senior teachers, whatever to differentiate the role and allow for progression of responsibilities and remuneration within the teaching ranks? Perhaps this could even save money if other variables like class size per individual or full-year calendars were employed as part of the overall strategy. Point is, the same old same old is ready for a fix.
- Given that a transformative change is challenging and even if desired will take time, we also suggest employing a hybrid pay model with some portion of salary increase dollars going towards credentials and years of experience, with the remaining funds distributed in a model determined by teachers and staff with school leadership. What that split should be isn't clear, but we suggest starting with some of the funds going to both buckets. Principals should have the final say regarding the pay for teachers in their schools. This way, overall salaries will continue to go up, but those performing better on the variables and factors locally identified get rewarded for their performance. Perhaps some portion of the performance-based measures should be local school, others district-wide. Whatever system is devised, it needs to be assessed every few years to determine how it is working, with adjustments made given the feedback, especially as needs, priorities, and personnel change.
- Teams of teachers should be part of the assessment model for their colleagues, providing guidance and support for their principals. Maybe this can be part of Berry et al.'s (2013) concept of teacher leadership. But just as Fullan (2016) called for teachers to drive

change in schools, his mantra of "let the group change the group" holds equal value for teachers in devising and carrying out remuneration policies that affect their lives.

- We believe that such systems should allow for some individualization for different teachers—much as we believe in individualized instruction and learning for students. Teachers should be able to contribute in varying ways to their school and classroom success. Multiple factors should be considered in developing systems for rewarding teacher importance.
- Finally, leaders need be cautious that this system turns out not to be just another way for everyone to continue to get the same level of salary raise each year. The goal is to reward best performance, and that needs to drive what is developed and implemented.

CHAPTER 17

Meta-Analysis

Statistics and certain statistical practices have dominated science and social science for decades. But within these fields, much controversy exists about the value of certain common statistics and practices. For example, Amrhein, Greenland, and McShane (2019), in a commentary in the highly respected journal *Nature,* called for the concept of statistical significance to be abandoned to avoid statistical abuses in decision making. Similarly, a special issue of the journal *The American Statistician* in 2019 was devoted to correcting the misuse of the concept of statistical significance, with the editors (Wasserstein et al., 2019), explaining "statistical methods do not rid data of their uncertainty" (p. 3). More broadly, as the British journalist Michael Blastland and economist Andrew Dilnot (2009) explained in their book *The Numbers Game,* numbers can "bamboozle not enlighten, terrorize not guide, and all too easily end up abused and distrusted. Potent but shifty, the role of numbers is frighteningly ambiguous" (p. xi). As researchers ourselves, we use statistics and numbers all the time, but as Wasserstein and his colleagues (2019) suggested for all researchers, there is a need to accept uncertainty, be thoughtful, be open, and be modest.

Education, like many other fields, has multiple subfields with numerous research studies performed and testimonies reported and published about how things work. For years scholars wishing to get a sense of the meaning of all the research and studies in a particular field would review the studies individually, likely categorize them across multiple components, and seek commonalities and themes in order to draw some kind of findings about the collective outcomes. No doubt, among the many studies and publications were reports of varying quality. In more recent decades, a very sophisticated approach to doing this involved a psychometric review known as meta-analysis, where studies are categorized in terms of their research sufficiency, then those deemed of high enough quality are somehow made equivalent enough to perform a quantitative review to discern collective findings. While there are approaches for doing meta-syntheses of qualitative studies, many meta-analyses don't include qualitative studies. Clearly a lot of issues with doing this, but it gave education and the other fields performing these analyses a quantitative way to conduct these mega reviews. The analysis elicited numbers, which in our culture gains a level of prominence beyond analyses that don't employ them as part of the formula. Mathematicians have come to understand, as Eriksson (2012) explained, that if math is held up too high in prominence, "its use is not subjected to sufficient levels of critical thinking" (p. 746). Or as Sperber (2010) described the phenomenon of accepting things not fully understood, "what readers do is judge profound what they have failed to grasp" (p. 583).

We see meta-analysis as a duck-and-cover approach to aid in influencing educational policy and practice. It is a really good idea to find a way to systematize the review of the large numbers of publications about educational work. It is incredibly seductive to have a way to produce a set of numbers that leads us on the path to the yellow-brick road. But just as Dorothy and Toto and the other characters in *The Wizard of Oz* faced mighty challenges along the way, meta-analysis elucidates challenges and results that deserve to be taken with caution before going out and changing what educators do. Perhaps okay as a guide for further consideration of practices, but duck and cover, it really evokes results that raise too many red flags to serve in the prominent role it has taken.

Meta-analysis perhaps never would have reached so many policy-makers and practitioners in education without *Visible Learning*. In 2008, Warwick Mansell of the U.K.-based education magazine, *Times Education Supplement*, or *TES*, wrote: "It is perhaps education's equivalent to the search for the Holy Grail—or the answer to life, the universe and everything" (Mansell, 2008). "Grappled with by teachers and educationists for millennia, the perennial question goes a bit like this: if you could change one thing about the way our schooling system is run, what would it be?" Mansell continued, "Now, what is believed to be the largest ever educational research study—covering more than 80 million pupils and bringing together more than 50,000 smaller studies—has come up with the answer."

The holy grail on teaching Mansell wrote about is a book called *Visible Learning: A Synthesis of Over 800 Meta-analyses Relating to Achievement* authored by John Hattie (Hattie, 2009), an education professor at the University of Auckland in New Zealand at the time. The book reports results of Hattie's synthesis of more than 800 meta-analyses of studies related to student achievement. Basically, Hattie conducted a meta-analysis of other meta-analytical studies, a meta-analysis of meta-analyses. Again, a meta-analysis is essentially a statistical approach to combine results of many studies.

After analyzing meta-analyzing over 800 meta-analytical studies in education, Hattie arrived at a list of over 130 influences that affect student achievement. He calculated the effect sizes for each. Hattie found that the average effect size of all intervention is 0.4 and he uses this "hinge point" to judge the effectiveness of the influences. He rank-ordered the influences according to their effective sizes, resulting in a list of what works best or better in education.

Hattie continued his line of work and published his updated findings in his 2011 book *Visible Learning for Teachers: Maximizing Impact on Learning* (Hattie, 2012) and his article "The Applicability of Visible Learning to Higher Education" (Hattie, 2015). Hattie and colleagues have also written books based on the visible learning framework for teachers, school leaders, and parents. The most recent is *10 Steps to Develop Great Learners: Visible Learning for Parents* (Hattie & Hattie, 2022), in which they claim to have "evidence from about a third of a billion students, over 100,000 studies, and over 300 influences" (p. 152).

The list of influences or factors was expanded from the original 138 to more than 300. Hattie arranged the influences into six areas: the student, the home, the school, the curricula, the teacher, and teaching and learning approaches. But since he was not interested in "what cannot be influenced in schools" (Hattie, 2008, p. iix), his book is about what schools, teachers, and parents can do to help students learn.

Visible learning has become a multi-million-dollar enterprise in education. Hattie's work, with lots of numbers, simple answers to complex problems, and impressive presentations, was exactly what education policymakers, school leaders, and practitioners had been looking for. Visible learning and John Hattie have been embraced by policymakers and practitioners around the world. Although Hattie stated in the book that he wanted to give "an explanatory story, not a 'what works' recipe" (Hattie, 2008, p. 3), the book turns out, or at least perceived by many readers, to be a list of what works best in education (Bergeron, 2017). "He is not the messiah," wrote Darren Evans in *TES*, the publication that called visible learning education's holy grail, "but for many policy makers he comes close. John Hattie, possibly the world's most influential education academic, has the ear of governments everywhere" (Evans, 2012). It has also reached hundreds of thousands of teachers around the globe.

Where did meta-analysis come from? Gene Glass, then a professor at the University of Colorado, has been credited as the modern founder of meta-analysis. Although the approach had been used by others decades before, it was in a 1976 article published in *Educational Researcher* with the title "Primary, Secondary, and Meta-analysis of Research" (Glass, 1976), Glass first used the term:

> My major interest currently is in what we have come to call—not for want of a less pretentious name—the meta-analysis of research. The term is a bit grand, but it is precise, and apt, and in the spirit of "meta-mathematics," "meta-psychology," and "meta-evaluation." Meta-analysis refers to the analysis of analyses. I use it to refer to the statistical analysis of a large collection of analysis results from individual studies for the purpose of integrating the findings. It connotes a rigorous alternative to the casual, narrative discussions of research studies which typify our attempts to make sense of the rapidly expanding research literature. (p. 3)

Meta-analysis has been advanced by many scholars. It has also become a common approach in educational research to extract and summarize common findings across studies. The American Educational Research Association (AERA), the leading research organization in the field of education, has a journal called "Review of Educational Research," that has essentially become a journal of meta-analyses of the many facets covered under the umbrella of education.

The primary approach for meta-analysis is relatively straightforward: 1. Define the question (for example: Does class size affect student academic achievement?); 2. Search the literature to find related studies; 3. Select appropriate and qualified studies to be included; 4. Decide which variables or summary measures are allowed; 5. Select a meta-analysis model to use; and 6. Examine sources of between-study heterogeneity.

A primary purpose of meta-analysis is to analyze the effect of certain interventions on certain outcomes. For example, there is a strong interest in the effect of class size on student achievement. As a result, numerous studies have investigated the impact of class size on learning. Some studies found it to be very powerful while others found it to have little impact. In quantitative studies, the effect is expressed in effect sizes. So we can imagine one study found the effect size of class size on student achievement, which can be standardized test scores, to be 0.4 but another study with similar sample size has an effect size of −0.4. Pulled together, the effect size is 0. Of course, meta-analysis covers many more than two studies. But the idea is similar despite the complicated statistical process and considerations.

While meta-analysis can be a very powerful tool for understanding the impact of certain programs or interventions in education, medicine, and other fields, the practice has its share of critics. It has specific methodological requirements and considerations. For example, it first requires that the studies included were conducted with high quality. Second, it also requires that all studies of the same topic are included so as to avoid bias. For instance, because of the bias for positive effects in publications, we need to be aware of studies that were not published for finding negative impact.

It is thus no surprise that the *visible learning* work done by John Hattie and colleagues has been criticized from a variety of different angles (Bergeron, 2017; Brown, 2013; Snook et al., 2009; Terhart, 2011). One of the biggest criticisms is Hattie's method. For example, Neil Brown, a computing education researcher at King's College London in the UK, pointed out many methodological flaws in Hattie's effect sizes in 2013. Brown charged that Hattie's averaging and comparison of effect sizes across different studies and interventions were inappropriate, essentially confusing apples as oranges (Brown, 2013). Ewald Terhart, a professor at the University of Münster in Germany, reviewed Hattie's work and concluded: "It is obvious that Hattie in fact has not found the Holy Grail of research on schooling, teaching, and teachers" (Terhart, 2011, p. 436).

Pierre-Jérôme Bergeron, a Canadian statistician at the University of Ottawa, accused Hattie of practicing pseudoscience. In the article "How to Engage in Pseudoscience with Real Data: A Criticism of John Hattie's Arguments in Visible Learning From the Perspective of a Statistician," Bergeron pointed out a number of methodological errors that threaten the foundation of Hattie's conclusions. For example, Bergeron asserts: "Hattie's method is not statistically sophisticated"; "he . . . is capable of using a formula that converts a correlation into Cohen's d . . ., without understanding the prerequisites for this type of conversion to be valid. He is guilty of many errors. . . ." After explaining Hattie's statistical errors in detail, Bergeron concluded: "It is clear that John Hattie and his team have neither the knowledge nor the competencies required to conduct valid statistical analyses. No one should replicate this methodology because we must never accept pseudoscience" (Bergeron, 2017).

But beyond the psychometric problems many point to, for a number of reasons, meta-analysis can be quite problematic in practice even when it is conducted properly. First, it is extremely difficult to conduct truly randomized studies in education, which means the settings of educational research can vary a great deal. As a result, findings from one study in one class, one school, or one school district may not be compared to findings from another study in another class, school, or school district. For example, a study of students in inner-city Chicago may not be treated the same as a study in the suburb of Chicago. A study of students in the United States cannot be accepted as equivalent to a study of students in China. Some interventions may work very well in one context but can have a negative impact in another context. Combining the results and finding the average can both ignore the positive and neglect the negative impact. It's just like averaging the impact of there being a fire engulfing people in a tropical area and in the Antarctic.

Second, no educational intervention works for all students equally. It may work well for some students but can be detrimental to others. This is one of the reasons that the effect sizes in educational studies are typically moderate. When meta-analyses pulled effect sizes together, they basically ignore the "side effects" on some students. While for policy purposes, it is reasonable to neglect the negative impact on some students, in practice, no student should be sacrificed for other students.

Third, educational studies typically research the effects of certain interventions on specific outcomes such as grades or test scores, which measure the degree to which students have learned the required content. There are many other outcomes that are not measured, for example, social-emotional capabilities, engagement with school, longer-term transfer, or creativity. The short-term outcomes may come at a cost of other outcomes. Meta-analysis does not help identify the impact of interventions on other outcomes (Zhao, 2018).

Fourth, if meta-analyses don't make a thorough analysis of the costs of adoption and implementation, the value to schools is rather limited. Many educational interventions and practices are quite costly, requiring buy-in, training, and ongoing support. Even if the meta-analysis happened to identify something appropriate for adoption, these other considerations have to be considered. Moreover, the interactions that any intervention may have with what is already in place, in essence, a thoughtful systemic consideration of adopting any new practice is necessary for anything to actually perform well in the real world.

Finally, leaving out well designed and conducted qualitative studies that explore the specifics and idiosyncrasies of any intervention, likely leaves the nuance present in any policy implementation out of the discussion. So most meta-analytic analyses have severe limits as to what they can say and offer practitioners.

In sum, while meta-analysis has its place as a technique in the education space, the inferential leaps made to moderating practice as a result of the forced matching of multiple research studies is fraught with problems. Going back to our comments at the beginning of this chapter, meta-analysis is fraught with uncertainty. Any results need be taken with a large dose of modesty. It is in this way that meta-analysis falls into the duck-and-cover fold. Good idea, certainly there is value to gaining a broad understanding about what is going on in terms of combining results of different studies. But this is incredibly problematic for a variety of reasons we identified when it comes to impacting practice. If it is the holy grail, as some have suggested, it is of the Monty Python variety!

RECONSIDER, REMOVE, REPLACE

As has been discussed regarding the practices and policies in multiple of our chapters, educational practitioners, policymakers, and the general public all have a vested interest in finding ways to improve education. Meta-analysis is seen as a tool to help educators and leaders find ways to adjust practice. But it is tragically flawed, putting together studies that many times are incredibly difficult to merge. It also leaves out many studies that may not be as psychometrically rigorous as needed for the analysis to work, but many of these could lend significant nuance and understanding to what is known about the practice under review.

In the end, we aren't necessarily calling for the end of meta-analysis and the search to find better ways to make sense out of multiple studies in a field or subfield in education. Instead, we call for a reconsidering of what is done and stepping back from accepting these large-scale sophisticated analyses as the end-all for what works. Instead, we believe that any review of studies, including meta-analyses, requires a further set of considerations prior to jumping to practice based on what in many cases is faulty. Meta-analysis is sophisticated and has the feel of hard science, but in the end, it potentially creates false hope for what truly works. As the statisticians we quoted at the outset of this chapter warned, it is important to remember what they called "ATOM: accept uncertainty, be thoughtful, open, and modest" (Wasserstein et al. 2019, p. 3).

We argue for another layer of analysis, where the real-world application of results from meta-analyses and individual studies is considered involving the great variety of people, places, implementation, financial considerations, utility, and situations we alluded to. The results of thoughtful qualitative studies need be considered. The larger view should help in pinpointing approaches that school people should try, rather than jumping on the results of meta-analyses without this further set of considerations. Remember, effect sizes and other statistics used are numbers created by statisticians to help in understanding what works in practice over a multitude of situations and studies. But what goes behind those numbers, and what actual effect sizes really make a difference in varying circumstances, has to be discerned by those in the field.

Think of it this way. New drugs in medicine go through multiple phases of studies, over many years, before being allowed to be sold on the open market. Most tested drugs don't make it through the process. Once drugs are approved, all prescriptions come with a laundry list of possible negative side effects that the drugs may have on humans, as we all may react differently. There also is a long list of possible interactions the drugs might have with other prescriptions people take. The bottom line is that there is a lot of study and a lot of care into approving drugs before releasing them to the public. Shouldn't we do the same with educational practices and interventions? For surely there are possible side effects and multiple potential interactions that the single numbers that meta-analyses elicit don't even consider. Reconsider the use of meta-analysis, let's come up with something better.

Conclusion

Looking Forward—Are There Better Ways?

One of our favorite TED talks was given in 2011 by economic writer Tim Harford, called "Trial, Error and the God Complex." In it Harford talks about Archie Cochrane, a Scottish physician in the middle part of the 20th century whose work over the years promoted randomized controlled trials (RCT) and systemic reviews. Harford's talk was about how Cochrane challenged current state-of-the-art thinking in various situations using RCT-like approaches, as a means to address what Harford referred to as a terrible affliction, what he called the "God Complex." In essence, no matter how complicated a problem or issue may be, the God Complex is that you are convinced that you understand the way the world works, that your set of solutions is correct. Harford describes several instances where that wasn't the case, explaining how the God Complex afflicts not just doctors, but economists, businesspeople, policymakers, even educators—leaders in many fields and endeavors. Harford explained how so many of us don't want our conclusions or approaches challenged or tested. He concluded by explaining how Cochrane understood "that uncertainty, that fallibility, that being challenged, they hurt. But sometimes you need to be shocked out of that." He ended by asserting how hard this is, how important this is, but also that "it is very difficult to make good mistakes" (Harford, 2011).

The education version of the God complex is what this book addressed. Duck-and-cover policies persist because they aren't questioned. Our intent isn't to criticize educational leaders or policymakers, but to point them in a direction to challenge their thinking and approaches, to find better ways to educate students and run schools and school systems. To think about what is being done, as difficult as Harford explains that is.

We need to be humble enough ourselves to listen to our own advice and examine what we've proposed in an ongoing way. Perhaps we are wrong about some of the duck-and-cover policies and practices we analyzed. We accept that and urge readers to set us straight. But we also urge that just implementing policies and practices without the necessary forethought, not constantly examining what is being done and assessing its value, will lead to a continuation of the duck-and-cover concerns we raised.

What we discovered through our analyses was that underlying the duck-and-cover policies and practices in schools are several erroneous assumptions. These assumptions are prevalent in education collectively despite the fact that individually we may not agree that they make sense. This is very much like racism in that we hear people say that they have friends from certain racial groups, but then they still hold negative racist views of those groups.

The first assumption underlying duck-and-cover policies is that students are the same and need the same curriculum and outcomes. The duck-and-cover policies and practices around kindergarten readiness, 3rd-grade reading readiness, closing the achievement gap, college and career readiness, SEL, and talented and gifted education are all driven by this assumption. We in this country hold firmly that all children must have the same outcomes, despite the reality that this is not possible. All children must study the same content, acquire the same skill and knowledge, develop the same attitude and perspective, and pass the same test at the same age. This belief is strengthened with another firm belief that all children will need the same knowledge, skills, and abilities to succeed in education and in life. Thus governments, policymakers, business leaders, and the public have all been working on creating the dream set of content, and school leaders, parents, teachers, and students have all been forced to make sure that students indeed master the prescribed dream content. Of course, regardless of the efforts, it is impossible for all students to achieve the same outcomes at the same time, which then results in approaches like talented and gifted programs for the more accomplished and remedial or sometimes special education programming for those who do poorly.

This assumption is far from the reality of the world and humanity. First, there is no dream set of knowledge and skills that work for all people in the world today. In our rapidly changing world, it is impossible to predict what talents, passions, skills, knowledge, and abilities may be most valuable and work well in what context in the future. What is needed is to support the development of individual talents and passions, cultivate creativity and entrepreneurial thinking, and foster the impact mindset so that students have the passion and talent to create impact for the world and others. Second, students are fundamentally different from each other. They are born with different aptitudes, interests, and personalities. They are born into different families, communities, and cultures. Their natural-born qualities interact with their post-birth experiences to create a unique jagged profile of qualities for each student. When they come to school and go through school, their differences interact with the homogenous school experiences and result in advanced, average, and poor performances in schools. Schools should be the place to provide experiences to support the development of their individual differences and guide them to utilize their differences to impact the world.

The second assumption underlying duck-and-cover policies is that students are compliant and willing recipients of information (or education). Thus, they are expected to follow whatever dream content policymakers create for them and whatever programs schools place them in. The message we adults give children when we want them to learn something is always "for your own good." As a result, policymakers and schools come up with all sorts of "readiness" standards, divide students into different tracks and groups, deliver foreign languages in secondary school, and provide remediation in reading and math for those who are behind. But the reality is that children are autonomous and intentional human beings. They have intentions, they want respect, they desire autonomy, and they pursue purpose in life. They then make decisions based on their own perspectives of their interests, abilities, and relationships. To quote that famous Frank Sinatra song, "I did it my way." The same is true for all of us, including students. So they do not blindly accept and exert all their energy into whatever schools want them to do. They can also suffer tremendously in schools, losing interest, developing low self-esteem, and/or resisting or rejecting schools. They may have multiple interests that schools never address. Today, it's unknown how to calculate the impact of social media and how often students are online and interacting, often to us in unfathomable ways. Point is, treating students as a homogeneous passive group is erroneous. It is this approach to students as simple passive recipients of whatever is offered that impacted the success of the effective schools movement of the 1980s and 1990s. It implied that certain characteristics of schools and teaching were needed for effectiveness, but ignored that students aren't passive, uninterested participants in the teaching and learning processes.

The third assumption beneath duck-and-cover fiascos is that the future world is the same as in the past. Based on this assumption, we can design the content, process, approach, and structure of learning based on what we knew from the past, even as long as 100 or 200 years ago. But the reality is that our world is ever changing and the changes are emerging more rapidly than ever before. What are the right things to teach? How should we do that? Much what students are required to learn and how schools are structured is based on what was meaningful before. Schools continue to force all students to learn the same outdated prepackaged content—despite the fact that traditional human jobs have been and continue to be replaced by smart machines, despite the fact that numerous individuals have created their own jobs, despite the fact that the future is uncertain, regardless of the incredible advances in technology and social media, and despite the fact the future world does not need a workforce with homogenous knowledge and skills, especially from what will soon be the past. Moreover, even though students today can learn via technology from various resources and sources, the overall teaching plan in schools remains pretty stagnant, that one teacher needs to be responsible for a group of students of similar age.

The fourth assumption regarding duck and cover is that teachers are a uniform workforce instead of live, purposeful, and autonomous individual human beings. As a result, the education system believes that teachers being mandated what to teach, how to act, how to be assessed, in other words, how to behave on all fronts, drives policy—sadly creating far too much constraint where leeway makes more sense. As some teachers explained to us, during the period leading up to state testing they tell their students and parents not to worry, that once the tests are over they can get back to what they are supposed to be doing. What a depressing sentiment and sad state of affairs.

And it follows and is assumed that whatever teachers are asked to do will happen as planned. Thus, for teachers, the numerous policies and curriculum changes that have been made, for example the teacher evaluation approaches (including the value-added models), are implicitly laden with assumptions that teachers could change their teaching and ultimately improve test scores for all students. These demands never worked but they have continued and will continue unless it is recognized that teachers need be treated more respectfully, and their individual differences need be seen as a strength for schools and students. Moreover, teachers need to be recognized as human beings, with their own interests and abilities, with their own emotions and life experiences, and with their strengths and weaknesses. It gets even more complicated. As Berliner (2014) highlighted, "teacher effects" can't simply be attributed to teachers, but must consider multiple interactions among many variables, among student peers, considering things like composition of classrooms, school climate, leadership, funding differentials, etc. Schools need to recognize this variability and give teachers autonomy so that they can become professionals and exercise their professional and human judgment in schools.

These four assumptions led to the mindset that drives the duck-and-cover policies and practices. In addition, through our analyses of the varying issues we addressed, we found multiple themes that transcended them and characterize the zeitgeist of living in a duck-and-cover world in schools.

First, we find it ironic that as an institution which has typically been characterized as uncreative and rejecting innovations, schools actually implement a lot of different things, and are at times responsive to new demands or policies and ideas as a bureaucratic unit of the education system. So they do change, but in prescribed ways that the systems control. It isn't so much complete continuity overall, but instead, continuity in core practices and approaches that characterize schools and schooling. While the fundamental structures and core content standards, as well as classroom teaching, are very resistant to change, schools do adopt new ideas imposed by the system or by social popularity, often resulting in what we refer to as the "cart before the horse syndrome." Just because an idea is promoted and popular, schools often accept that and implement the new practice or program before they should, without necessarily knowing what they mean or what teachers may do with them. There often is little good evidence regarding effectiveness. This is why ideas such SEL, meta-analysis, class size, educational technology, and class scheduling have been accepted and integrated into schools, with very few questioning or worrying about the effectiveness, benefits, or impact of these practices. The most significant concern related to the cart-before-the-horse problem is going to educational practice before there is sufficient research, field-level practice, and testing to support what is being done. There is no generally accepted stamp of approval to guide schools and their leaders.

Related to this is a second theme we refer to as the "implementation blues." For decades, research has lamented issues with implementing reforms well into schools. Schools copy what their colleague districts do without understanding the differences among multiple settings. Schools respond to local political pressure or demands often with little sense of what research really suggests, leaving the science behind. Fidelity of implementation of any reform is always a challenge, given how isolated teachers are and the inability for schools and districts to provide guidance or oversight to determine if the proposed changes are being implemented appropriately. We sensed this in the implementation of dress and grooming policies, SEL, 3rd-grade reading, kindergarten readiness, and other policies. How time is used in schools has proven remarkably resistance to alteration. But to us, we offer the caution derived from the medical world, where despite their many problems, they go about implementation in a far more careful and deliberate way.

Indeed, those studying medical interventions suggest that it takes up to 17 years to move from evidence into practice, including clinical practices, treatments, and new drugs. These time lags are due to multiple variables, such as the need for clinical trials, astounding financial and personnel costs, and gathering and assessing all the evidence. Clinical guidelines are established for moving to practice (Morris et al., 2011; Munro & Savel, 2016). We aren't suggesting a 17-year lag time is a good thing, and in the political world of education, where parents, politicians, and others often promote their favorite idea for schools, such a time delay probably isn't even feasible. But in education, little of this formality in the adoption and implementation processes is present, so the lag isn't nearly as pronounced. However, it results in implementing far more questionable practices that somehow become institutionalized to a much higher degree than would likely be the case if some version of the medical approach were utilized. The notion of the onslaught of fads and frills we mentioned in the Introduction to this book, where new reforms come and go frequently in education, is the outcome of educators and leaders not being more deliberate when implementing interventions.

We need to add here that part of the challenge of implementation of anything new in schools, especially anything dramatically new, involves changing what is done with students, and asking teachers and leaders who have spent decades in schools—ostensibly liking what they experienced (or else why enter the field as a professional?), to change what is comfortable and known. And how many parents will willingly put up with changing what they expect based on their understanding and experiences, and allowing their kids to serve as guinea pigs for the latest new idea? Strong science might help, but these realities add to the implementation blues, along with what we described in Chapter 7 as the equivalent of expecting a religious conversion to happen among those responsible for carrying out the latest idea.

In addition, there are often interactions among these themes. Sometimes, for example, the latest reform or fad is implemented too soon before it is tested well enough at scale, the cart-before-the-horse syndrome, and at the same time the implementation is lousy, too. When this happens, it is hard to determine if the new idea really stinks, or if it was never really tried appropriately and tested because the implementation was so screwed up.

Third, to some degree, it is impressive how schools mimic their neighbors. A play on NCLB's name with a slight twist could easily apply here, "no district left behind" (NDLB)! If something seems to be making a difference in one locale, educators and policymakers often jump to adopt it or attempt to implement these to scale—we understand why this happens given the pressure to perform well on the standardized measures employed. But there is a great likelihood of a real dearth of evidence that these specific practices work all that well in the first place, but certainly little data suggesting it translates anywhere else. This is where well-designed clinical trials might be of assistance. We appreciate the pressures leaders face to improve schools, and understand that elected school board members are politicians who have to show something for their time in the limelight if they want to be re-elected. As a result, too often new things are suggested just after some leaders or policymakers attend a conference where the latest "magic bullet" was promoted. Or state officials push something new without it having been vetted properly. In the case of schools, these mandates can often come from legislatures or state governing bodies for schools, were the likelihood of full scientific support being necessary for promoting a practice is rather slim. Institutional sociologists refer to this instinct to copy as institutional isomorphism, and it is common in schools. It is why nearly all the policies and practices we examined are so prevalent, despite the weak research support for their use.

Fourth, we weren't particularly surprised, but the prevalence and dominance of tests ungirding most everything that happens in schools was stark. We refer to this as "the tyranny of the metrics." Nearly every issue we analyzed referred to improving test scores as the basis for introducing or keeping the practice or replacing something already being done. Third grade proficiency, test based. Kindergarten readiness, test-based. We expect for SEL that standardized tests are on the horizon, as the lack of good assessments was a common concern among those studying SEL. Only time will tell how good those assessments will be. We certainly know that the experts promoting SEL suggest one of its main promises is that students strong in SEL will raise their academic standardized test scores. But go down the list of duck-and-cover policies and practices we reviewed. Test scores show up a lot. Interestingly, even when non-test-based approaches to solving problems are suggested, for example, classroom observations in lieu of test-based teacher evaluations, tests pop their ugly heads. Many new systems tie the validity of their results on these differing approaches to, guess what, higher student test scores. So we develop schemes to replace tests, then validate them with the tests we just replaced. Again, as stated in our chapter on standardized tests, we recognize that assessments are important and good tests need prevail. But the world of assessment of students and teachers and schools themselves need better measures. The metrics that have prevailed for a long time continue to dominate.

Related to this, our review of meta-analysis underscores the statistical and quantitative envy that is part of the "tyranny of the metrics" syndrome. If we can quantify something, it must be good. This, of course, flies in the face of the reality of uncertainty in education. Moreover, so many of the statistical experts we cited caution about this envy for sophisticated numbers and formulas.

Education is at a very interesting crossroads. Since the first George Bush and Bill Clinton Goals 2000 drive, through second Bush NCLB and Obama administration's Race to the Top initiatives, and most recently the unnamed education efforts of the Trump administration, we have at least wasted three decades from the highest levels of government in pushing education forward. Certainly some positive initiatives have been introduced and implemented. Our analysis reveals insights as to policies and practices that were adopted, often with much fanfare, but have exhausted their shelf-life. In recent decades especially, dramatic changes have taken shape, in technology, demographics, societal needs. COVID-19 has become part of our everyday reality. There have been many calls for education to change, to teach students different skills and knowledge, to change structure and approaches for teachers and student learning. Demands have emerged to teach students differently. But schools have been stuck with and constrained by many duck-and-cover policies and practices, without much challenge or real meaningful and productive alterations. Certainly, nothing transformative has transpired.

Since March 2020, as COVID-19 became a part of life (and still lingers, seemingly ready to pounce again at any moment), a universal period of experiment in education emerged that pushed all schools and teachers to teach differently. Schools flashed their potential for significant change. But they need to examine their practices and let go of the dinosaurs that still roam the systems, hallways, and classrooms in schools. Schools need to move forward and come up with different and better ideas to teach our independent human learners in a world that is unpredictably transformed by technology, politics, climate change, globalization, and other forces bearing down on the school buildings, much as the imagined atomic bombs ready to pounce on schools that led to the original duck-and-cover movement. The emerging field of complexity science teaches us that linearity and predictability don't exist in complex, open systems like schools, and success derives from being adaptable and evolving with the circumstances (e.g., see Waldrop, 1992; Wheatley, 1992). If we let this moment pass us by, if we don't look at what we do and make the appropriate changes, then duck and cover, we'll remain under our desks for another generation.

A DUCK-AND-COVER AUDIT GUIDE FOR SCHOOLS

We close with a suggestion for ways practitioners might employ an anti–duck and cover strategy in examining their policies and practices. Think of this as our duck-and-cover audit guide. It uses elements of backward design in framing a series of guiding questions for school leaders, policymakers, and practitioners to think about as they examine their practices and policies.

1. What was the original intent of the policy or practice, or what is the intent for something being considered?
    a. Be sure to fully understand what policy or practice is being suggested, and if already in pace, why it was originally adopted?
    b. If the policy or program is long standing, does it still fit with current needs?
2. What are/were the specific outcomes expected? And what are the side effects; what possible negative and damaging effects are/were there that accompany the outcomes?
3. Is there any evidence that it met these outcomes, and if something new or recent, what is the basis for believing it will work, has worked, continues to work? Be honest!
4. Assess the evidence. Is the evidence solid or is it opinion, part of the folklore of the district, state, or country? Do any data actually exist that substantiate its effectiveness and reason for continuation? If not, get out there and collect some in order to do some evaluation and assessment.
5. Be brave, dump what deserves to be dumped, make adjustments if the policy or practice still has value. Don't start what shouldn't be started (e.g., just because the neighboring district does it, doesn't mean you should).
6. Involve the whole school community in this assessment. The voice of leaders, teachers, students, parents, and the broader community all have a place, especially on sacred concepts like school board governance, dress and grooming codes, etc.
7. Remember that as a student, feedback and correctives were the only way to learn. As leaders, you are learners, too—so ongoing feedback, assessment, and adjustment should be at the core of your practice. That process, that version of trial and error, is what is known as science. Be scientifically savvy leaders.

We invite those who read this book to join us in the anti–duck and cover movement to transform schools. Send us your stories and ideas, and we'll use them to continue to promote the kinds of changes schools deserve. E-mail us at duckandcoverbook@gmail.com with your thoughts.

References

Introduction

Callahan, R. E. (1962). *Education and the cult of efficiency*. The University of Chicago Press.

Cohen, D. K., & Mehta, J. D. (2017). Why reform sometimes succeeds: Understanding the conditions that produce reforms that last. *American Educational Research Journal, 54*(4), 644–690.

De Gruchy, J. W. (2009). *Dietrich Bonhoeffer works, Vol. 8: Letters and paper from prison*. Fortress Press.

DiMaggio, P. J., & Powell, W. W. (1983). The iron cage revisited: Institutional and collective rationality in organizational fields. *American Sociological Review, 48*, 147–160.

DiMaggio, P. J., & Powell, W. W. (1991). Introduction. In W. W. Powell & P. J. DiMaggio (Eds.), *The new institutionalism in organizational analysis*. University of Chicago Press.

Downs, A. (1957). *An economic theory of democracy*. Addison Wesley.

Fullan, M. (2016). Amplify change with professional capital. *JSD, 37*(1), 44–56.

Fullan, M. (2007). *The new meaning of educational change* (4th ed.). Teachers College Press.

Kruglanski, A. W., & Peri, N., & Zakai, D. ((1991). Interactive effects of need for closure and initial confidence on social information seeking. *Social Cognition, 9*(2), 127–148.

Marris, P. (1974). *Loss and change*. Anchor.

Neustadt, R. E., & May, E. R. (1988). Thinking in time: The uses of history for decision-makers. The Free Press.

Nickerson, Raymond S. (1998), Confirmation bias: A ubiquitous phenomenon in many guises. *Review of General Psychology, 2*(2): 175–220.

Popper, Sir K. R. (1966). *Of clouds and clocks*. Arthur Holly Compton Memorial Lecture. Washington University Press.

Pressman J. L., & Wildavsky, A. (1973). *Implementation*. University of California Press.

Ramirez, A. (2013). *Save our science: How to inspire a new generation of scientists*. TED Books.

Schultz, K. (2010). *Being wrong*. HarperCollins.

Scriven, M. (1983). *Evaluation ideologies*. In G. F. Madaus, M. Scriven, & D. L. Stufflebeam (Eds.), *Evaluation models*. Kluwer-Nijhoff Publishing.

Sperber, D. (2010). The guru effect. *Review of Philosophy and Psychology, 1*, 583–592.

Tower, W. E. (1932). The truth about "fads and frills." *The Journal of Education, 115*(12), 346–348.

Trout, J. D. (2002). Scientific explanation and the sense of understanding. *Philosophy of Science, 69*, 212–233.

Tyack, D., & Cuban, L. (1995). *Tinkering towards utopia: A century of public school reform.* Harvard University Press.

Waldrop, M. M. (1992). *Complexity: The emerging science at the edge of order and chaos.* A Touchstone Book, Simon and Schuster.

Watzlawick, P., Weakland, J. H., & Fisch, R. (1974). *Change: Principles of problem formation and problem resolution.* W.W. Norton & Co.

Webster, D. M., & Kruglanski, A. W. (1994). Individual differences in need for cognitive closure. *Journal of Personality and Social Psychology, 67*(6), 1049–1062.

Zhao, Y. (2018). *What works may hurt: Side effects in education.* Teachers College Press.

Chapter 1

Ackerman, D. J. (2018). *Real world compromises: Policy and practice impacts of kindergarten entry assessment-related validity and reliability challenges.* Education Testing Service: Policy Information Report and ETS Research Report Series No. RR-18–13.

Cameron, K., & Boyles, D. (2022). Learning and teaching in a neoliberal era: The tensions of engaging in Froebelian-informed pedagogy while encountering quality standards. *Global Education Review, 9*(2), 99–117.

Education Commission of the States (2020). 50-state comparison: State K-3 policies. Retrieved June 8, 2022, from https://www.ecs.org/kindergarten-policies/

Elkind, D. (2009). *The hurried child.* Da Capo Lifelong Books.

Gardner, H. (1983). *Frames of mind: The theory of multiple intelligences.* Basic Books.

Gardner, H. E. (2006). *Multiple intelligences: New horizons in theory and practice.* Basic Books.

Grodsky, E., Huangfu, Y., Miesner, H. R., & Packard, C. (2017). Kindergarten readiness in Wisconsin. WCER Working Paper No. 2017.3, University of Wisconsin: Wisconsin Center for Education Research.

Jeynes, W. H. (2006). Standardized tests and Froebel's original kindergarten model. *Teachers College Record, 108*(10), 1937–1959.

Johnson, I. (2019). *"We're trying to have a childhood": Parent notions of kindergarten readiness* [Ed.D. dissertation thesis]. University of New England.

John, O. P., Robins, R. W., & Pervin, L. A. (2008). *Handbook of personality: Theory and research* (3rd ed.). Guilford Press.

Oregon Department of Education. (2017). What is kindergarten assessment? Retrieved from https://oregonearlylearning.com/parents-families/kindergarten -ready/kindergarten-assessment/

Pierson, A. (2018). Exploring state-by-state definitions of kindergarten readiness to support informed policymaking. Retrieved from https://ies.ed.gov/ncee/edlabs /regions/northwest/blog/kindergarten-readiness.asp

Reiss, S. (2000). *Who am I?: The 16 basic desires that motivate our behavior and define our personality.* Jeremy P. Tarcher/Putnam.

Ridley, M. (2003). *Nature via nurture: Genes, experience, and what makes us human* (1st ed.). HarperCollins.

Weisenfeld, G. G. (2017). *Assessment tools used in kindergarten entry assessments (KEAs): State scan*. Center on Enhancing Early Learning Outcomes.

Wyoming Department of Education. (2003). Early childhood readiness standards. Retrieved from https://files.eric.ed.gov/fulltext/ED480653.pdf

Chapter 2

Achieve Inc. (n.d.). College and career readiness. Retrieved from https://www.achieve.org/college-and-career-readiness

Ambur, E. (2021). Jobs of the future today: 20 occupations that will change the job market and the world by 2025. Retrieved July 4, 2022, from https://www.forbes.com/sites/eliamdur/2021/02/01/jobs-of-the-future-today-20-occupations-that-will-change-the-job-market-and-the-world-by-2025/?sh=4699020e10e8

Burton, N. W., & Ramist, L. (2001). *Predicting success in college: SAT® studies of classes graduating since 1980*. Retrieved from http://research.collegeboard.org/sites/default/files/publications/2012/7/researchreport-2001-2-predicting-college-success-sat-studies.pdf

Conley, D. T. (2013). *Getting ready for college, career and the common core: What every educator needs to know*. Jossey-Bass.

Geiser, S., & Studley, R. (2001). *UC and the SAT: Predictive validity and differential impact of the SAT I and SAT II at the University of California*. Retrieved from http://web.stanford.edu/~rag/ed351B/sat_study.pdf

Heckman, J. J., & Kantz, T. (2012). Hard evidence on soft skills. *Labour Economics, 19*, 451–464.

Kamanetz, A. (2016). Most high school seniors aren't college or career ready, says "Nation's Report Card." nprED. Retrieved July 4, 2022, from https://www.npr.org/sections/ed/2016/04/27/475628214/most-high-school-seniors-arent-college-or-career-ready-says-nations-report-card

Kobrin, J. L., Patterson, B. F., Shaw, E. J., Mattern, K. D., & Barbuti, S. M. (2008). *Validity of the SAT® for predicting first-year college grade point average*. Retrieved from http://research.collegeboard.org/sites/default/files/publications/2012/7/researchreport-2008-5-validity-sat-predicting-first-year-college-grade-point-average.pdf

Malin, J. R., Bragg, D. D., & Hackman, D. G. (2017). College and career readiness and the Every Student Succeeds Act. *Educational Administration Quarterly, 53*(5), 809–838.

Mattern, K., Burrus, J., Camara, W. O'Conner, R., Hansen, M. A., Gambrell, J., Casilla, A., & Bobek, B. (2014). *Broadening the definition of college and career readiness: A holistic approach*. ACT Research Report Series, No. 5. Retrieved July 3, 2022, from https://www.act.org/content/act/en/research/pdfs/broadening-the-definitionofcollegeandcareerreadinessaholisticapp.html

McDiarmid, G. W., & Zhao, Y. (2022). *Learning for uncertainty: Teaching students how to thrive in a rapidly evolving world*. Routledge.

Mishkind, A. (2014). Overview: State definitions of college and career readiness. College & Career Readiness & Success Center, American Institutes for Research.

Whiting, K. (2020). These are the top 10 job skills of tomorrow—and how long it takes to learn them. World Economic Forum. Retrieved July 3, 2022, from https://www.weforum.org/agenda/2020/10/top-10-work-skills-of-tomorrow-how-long-it-takes-to-learn-them/

U.S. Department of Education. (n.d.). K-12 reform standards. Retrieved from https ://www.ed.gov/k-12reforms/standards

Chapter 3

Andrew, M. (2014). The scarring effects of primary-grade retention? A study of cumulative advantage in the educational career. *Social Forces, 93*(2), 653–685. doi:10.1093/sf/sou074

Elkind, D. (1988). *The hurried child. Growing up too fast too soon.* Addison-Wesley.

Elkind, D. (2007). *The power of play: Learning what comes naturally.* Hachette Books.

Elkind, D. (2012). Knowing is not understanding: Fallacies and risks of early academic instruction. *Young Children, 67*(1), 84–87.

Faverio, M., & Perrin, A. (2022). *Three in ten Americans now read e-books.* Pew Research Center. Retrieved August 6, 2022, from https://www.pewresearch.org/fact-tank/2022/01/06/three-in-ten-americans-now-read-e-books/

Grand View Research. (2022). Audiobooks market size, share & trends analysis report by genre, by preferred device, by distribution channel, by target audience, by region, and segment forecasts, 2022–2030. Retrieved August 6, 2022, from https://www.grandviewresearch.com/industry-analysis/audiobooks-market

Hernandez, D. J. (2012). *Double jeopardy: How third-grade reading skills and poverty influence high school graduation.* Annie E. Casey Foundation.

Konstantopoulos, S., & Borman, G. (2011). Family background and school effects on student achievement: A multilevel analysis of the Coleman data. *Teachers College Record, 113*(1), 97–132.

Kozlowski, M. (2020). *Audiobook trends and statistics for 2020.* Good E Reader. Retrieved August 1, 2022, from https://goodereader.com/blog/audiobooks/audiobook-trends-and-statistics-for-2020

Lindo, E. J. (2014). Family background as a predictor of reading comprehension performance: An examination of the contributions of human, financial, and social capital. *Learning and Individual Differences, 32*, 287–293.

Hansen, M., Levesque, E., Valant, J., & Quintero, D. (2018). *The 2018 Brown Center Report on American education: How well are American students learning?* Retrieved from https://www.brookings.edu/wp-content/uploads/2018/06/2018-Brown-Center-Report-on-American-Education_FINAL1.pdf

National Conference of State Legislatures. (2019). Third-grade reading legislation. Retrieved from https://www.ncsl.org/research/education/third-grade-reading-legislation.aspx

Pagani, L. Trembley, R. E., Vitaro, F. Boulerice, B., & McDuff, P. (2001). Effects of grade retention on academic performance and behavioral development. *Development and Psychopathology, 13*, 297–315.

Reiff, H. B., Gerber, P. J., & Ginsberg, R. (1997). *Exceeding expectations: Successful adults with learning disabilities.* Pro Ed.

The Annie E. Casey Foundation. (2010). *Early warning: Why reading by the end of third grade matters.* Retrieved from http://www.aecf.org/m/resourcedoc/AECF -Early_Warning_Full_Report-2010.pdf

The Annie E. Casey Foundation. (2013). *Early warning confirmed: A research update on third grade reading.* Retrieved from http://www.aecf.org/m/resourcedoc /AECF-EarlyWarningConfirmed-2013.pdf

Tienken, C. H., & Zhao, Y. (2013). How common standards and standardized testing widen the opportunity gap. In P. L. Carter & K. G. Welner (Eds.), *Closing the opportunity gap: What America must do to give every child an even chance* (pp. 113–122). Oxford University Press.

Valbuena, J., Mediavilla, M., Choi, A., & Gil, M. ((2020). Effects of grade retention policies: A literature review of empirical studies applying causal inference. *Journal of Economic Surveys, 35*(2), 408–451.

Chapter 4

Anderson, J. D. (1989). *The education of blacks in the south, 1860–1935.* University of North Carolina Press.

Cobbold, T. (2010). *Closing the achievement gaps in Australian schools.* Paper presented at the Presentation to the Independent Scholars Association of Australia Annual Conference. National Library, Canberra.

Emler, T. E., Zhao, Y., Deng, J., Yin, D., & Wang, Y. (2019). Side effects of large -scale assessments in education. *ECNU Review of Education, 2*(3), 279–296.

Every Student Succeeds Act. (2015). Congress (pp. 114–195).

Ford, M. (2013). Achievement gaps in Australia: What NAPLAN reveals about education inequality in Australia. *Race Ethnicity and Education, 16*(1), 80–102.

Gamoran, A. (2007). *Standards-based reform and the poverty gap: Lessons for No Child Left Behind.* Brookings Institution Press.

Haney, W. (2000). The myth of the Texas miracle in education. *Education Policy Analysis Archives, 8*(41).

Hansen, M., Levesque, E. M., Quintero, D., & Valant, J. (2018). Have we made progress on achievement gaps? Looking at evidence from the new NAEP results. Retrieved from https://www.brookings.edu/blog/brown-center-chalkboard /2018/04/17/have-we-made-progress-on-achievement-gaps-looking-at -evidence-from-the-new-naep-results/

Hanushek, E. A., Peterson, P. E., Talpey, L. M., & Woessmann, L. (2019). The achievement gap fails to close. *Education Next, 19*(3), 8–17.

Heckman, J. J., & Kautz, T. (2012). Hard evidence on soft skills. *Labour Economics, 19,* 451–464.

Hess, F. M. (2011). Our achievement-gap mania. *National Affairs, Fall 2011*(9), 113–129.

Ladson-Billings, G. (2006). From the achievement gap to the education debt: Understanding achievement in U.S. schools. *Educational Researcher, 35*(7), 3–12.

Kozol, J. (1991). *Savage inequalities: Children in America's schools.* Harper Perennial.

Mann, H. (1848). *Twelfth annual report to the secretary of the Massachusetts State Board of Education.* Retrieved from https://genius.com/Horace-mann-twelfth

-annual-report-to-the-secretary-of-the-massachusetts-state-board-of-education
-1848-annotated

National Assessment of Educational Progress. (2021). Explore NAEP long-term trends in reading and mathematics. Retrieved from https://www.nationsreportcard.gov /ltt/?age=9

No Child Left Behind Act of 2001. (2002). Congress (pp. 107–110).

OECD. (2016). *PISA 2015 results (Vol. I): Excellence and equity in education.* Retrieved from http://dx.doi.org/10.1787/9789264266490-en

Perkinson, H. J. (1977) *The imperfect panacea: American faith in education 1865–1976* (2nd ed.). McGraw-Hill College.

Sahlberg, P. (2012, June 29). How GERM is infecting schools around the world. Retrieved from http://www.washingtonpost.com/blogs/answer-sheet/post/how -germ-is-infecting-schools-around-the-world/2012/06/29/gJQAVELZAW_blog .html#comments

Schaeffer, K. (2020). *6 facts about economic inequality in the U.S.* Pew Research Center. Retrieved on July 14, 2022, from https://www.pewresearch.org /fact-tank/2020/02/07/6-facts-about-economic-inequality-in-the-u-s/

Tienken, C. H., & Zhao, Y. (2013). How common standards and standardized testing widen the opportunity gap. In P. L. Carter & K. G. Welner (Eds.), *Closing the Opportunity Gap: What America Must Do to Give Every Child an Even Chance* (pp. 113–122). Oxford University Press.

Tyack, D. (2004). *Seeking common ground. Public schools in in a diverse society.* Harvard University Press.

Wilson, W. J. (2009). *More than just race: Being black in the inner city.* W.W. Norton and Company.

Zhao, Y. (2016). From deficiency to strength: Shifting the mindset about education inequality. *Journal of Social Issues, 72*(4), 716–735.

Chapter 5

Biesta, G. J. (2010). Why "what works" still won't work: From evidence-based education to value-based education. *Studies in Philosophy and Education, 29*(5), 491–503.

Boncu, A., Costea, J., & Minulescu, M. (2017). A meta-analytic study investigating the efficiency of socio-emotional learning programs on the development of children and adolescents. *Romanian Journal of Applied Psychology, 19*(2), 35–41.

CASEL. (2019). Collaborative states initiative. *Collaborative for Academic, Social, and Emotional Learning (CASEL).* Retrieved from https://casel.org /collaborative-state-initiative/

Cochoran, R. P., Cheung, A. C. K., Kim, E., & Wie, C. (2018). Effective universal school-based social and emotional learning programs for improving academic achievement: A systematic review and meta-analysis of 50 years of research. *Educational Research Review, 25*, 56–72.

Duckworth, A. L., & Yeager, D. S. (2015). Measurement matters: Assessing personal qualities other than cognitive ability for educational purposes. *Educational Researcher, 44*(4), 237–251.

Durlak, J. A., Weissberg, R. P., Dymnicki, A. B., Taylor, R. D., & Schellinger, K. B. (2011). The impact of enhancing students' social and emotional learning: A meta-analysis of school-based universal interventions. *Child Development, 82*(1), 405–432.

Dweck, C. S. (2008). *Mindset: The new psychology of success*. Ballantine Books.

EASEL. (2020). Look inside frameworks. *EASEL*. Retrieved from http://exploresel .gse.harvard.edu/frameworks/

Effrem, K., & Robbins, J. (2019). *Social-emotional learning: K–12 education as new age nanny state*. Retrieved from Pioneer Institute https://files.eric.ed.gov /fulltext/ED593789.pdf

Elias, M. J. (2019). What if the doors of every schoolhouse opened to social-emotional learning tomorrow: Reflections on how to feasibly scale up high-quality SEL. *Educational Psychologist, 54*(3), 233–245.

Finn Jr., C. E. (2017). Why are schools still peddling the self-esteem hoax? Social-emotional learning is rooted in "faux psychology." *Education Week, 36*(36), 22. Retrieved from https://www.edweek.org/ew/articles/2017/06/21/why-are -schools-still-peddling-the-self-esteem.html

Greenberg, M. T., Domitrovich, C. E., Weissberg, R. P., & Durlak, J. A. (2017). Social and emotional learning as a public health approach to education. *The Future of Children*, 13–32.

Greene, J. P. (2019). *The moral and religious roots of social and emotional learning*. Retrieved from https://www.aei.org/wp-content/uploads/2019/06/The-Moral -and-Religious-Roots-of-Social-and-Emotional-Learning.pdf

Hallanan, M. T. (2008). Teacher influences on students' attachment to school. *Sociology of Education, 81*, 271–283.

Hess, F. (2017). Some advice for champions of social and emotional learning. *Education Next*. Retrieved from https://www.educationnext.org /advice-champions-social-emotional-learning/

Hoffmann, D. M. (2009). Reflecting on social emotional learning: A critical perspective on trends in the United States. *Review of Educational Research, 79*(2), 533–556.

Immordino-Yang, M. H., Darling-Hammond, L., & Krone, C. R. (2019). Nurturing nature: How brain development is inherently social and emotional, and what this means for education. *Educational Psychologist, 54*(3), 185–204.

Jagers, R. J., Rivas-Drake, D., & Williams, B. (2019). Transformative social and emotional learning (SEL): Toward SEL in service of educational equity and excellence. *Educational Psychologist, 54*(3), 162–184.

Jones, S.M., Brush, K.E., Ramirez, T., Zoe, X.M., Marenus, M., Wettje, S., Finney, K. Raisch, N., Podoloff, N., Kahn, J., Barnes, S., Stickle, L., Brion-Meisels, G., McIntyre, J., Cuartas, J., & Bailey, R. (2017). *Navigating SEL from the inside out: Looking inside & across 25 leading SEL programs: A practical resource for schools and OST providers*. Retrieved from https://www.wallacefoundation .org/knowledge-center/Documents/Navigating-Social-and-Emotional-Learning -from-the-Inside-Out.pdf

Jones, S. M., & Doolittle, E. J. (2017). Social and emotional learning: Introducing the issue. *The Future of Children*, 3–11.

Kamenetz, A. (2017). Social and emotional skills: Everybody loves them, but still can't define them. *NPR*. Retrieved from https://www .npr.org/sections/ed/2017/08/14/542070550/social-and-emotional-skills -everybody-loves-them-but-still-cant-define-them

Mahoney, J. L., Durlak, J. A., & Weissberg, R. P. (2018). An update on social and emotional learning outcome research. *Phi Delta Kappan, 100*(4), 18–23. doi:10.1177/0031721718815668

McKown, C. (2019). Challenges and opportunities in the applied assessment of student social and emotional learning. *Educational Psychologist, 54*(3), 205–221.

National Commission on Social, E. A. L. (2019). *From a nation at risk to a nation at hope.* Retrieved from ASPEN Institute http://nationathope.org/report-from-the-nation/

Nichols, S. L., & Berliner, D. C. (2007). *Collateral damage: How high-stakes testing corrupts America's schools.* Harvard Education Press.

Nichols, S. L., & Berliner, D. C. (2008). Testing the joy out of learning. *Educational Leadership, 65*(6), 14–18.

Ryan, K. (2019). Foreword. In *social-emotional learning: K–12 education as new age nanny state pioneer institute* (pp. 4–6). Pioneer Institute.

Schonert-Reichl, K. A. (2019). Advancements in the landscape of social and emotional learning and emerging topics on the horizon. *Educational Psychologist, 54*(3), 222–232.

Schwartz, H. L., Erin, M. B., Bogan, D., Boyle, A. E., Meyers, D. C., & Jagers, R. J. (2022). Social and emotional learning in schools nationally and in the collaborating districts initiative: Selected findings from the American teacher panel and American school leader panel surveys. Retrieved from https://www.rand.org/pubs/research_reports/RRA1822-1.html

Sklad, M., Diekstra, R., Ritter, M. D., Ben, J., & Gravesteijn, C. (2012). Effectiveness of school-based universal social, emotional, and behavioral programs: Do they enhance students' development in the area of skill, behavior, and adjustment? *Psychology in the Schools, 49*(9), 892–909.

Taylor, R. D., Oberle, E., Durlak, J. A., & Weissberg, R. P. (2017). Promoting positive youth development through school-based social and emotional learning interventions: A meta-analysis of follow-up effects. *Child Development, 88*(4), 1156–1171.

Wigelsworth, M., Lendrum, A., Oldfield, J., Scott, A., ten Bokkel, I., Tate, K., & Emery, C. (2016). The impact of trial stage, developer involvement and international transferability on universal social and emotional learning programme outcomes: A meta-analysis. *Cambridge Journal of Education, 46*(3), 347–376.

Zhao, Y. (2009). *Catching up or leading the way: American education in the age of globalization.* ASCD.

Zhao, Y. (2012). *World class learners: Educating creative and entrepreneurial students.* Corwin.

Zhao, Y. (2018a). *Reach for greatness: Personalizable education for all children.* Corwin.

Zhao, Y. (2018b). *What works may hurt: Side effects in education.* Teachers College Press.

Zhao, Y. (2020). Another education war? The coming debates over social and emotional learning. *Phi Delta Kappan, 101*(8), 42–48.

Zhao, Y., Wehmeyer, M., Basham, J., & Hansen, D. (2019). Tackling the wicked problem of measuring what matters: Framing the questions. *ECNU Review of Education, 2*(3), 262–278.

Chapter 6

American Academy of Arts and Sciences. (2017). *America's languages: Investing in language education for the 21st century*. Commission on Language Learning. https://www.amacad.org/sites/default/files/publication/downloads/Commission-on -Language-Learning_Americas-Languages.pdf

Bialystok, E (2009). Components of executive control with advantages for bilingual children in two cultures. *Cognition, 112*(3), 494–500. http://www.sciencedirect .com/science/article/pii/S0010027709001577

Chamot, A. U. (2004). Issues in language learning strategy research and teaching. *Electronic Journal of Foreign Language Teaching, 1*(1), 14–26.

Conant, J. B. (1959). *The American high school today*. McGraw-Hill Book Company.

DeKeyser, R. M. (2018). *Age in learning and teaching grammar*. In John. I. Liontas (Ed.), *TESOL Encyclopedia of English Language Teaching*. John Wiley and Sons.

Diekhoff, J. S. (1965). NDEA and modern foreign languages. Modern Foreign Languages Association. https://files.eric.ed.gov/fulltext/ED021499.pdf

Fan, S. P., Libermen, Z., Keysar, B., & Kinzler, K. D. (2015). The exposure advantage: Early exposure to a multilingual environment promotes effective communication. *Psychological Science, 26*(7), 1090–1097.

Hartshorne, J. K., Tennenbaum, J. B., & Pinker, S. (2018). A critical period for second language acquisition: Evidence from 2/3 million English speakers. *Cognition, 177*, 263–277.

Lichtman, K. (2016). Age and learning environment: Are children implicit second language learners. *Journal of Child Language, 43*, 707–730.

McGinn, G. H. (2015). Foreign language, cultural diplomacy, and global history. https://www.amacad.org/sites/default/files/media/document/2019-02/Foreign -language-Cultural-Diplomacy-Global-Security.pdf

Mirel, J. (2006). The traditional high school. *Education Next, 6*(1), 14–21.

Morales, J., Calvo, A., & Bialystok, E. (2013). Working memory development in monolingual and bilingual children. *Journal of Experimental Child Psychology, 114*(2), 187–202. https://www.ncbi.nlm.nih.gov/pubmed/23059128

National Education Association (1895). *Report of the committee of fifteen*. National Education Association.

National Education Association (1893). *Report of the committee of ten*. National Education Association.

National Education Association (1918). Cardinal principles of education. Commission of the Reorganization of Secondary Education, National Education Association.

Nikolov, M., & Djigunovic (2006). Recent research on age, second language acquisition, and early foreign language learning. *Annual Review of Applied Linguistics, 26*, 234–260.

Pufahl, I., & Roades, N. C. (2011). Foreign language instruction in U.S. schools: Results of a national survey of elementary and secondary schools. *Foreign Language Annals, 44*(2), 258–288.

Report to the President from the President's Commission on Foreign Language and International Studies (1979). *Strength through wisdom: A critique of U.S. capability*. Government Printing office.

Renandya, W. A. (2013). Essential factors affecting EFFL learning outcomes. *English Teaching*, 68(4), 23–41.

Santiestevan, S. (1991). Use of the Spanish language in the United States: Trends, challenges, and opportunities. *ERIC Digest*, ED335176. https://eric.ed.gov/?id=ED335176

Singleton, D., & Ryan, L. (2004). *Language acquisition: The age factor*. Multilingual Matters.

Stearns, P. N. (2009). *Educating global citizens in colleges and universities: Challenges and opportunities*. Routledge.

Statistica (2021). Elementary schools in the U.S.—Statistics & facts.

Sun, Y. (2019). An analysis on the factors affecting second language acquisition and its implications for teaching and learning. *Journal of Language Teaching and Research*, 10(5), 1018–1022.

The Language Flagship. (2017). The national K-12 foreign language enrollment survey. The Language Flagship at the Defense Language and national Security Education Office (DLNSEO). American Council for International Education.

Uslu, B. (2020) The effect of foreign language acquisition on preschool children's self-regulation and social skills. *European Early Childhood Education Research Journal*. DOI: 10.1080/1350293X.2020.1724612

Utah State Office of Education. (2013). Critical languages: Dual language immersion education appropriations report. Utah State Board of Education.

Vocolo, J. M. (1974). What went wrong with foreign language teaching in high school? *Educational Leadership, 31*, 294–297.

Wiley, T. G., Moore, S. C., & Fee, M. S. (2012). A "languages for jobs" initiative. Council on Foreign Relations. Renewing America. Policy Innovation Memorandum, No. 24. https://www.cfr.org/report/languages-jobs-initiative

Zeigler, K., & Camarota, S. A. (2019). 67.3 million in the U.S. spoke a foreign language in the home in 2018. Center for Immigration Studies. https://cis.org/Report/673-Million-United-States-Spoke-Foreign-Language-Home-2018

Chapter 7

Aragon, C. R., Davis, K., & Fiesler, C. (2019). *Writers in the secret garden: Fanfiction, youth, and new forms of mentoring*. The MIT Press.

Cuban, L. (1986). *Teachers and machines: The classroom uses of technology since 1920*. Teachers College Press.

Cuban, L. (1993). Computers meet classroom: Classroom wins. *Teachers College Record, 95*(2), 185–210.

Elmore, R. (2011). What happens when learning breaks out in rural Mexico? Retrieved from http://blogs.edweek.org/edweek/futures_of_reform/2011/05/what_happens_when_learning_breaks_out_in_rural_mexico.html

Ginsberg, R. (1995). The new institutionalism, the new science, persistence and change: The power of faith in schools. In R. L. Crowson, W. L. Boyd, & H. B. Mawhinney (Eds.), *The Politics of Education and the New Institutionalism* (pp. 153–166). Falmer Press, Taylor and Francis.

Lortie, D. C. (1975). *Schoolteacher*. University of Chicago Press.

Papert, S. (1993a). *The children's machine: Rethinking school in the age of the computer*. Basic Books.

Papert, S. (1993b). *Mindstorms: Children, computers, and powerful ideas* (2nd ed.). Basic Books.

Papert, S. (1999). *Technology in schools—To support the system or render it obsolete?* Milken Exchange. Retrieved from http://www.milkenexchange.org/article.taf?_function=detail&Content_uid1=106

Perelman, L. J. (1992). *School's out.* Avon.

Pew Research Center. (2021). *Mobile fact sheet.* Demographics of Mobile Device Ownership and Adoption in the United States, Pew Research Center.

Rideout, V., & Robb, M. B. (2019). *The common sense census: Media use by tweens and teens, 2019.* Common Sense Media.

Sahlberg, P. (2018). *When is the best age to start school?* Retrieved from https://pasisahlberg.com/when-is-the-best-age-to-start-school/#:~:text=An%20important%20element%20is%20%E2%80%9Cschool,and%20in%20other%20Nordic%20countries

The Associated Press. (1923). Edison predicts film will replace teacher, books. Retrieved December 4, 2022, from https://virginiachronicle.com/?a=d&d=HR19230518.2.11&e=-------en-20--1--txt-txIN--------

Twente, J. M. (2018). *iGen: Why today's super-connected kids are growing up less rebellious, more tolerant, less happy—and completely unprepared for adulthood—and what that means for the rest of us.* Atria paperback.

Tyack, D., & Tobin, W. (1994). The "grammar" of schooling: Why has it been so hard to change? *American Educational Research Journal, 31*(3), 453–479.

Tyack, D. B., & Cuban, L. (1995). *Tinkering toward utopia: A century of public school reform.* Harvard University Press.

Zhao, Y. (2018). The changing context of teaching and implications for teacher education. *Peabody Journal of Education,* 1–14.

Zhao, Y. (2020). Social learning and learning to be social: From online instruction to online education. *American Journal of Education, 127*(1), 137–142.

Zhao, Y. (2021a). Could the pandemic change education for the better? *Educational Leadership, 79*(1), 26–31.

Zhao, Y. (2021b). *Learners without borders: New learning pathways for all students.* Corwin.

Chapter 8

Birman, B. F., Desimone, L., Porter, A. C., & Garet, M. S. (2000). Designing professional development that works. *Educational Leadership, 57*(8), 28–33.

Bolam, R., McMahon, A., Stoll, L., Thomas, S., & Wallace, M. (2005). *Creating and sustaining professional learning communities.* Research report number 637. General Teaching Council for England, Department for Education and Skills.

Brinson, J. R. (2015). Learning outcome achievement in non-traditional (virtual and remote) versus traditional (hands-on) laboratories: A review of empirical research. *Computers and Education, 8*(7), 218–237.

Cornett, J., Ellison, J., Hayes, C., Killion, J., Kise, J., Knight, J., Reinke, W., Reiss, K., Sprick, R., Toll, C., & West, L., (2009). *Coaching approaches and perspectives.* Corwin Press.

Desimone, L. M. (2009). Improving impact studies of teachers' professional development: Toward better conceptualizations and measures. *Educational Researcher, 38*(3), 181–199.

Desimone, L. M., Porter, A. C., Garet, M. S., Yoon, K. S., & Birman, B. F. (2002). Effects of professional development on teachers' instruction: Results from a three-year longitudinal study. *Educational Evaluation and Policy Analysis*, 24(2), 81–112.

Dufour, R. (2004). What is a professional learning community? *Educational Leadership*, 61(8), 6–11.

Garet, M. S., Porter, A. C., Desimone, L., Birman, B. F., & Yoon, K. S. (2001). What makes professional development effective? Results from a national sample of teachers. *American Educational Research Journal*, 38(4), 915–945.

Ginsberg, R., & Herrmann-Ginsberg, L. (2005). Accomplished teachers and their interactions with parents: A comparative analysis of strategies and techniques. *Research Digest—Family Involvement Network of Educators*. Harvard Family Research Project. Retrieved from http://www.hfrp.org/publications-resources/browse-our-publications/accomplished-teachers-and-their-interactions-with-parents-a-comparative-analysis-of-strategies-and-techniques

Guskey, T. (2000). *Evaluating professional development*. Corwin.

Guskey, T., & Yoon, K. S. (2009). What works in professional development? *Phi Delta Kappan*, 90(7), 495–500.

Hattie, J. (2012). *Visible learning for teachers: Maximizing impact on learning*. Routledge.

Heineke, S. F., (2013). Coaching discourse: Supporting teachers' professional learning. *The Elementary School Journal*, 113(3), 409–433.

Hill, H. C. (2009). Fixing professional development. *Phi Delta Kappan*, 90(7), 470–476.

Killion, J., & Harrison, C. (2006). *Taking the lead: New roles for teachers and school-based coaches*. National Staff Development Council.

Knight, J. (2007) *Instructional coaching. A partnership approach to improving instruction*. Corwin Press.

Knight, J. (2014). *Focus on teaching: Using video for high-impact instruction*. Corwin Press.

Knight, J., Elford, M., Hock, M., Dunekack, D., Bradley, B., Deshler, D., & Knight, D. (2015). 3 steps to great coaching. *JSD—The Learning Forward Journal*, 36(1), 11–18.

Kraft, M., A., Blazar, D., & Hogan, D. (2018). The effect of teacher coaching on instruction and achievement: A meta-analysis of the causal evidence. *Review of Educational Research*, 88(4), 547–588.

Little, J. W. (1987). Teachers as colleagues. In V. Richardson-Koehler (ed.), *Educators' handbook: A research perspective* (pp. 491–518). Longman.

Lustick, D., Sykes, G. (2006). National Board Certification as professional development: What are teachers learning? *Education Policy Analysis Archives*, 14(5), 1–46. http://epaa.asu.edu/ojs/article/view/76

Richardson, J. (2003). The dilemmas of professional development. *Phi Delta Kappan*, 84, 401–406.

Thomas, K. (2013). Changing mathematics teaching practices and improving student outcomes through collaborative evaluation. *Teacher Education and Practice*, 26(4), 779–796.

Timperley, H. S. (2005). Instructional leadership challenges: The case of using student achievement information for instructional improvement. *Leadership and*

Policy in Schools, 4(1), 3–22. http://www.tandfonline.com/doi/pdf/10.1080/15 700760590924591?needAccess=true

Torff, R., & Sessions, D. (2009). Teachers' attitudes about professional development in high-SES and low-SES communities. *Learning Inquiry, 3*, 67–77.

TNTP (2015). *The mirage: Confronting the hard truth about our quest for teacher development.* Retrieved August 4, 2022, from TNTP-Mirage_2015.pdf

Vescio, V., Ross, D., & Adams, A. (2008). A review of research on the impact of professional learning communities on teaching practice and student learning. *Teaching and Teacher Education, 24*, 80–91.

Yoon, K. S., Duncan, T., Lee, S. W Y, Scarloss, B., & Shapley, K. L. (2007). *Reviewing the evidence on how teacher professional development affects student achievement. Issues and answers.* U.S. Department of Education, Institute of Education Sciences, National Center for Education Evaluation and Regional Assistance, Regional Educational Laboratory, Southwest. http://ies.ed.gov /ncee/edlabs

Chapter 9

Bailyn, B. (1972). *Education in the forming of American society.* W.W. Norton & Co., Inc.

Biddle, B. J., & Berliner, D. C. (2002). Small class size and its effects. *Educational Leadership, 59*(5), 12–23.

Chingos, M. M., & Whitehurst, G. J. R. (2011). Class size: What research says and what it means for state policy. Retrieved July 14, 2022, from https://www.brookings .edu/research/class-size-what-research-says-and-what-it-means-for-state-policy/

Darling-Hammond, L. (2009). Recognizing and enhancing teacher effectiveness. *The International Journal of Educational and Psychological Assessment, 3*(1).

Finn, J. D., & Achilles, C. M. (1990). Answers about questions about class size: A statewide experiment. *American Educational Research Journal, 27*, 557–577.

Fredriksson, P., Öckert, B., & Oosterbeek, H. (2013). Long-term effects of class size. *The Quarterly Journal of Economics, 128*(1), 249–285.

Hanushek, E. A. (1999). Some findings from an independent investigation of the Tennessee STAR experiment and from other investigations of class size effects. *Educational Evaluation and Policy Analysis, 21*(2), 143–163.

Lortie, D. (1975). *Schoolteacher.* University of Chicago Press.

McDiarmid, G. W., & Zhao, Y. (2022). *Learning for uncertainty: Teaching students how to thrive in a rapidly evolving world.* Routledge.

PPTA (2022). *Class size, average class size, and pupil-teacher ratio: Truth, lies and government statistics.* Retrieved July 14, 2022, from https://www.ppta.org.nz /news-and-media/class-size-average-class-size-and-pupil-teacher-ratio-truth -lies-and-government-statistics/

Shen, T., & Konstantopoulos, S. (2021). Estimating causal effects of class size in secondary education: Evidence from TIMSS. *Research Papers in Education, 36*(5), 507–541.

Woessmann, L., & West, M. (2006). Class-size effects in school systems around the world: Evidence from between-grade variation in TIMSS. *European Economic Review, 50*(3), 695–736.

Zhao, Y. (2018a). The changing context of teaching and implications for teacher education. *Peabody Journal of Education,* 1–14.

Zhao, Y. (2018b). *Reach for greatness: Personalizable education for all children.* Corwin.

Chapter 10

Alexander, K. L., Entwisle, D. R., & Olson, L. S. (2007). Lasting consequences of the summer learning gap. *American Sociological Review, 72,* 167–180.

Anderson, L. W. (1976). An empirical investigation of individual differences in time to learn. *Journal of Educational Psychology, 68*(2), 226–233.

Bailey, D., Duncan, G. J., Murname, R. J., & Yeung, N. A. (2021). Achievement gaps in the wake of Covid-19. *Educational Researcher, 50*(5) 266–275. Retrieved from https://doi.org/10.3102/0013189X211011237

Ballinger, C (n.d.). *NAYRE.* Slide 1, nayre.org.

Berliner, D. C. (1990). What's all the fuss about instructional time? In Ben-Peretz, M. (ed.), *The Nature of Time in Schools: Theoretical Concepts, Practitioner Perceptions.* Teachers College Press.

Bloom, B. S. (1974). Time and learning. *American Psychologist, 29*(9), 682–688.

Callahan, R. E. (1962). *Education and the cult of efficiency.* The University of Chicago Press.

Canady, R. L., & Rettig, M. D. (1995). *Block scheduling: A catalyst for change in high schools.* Eye on Education.

Dorn, E., Hancock, B., Sarakatsannis, J., & Viruleg, E. (2021). *Covid-19 and education: The lingering effects of unfinished learning.* McKinsey & Company. Retrieved from https://www.mckinsey.com/industries/education/our-insights/covid-19-and-education-the-lingering-effects-of-unfinished-learning#

Education Commission of the States. (2005). Reprint of the 1994 report of the National Commission on Time and Learning.

Farbman, D. A. (2015). *The case for improving and expanding time in school: A review of key research and practice.* National Center on Time and Learning. https://www.timeandlearning.org/sites/default/files/resources/caseformorelearningtime.pdf

Fisher, C. W., Berliner, D. C., Filby, N. N., Marliave, R., Cahen, L. S., & Dishaw, M. M. (1981). Teaching behaviors. Academic learning time and student achievement: An overview. *The Journal of Classroom Interaction, 17*(1), 2–15.

Fitzpatrick, D., Burns, J. (2019). Single-track year-round education for improving academic achievement in U.S. K-12 schools: Results of a meta-analysis. *Campbell Systematic Reviews, 15,* e1053. https://doi.org/10.1002/cl2.1053

Ginsberg, R. (1997) Complexity science at the schoolhouse gate? A call to arms! *Complexity, 2,* 9–13.

Gold, K. M. (2018). The myth behind summer break and the challenge it creates for school reformers. *Washington Post.* https://www.washingtonpost.com/outlook/2018/09/04/myth-behind-summer-break/

Gold, K. M. (2002). *School's in: The history of summer education in American public schools.* P. Lang.

Hansen, M, Janseen, I., Schiff, A., Zee, P. C., & Dubocovich, M. L. (2005). The impact of school daily schedule on adolescent sleep. *Pediatrics, 115*(6), 1555–1561.

Lewis, L. L. (2022). *The sleep-deprived teen: Why our teenagers are so tired, and how parents and schools can help them thrive.* Mango Publishers.

National Commission on Excellence in Education (1983). A nation at risk: The imperative for educational reform. Washington, DC: U.S. Department of Education.

National Education Commission on Time and Learning. (1994). Prisoners of time. Author.

Patall, E. A., Cooper, H., & Allen, A. B. (2010). Extending the school day or school year: A systematic review of research (1985–2009). *Review of Educational Research, 80*(3), 401–436.

Sahlberg, P. (2010). *Finnish lessons: What can the world learn from educational change in Finland.* Teachers College Press.

Stallings, J. (1980). Allocated learning time revisited, or beyond time on task. *Educational Researcher, 9*(11), 11–16.

Thomas, C. (2001). What is wrong with block scheduling? *NASSP Bulletin, 85*(628), 74–77.

Tyack, D. B. (1974). *The one best system.* Harvard University Press.

Veal, W. R., & Schreiber, J. (1999). Block scheduling effects of a state-mandated test of basic skills. *Educational Policy Analysis Archives, 7*(29), 1–14.

Von Hippel, P. T., & Hamrock, C. (2019). Do test score gaps grow before, during, or between school years? Measurement artifacts and what we can know in spite of them. *Sociological Science, 6,* 43–80. https://sociologicalscience.com /download/vol-6/january/SocSci_v6_43to80.pdf

Worthen, B. R., & Zsiray, S. W., Jr. (1994). *What twenty years of educational studies reveal about year-round education.* Commissioned by the North Carolina Educational Policy Center, University of North Carolina.

Zepeda, S. J., & Mayers, R. S. (2006). An analysis of research on block scheduling. *Review of Educational Research, 76*(1), 137–170.

Chapter 11

Bredice, S. (1988). School librarian bans "Spuds MacKenzie" t-shirts. *UPI Archives.* Retrieved January 17, 2022, from https://www.upi.com/Archives/1988/03/28 /School-librarian-bans-Spuds-McKenzie-T-shirts/9906575528400/

Friedman, J. R. (2019). A girl's right to bare arms: An equal protection analysis of public school dress codes. *Boston College Law Review, 60,* 2547–2580.

Martin, J. L., & Brooks, J. N. (2020). Loc'd and faded, yoga pants, and spaghetti straps: Discrimination in dress codes and school pushout. *International Journal of Education Policy and Leadership, 16*(19), 1–19.

National Women's Law Center. (2018). Dress coded. Black girls, bodies, and bias in D.C. schools. Retrieved June 25, 2022, from https://nwlc.org/wp-content /uploads/2018/04/5.1web_Final_nwlc_DressCodeReport.pdf

Pavlakis, A., & Roegman, R. (2018). How dress codes criminalize males and sexualize females of color. *Phi Delta Kappan, 100*(2), 54–58.

Perry, A. (2020). Dress codes are the new "whites only" signs: How else to interpret the policing and controlling of black bodies? *The Hechinger Report.* Retrieved January 30, 2022, from https://hechingerreport.org/dress-codes-are-the -new-whites-only-signs/

Whitman, G. M. (2020). A curricular critique of school dress codes. *The Clearing House, 93*(2), 72–77.

Chapter 12

American Statistical Association. (2014). *ASA statement for using value-added models for educational assessment.* Retrieved from https://www.amstat.org/asa/files/pdfs/POL-ASAVAM-Statement.pdf

Baker, E. L., Barton, P. E., Darling-Hammond, L., Haertel, E., Ladd, H. F., Linn, R. L., Ravitch, D., Rothstein, R., Shavelson R.J., & Shepard, L.A. (2010). Problems with the use of student test scores to evaluate teachers. EPI Briefing Paper #278. Washington, DC: Economic Policy Institute.

Baum, S., Owen, S.V., & Oreck, B.A. (2004). Talent beyond words: Identification of potential talent in dance and music in elementary students. *Artistically and Musically Talented Students, 40*(2), 57–72.

Berry, B. Byrd, A., & Wieder, A. (2013). *Teacherpreneurs: Innovative teachers who lead but don't leave.* Jossey-Bass.

Bleiberg, J., Brunner, E., Harbatkin, E., Kraft, M. A., & Springer, M. G. (2021). *The effect of teacher evaluation on achievement and attainment: Evidence from statewide reforms.* EdWorkingPaper No. 21-496. Annenberg, Brown University. https://www.edworkingpapers.com/ai21-496

Brill, S. (2009). The rubber room. *The New Yorker.*

Darling-Hammond, L., Amrein-Beardsley, A., Hartel, E., & Rothstein, J. (2012). Evaluating teacher evaluation. *Kappan, 93*(6), 8–15.

Foley Nicpon, M., Allmon, A., Sieck, B., & Stinson, R.D. (2011). Empirical investigation of twice-exceptionality: Where have we been and where are we going? *Gifted Child Quarterly, 55*(1), 3–17.

Hallanan, M. T. (2008). Teacher influences on students' attachment to school. *Sociology of Education, 81,* 271–283.

Heckman, J. J., & Kautz, T. (2012). Hard evidence on soft skills. *Labour Economics, 19,* 451–464.

Johnson, S. M. (2015). Will VAMS reinforce the walls of the egg-crate school? *Educational Researcher, 44*(2), 117–126.

Kraft, M., Brunner, E. J., Dougherty, S. M., & Schwegman, D. J. (2020). Teacher accountability reforms and the supply and quality of new teachers. *Journal of Public Economics, 188,* 104212. https://doi.org/10.1016/j.jpubeco.2020.104212

Morris, V. C., Crowsan, R. L., Porter-Gehrie, C., & Hurwitz, Jr., E. (1984). *Principals in action: The reality of managing schools.* Charles E. Merrill.

Neumerski, C. M., Grissom, J. A., Goldring, E., Rubin, M., Cannata, M., Schuermann, P., & Drake, T. A. (2018). Restructuring instructional leadership: How multiple-measure teacher evaluation systems are redefining the role of the school principal. *The Elementary School Journal, 119*(2), 270–297.

Ravitch, D., Rothstein, R. Shavelson, R. J., & Shepard, L. A. (2010). Problems with the use of student test scores to evaluate teachers. EPI Briefing Paper #278. Economic Policy Institute.

Rich, M. (2012). National school debate is on in Chicago. *New York Times.*

Scriven, M. (1983). Evaluation ideologies. In, G. F. Madaus, M. Scriven, & D. L. Stufflebeam, (Eds.), *Evaluation Models.* Kluwer-Nijhoff Publishing.

Shulman, L. S. (1988). A union of insufficiencies: Strategies for teacher assessment in a period of educational reform. *Educational Leadership, 46*(3), 36–41.

Schweig, J. (2019). Measuring teaching effectiveness. Rand Corporation. Retrieved from https://www.rand.org/education-and-labor/projects/measuring-teacher-effectiveness.html#:~:text=Teachers'%20effectiveness%20is%20often%20measured,such%20as%20math%20and%20reading

Stodolsky, S. S. (1984). Teacher evaluation: The limits of looking. *Educational Researcher, 13*(9), 11–18.

Trail, B.A. (2012). *Twice-exceptional gifted children: Understanding, teaching, and counseling gifted students.* Routledge.

Weisberg, D., Sexton, S. Mulhern, J., & Keeling, D. (2009). *The widget effect: Our national failure to acknowledge and act on differences in teacher effectiveness.* The New Teacher Project. Retrieved from https://files.eric.ed.gov/fulltext/ED515656.pdf

Wise, A. E., Darling-Hammond, L., McLaughlin, M. W. & Bernstein, H. T. (1984). *Teacher evaluation: A study of effective practices.* Rand Corporation.

Chapter 13

Assouline, S. G., Colangelo, N., & VanTassel-Baska, J. (2015). *A nation empowered: Evidence trumps the excuses holding back America's brightest students.* The Connie Belin & Jacqueline N. Blank International Center for Gifted and Talented Development, University of Iowa.

Beard, A. (2018). *Natural born learners: Our incredible capacity to learn and how we can harness it.* Hachette UK.

Chua, A. (2007). *Days of empire: How hyperpowers rise to global dominance and why they fall.* Doubleday.

Colangelo, N., Assouline, S. G., & Gross, M. U. M. (2004). *A nation deceived: How schools hold back America's brightest students.* The Connie Belin & Jacqueline N. Blank International Center for Gifted and Talented Development, University of Iowa.

Coyle, D. (2009). *The talent code: Greatness isn't born. It's grown. Here's how.* Bantam Books.

Ekoko, B. E., & Ricci, C. (2014). *Natural born learners: Unschooling and autonomy in education.* CreateSpace.

Florida, R. (2002). *The rise of the creative class and how it's transforming work, leisure, community & everyday life.* Basic Books.

Florida, R. (2012). *The rise of the creative class: Revisited* (2nd ed.). Basic Books.

Gardner, H. E. (2006). *Multiple intelligences: New horizons in theory and practice.* Basic Books.

John, O. P., Robins, R. W., & Pervin, L. A. (2008). *Handbook of personality: Theory and research* (3rd ed.). Guilford Press.

Marland, S. P., Jr. (1972). *Education of the gifted and talented: Report to the Congress of the United States by the US Commissioner of Education.* U.S. Government Printing Office.

National Association of Gifted Children. (n.d.). Frequently asked questions about gifted education. Retrieved August 3, 2022, from https://www.nagc.org/resources-publications/resources/frequently-asked-questions-about-gifted-education

National Center for Education Statistics. (2022). Students with disabilities. *Condition of Education*. U.S. Department of Education, Institute of Education Sciences. Retrieved December 4, 2022 from https://nces.ed.gov/programs/coe/indicator/cgg

National Commission on Excellence in Education. (1983). *A nation at risk*. U.S. Department of Education.

Page, S. E. (2007). *The difference: How the power of diversity creates better groups, firms, schools and societies*. Princeton University Press.

Reis, S. M., Baum, S. M., & Burke, E. (2014). An operational definition of twice-exceptional learners: Implications and applications. *Gifted Child Quarterly, 58*(3), 217–230.

Reiss, S. (2000). *Who am I?: The 16 basic desires that motivate our behavior and define our personality*. Jeremy P. Tarcher/Putnam.

Ridley, M. (2003). *Nature via nurture: Genes, experience, and what makes us human* (1st ed.). HarperCollins.

Rose, T. (2016). *The end of average: How we succeed in a world that values sameness* (1st ed.). HarperOne.

Sahlber, P. (2011). *Finnish lessons: What can the world learn from educational change in Finland?* Teachers College Press.

Zhao, Y. (2018a). The changing context of teaching and implications for teacher education. *Peabody Journal of Education*, 1–14.

Zhao, Y. (2018b). Personalizable education for greatness. *Kappa Delta Pi Record, 54*(3), 109–115.

Zhao, Y. (2018c). *Reach for greatness: Personalizable education for all children*. Corwin.

Zhao, Y. (2018d). The rise of the useless: The case for talent diversity. *Journal of Science Education and Technology*, 1–7.

Zhao, Y. (2020a). COVID-19 as a catalyst for educational change. *Prospects*. doi:10.1007/s11125-020-09477-y

Zhao, Y. (2020b). Tofu is not cheese: Rethinking education amid the COVID-19 pandemic. *ECNU Review of Education, 3*(2), 189–203. doi:10.1177/2096531120928082

Zhao, Y., Basham, J., & Travers, J. (2022). Redefining human talents: Gifted education in the age of smart machines. *The Palgrave Handbook of Transformational Giftedness for Education*, 403.

Chapter 14

Adams, D., & Hamm, M. (2013). *Tomorrow's innovators: Essential skills for a changing world*. Rowman & Littlefield Education.

Baker, K. (2007). Are international tests worth anything? *Phi Delta Kappan, 89*(2), 101–104.

Campbell, D. T. (1976). *Assessing the impact of planned social change*. Paper no. 8, Occasional Paper Series, Dartmouth College: Public Affairs Center.

Duckworth, A. L., & Yeager, D. S. (2015). Measurement matters: Assessing personal qualities other than cognitive ability for educational purposes. *Educational Researcher, 44*(4), 237–251.

Emler, T. E., Zhao, Y., Deng, J., Yin, D., & Wang, Y. (2019). Side effects of large-scale assessments in education. *ECNU Review of Education, 2*(3), 279–296.

Every Student Succeeds Act. (2015). Congress (pp. 114–195).

Fernandez, M. (2012). El Paso schools confront scandal of students who "disappeared" at test time. *New York Times*. Retrieved July 7, 2022, from https://www

.nytimes.com/2012/10/14/education/el-paso-rattled-by-scandal-of-disappeared-students.html

Ginsberg, R. (1995). State-driven reforms and productivity: Lessons from South Carolina. In H. Walberg, B. Levin, & W. Fowler (Eds.), *Organizational Influences on Educational Productivity*. JAI Press.

Haertel, E., & Herman, J. (2005). *A historical perspective on validity arguments for accountability testing*. CSE Report 654. *Center for the Study of Evaluation/National Center for Research on Evaluation, Standards, and Student Testing*.

Heckman, J. J., & Kautz, T. (2012). Hard evidence on soft skills. *Labour Economics, 19*, 451–464.

Hout, M., & Elliott, S. W. (Eds.). (2011). *Incentives and test-based accountability in education*. National Academies Press.

Kingston, N. M., Karvonen, M., Bechard, S., & Erickson, K. A. (2016). The philosophical underpinnings and key features of the dynamic learning maps alternate assessment. *Teachers College Record, 118*, 1–30.

Kirst, M. (1990). *Accountability: Implications for state and local policy makers*. U.S. Department of Education. Office of Educational Research and Improvement, Information Services.

Koretz, D. (2017). *The testing charade: Pretending to make schools better*. University of Chicago Press.

Lemann, N. (2000). *The big test: The secret history of the American meritocracy*. Farber, Strauss and Giroux.

McCray, V. (2018). Altered test scores years ago altered lives, stained Atlanta schools. *The Atlanta Journal-Constitution*. Retrieved from https://www.ajc.com/news/local-education/altered-test-scores-altered-lives-stained-atlanta-schools/nFHhI3jPSQ7MjIS9dRuCNM/

National Commission on Excellence in Education. (1983). *A nation at risk: The imperative for educational reform*. U.S. Department of Education.

Nichols, S. L., & Berliner, D. C. (2007). *Collateral damage: How high-stakes testing corrupts America's schools*. Harvard Education Press.

No Child Left Behind Act of 2001. (2002). Congress (pp. 107–110).

Ramirez, A. (2013). *Save our science*. TED Books.

Sanchez, C. (Writer). (2013). El Paso schools cheating scandal: Who's accountable? NPR, All Things Considered. Retrieved July 7, 2022, from https://www.npr.org/2013/04/10/176784631/el-paso-schools-cheating-scandal-probes-officials-accountability#:~:text=Lorenzo%20Garcia%2C%20the%20former%20superintendent,test%20scores%20for%20financial%20gain

Strauss, V. (2022, Feb 1). Remember the Atlanta schools' cheating scandal? It isn't over. *The Washington Post*. Retrieved from https://www.washingtonpost.com/education/2022/02/01/atlanta-cheating-schools-scandal-teachers/

Tienken, C. H. (2008). Rankings of international achievement test performance and economic strength: Correlation or conjecture? *International Journal of Education Policy & Leadership, 3*(4), 1–15. Retrieved from http://journals.sfu.ca/ijepl/index.php/ijepl/article/view/110/44

Tienken, C. H., & Zhao, Y. (2013). How common standards and standardized testing widen the opportunity gap. In P. L. Carter & K. G. Welner (Eds.), *Closing the opportunity gap: What America must do to give every child an even chance* (pp. 113–122). Oxford University Press.

Trilling, B., & Fadel, C. (2009). *21st century skills: Learning for life in our times.* John Wiley & Sons.

Wagner, T. (2012). *Creating innovators: The making of young people who will change the world.* Scribner.

Woolever, J. L. (2019). *Student perceptions toward mandated tests* [Ed.D. Dissertation]. University of Kansas.

Zhao, Y. (2012). *World class learners: Educating creative and entrepreneurial students.* Corwin.

Zhao, Y. (2014). *Who's afraid of the big bad dragon: Why China has the best (and worst) education system in the world.* Jossey-Bass.

Zhao, Y. (2018). *What works may hurt: Side effects in education.* Teachers College Press.

Zhao, Y. (2020). Two decades of havoc: A synthesis of criticism against PISA. *Journal of Educational Change,* 1–22. doi:10.1007/s10833-019-09367-x

Zhao, Y., Wehmeyer, M., Basham, J., & Hansen, D. (2019). Tackling the wicked problem of measuring what matters: Framing the questions. *ECNU Review of Education, 2*(3), 262–278.

Chapter 15

Berry, B., Byrd, A., & Wieder, A. (2013). *Teacherpreneurs.* Jossey-Bass.

Cai, J. (2020). *Public voice: Uncontested candidates and low voter turnout are concerns in board elections.* National School Board Association. Retrieved June 30, 2022, from https://www.nsba.org/ASBJ/2020/April/the-publics-voice

Callahan, R. E. (1962). *Education and the cult of efficiency.* University of Chicago Press.

Cubberley, E. (1929). *Public school administration: A statement of the fundamental principles underlying the organization and administration of public education.* Houghton Mifflin.

DeSilver, D. (2020). In past elections, U.S. trailed most developed countries in voter turnout. Pew Research Center. Retrieved July 7, 2022, from https://www.pewresearch.org/fact-tank/2020/11/03/in-past-elections-u-s-trailed-most-developed-countries-in-voter-turnout/

Durfin, E. (2022). *Educational attainment distribution in the United States from 1960–2021.* Statista. Retrieved July 4, 2022, from https://www.statista.com/statistics/184260/educational-attainment-in-the-us/

Eden, M. (2021). *Move school board elections on-cycle to restore local control.* American Enterprise Institute. Retrieved July 2, 2022, from https://www.aei.org/research-products/report/move-school-board-elections-on-cycle-to-restore-local-control/

Hess, F. M. (2010). Weighing the case for school boards. *Kappan, 91*(6), 15–19.

Hess, F. M., & Meeks, O. (2010). *Governance in the accountability era.* National School Boards Association, the Fordham Foundation, and the Iowa School Board Foundation. Retrieved July 3, 2022, from https://files.eric.ed.gov/fulltext/ED515849.pdf

Honingh, M., Ruiter, M., & van Thiel, S. (2020). Are school boards and educational quality related? Results of an international literature review. *Educational Review, 72*(2), 157–172.

Land, D. (2002). Local school boards under review: Their role and effectiveness in relation to students' academic achievement. *Review of Educational Research, 72*(2), 229–278.

National School Boards Association. (2018). *Today's school boards and their priorities for tomorrow.* NSBA and K12 Insight. Retrieved July 2, 2022, from https://cdn-files.nsba.org/s3fs-public/reports/K12_National_Survey.pdf

NCES. (2018). Bar chart races: Changing demographics in K-12 public school enrollment. *NCES Blog.* Retrieved July 4, 2022, from https://nces.ed.gov/blogs/nces/post/bar-chart-races-changing-demographics-in-k-12-public-school-enrollment

Sell, S. (2005). Running an effective school district: School boards in the 21st century. *The Journal of Education, 186*(3), 71–97.

Twentieth Century Fund (1992). *Facing the challenge: The report of the twentieth century fund task force on school governance.* Twentieth Century Fund Press.

Tyack, D. B. (1974). *The one best system.* Harvard University Press.

Tyack, D. B., & Cuban, L. (1995). *Tinkering toward utopia.* Harvard University Press.

U.S. Census Bureau. (2021) Income and poverty in the United States: 2020. Retrieved July 1, 2022, from https://www.census.gov/library/publications/2021/demo/p60-273.html

Vitteritti, J. P. (1983). *Across the river: Politics and education in the city.* Holmes & Meier.

Chapter 16

Allegretto, S. (2022). *The teacher pay penalty has hit a new high.* Economic Policy Institute. Retrieved August 22, 2022, from https://www.epi.org/publication/teacher-pay-penalty-2022/

Allegretto, S., & Mishel, L. (2018). *The teacher pay penalty has hit a new high.* The Economic Policy Institute. Retrieved July 20, 2022, from https://www.epi.org/publication/teacher-pay-gap-2018/

Armenin-Beardley, A., & Close, K. (2021). Teacher-level value-added models on trial: Empirical and pragmatic issues of concern across five court cases. *Educational Policy, 35*(6), 866–907.

Armein-Beardsley, A. (2008). Methodological concerns about value-added assessment system. *Educational Researcher, 37*(2), 65–75.

Baker, B. D. (2016). *Does money matter?* (2nd Ed.). The Albert Shanker Institute. Retrieved from https://files.eric.ed.gov/fulltext/ED563793.pdf

Berry, B., Byrd, A., & Wieder, A. (2013). *Teacherpreneurs: Innovative teachers who lead but don't leave.* Jossey Bass.

Burnette, II, D. (2019). Student outcomes: Does more money really matter. *Educational Week.* Retrieved June 15, 2022, from https://www.edweek.org/policy-politics/student-outcomes-does-more-money-really-matter/2019/06

CDC Foundation (2021). Mental health impact of the Covid-19 pandemic on teachers and parents of K-12 students. https://www.cdcfoundation.org/mental-health-triangulated-report?inline

Darling-Hammond, L., Furger, R., Shields, P. M., & Sutcher, L. (2016). *Addressing California's emerging teacher shortage: An analysis of sources and solutions.* Learning Policy Institute.

Eckert, J. M., & Dabrowski, J. (2010). Should value-added measures be used for performance pay? *Kappan, 91*(8), 88–92.

Ellsbree, W. S. (1928). An evaluation of the single salary schedule. *Teachers College Record, 30*(3), 227–232.

Etzioni, A. (ed.) (1969). *The semi-professions and their organization.* Free Press.

Fullan, M. (2016). Amplify change with professional capital. *JSD, 37*(1), 44–56.

Hansen, M., & Quintero, D. (2017). Scrutinizing equal pay for equal work among teachers. The Brookings Institution. https://www.brookings.edu/research /scrutinizing-equal-pay-for-equal-work-among-teachers/

Hanushek, E. A. (1997). Assessing the effects of school resources on student performance: An update. *Educational Evaluation and Policy Analysis, 19*(2), 141–164.

Hanushek, E. A. (2016). School human capital and teacher salary policies. *Journal of Professional Capital and Community, 1*(1), 23–40. https://hanushek .stanford.edu/sites/default/files/publications/Hanushek%202016%20J%20 ProfCapitalandCommunity%201(1).pdf

Help! Teacher can't teach. (1980, June 16). *Time, 115*(24), 58–62.

National Center for Educational Statistics. (2021). Characteristics of public school teachers. Retrieved from https://nces.ed.gov/programs/coe/indicator/clr /public-school-teachers

National Center for Educational Statistics. (2021a). Digest of educational statistics. Retrieved from https://nces.ed.gov/programs/digest/d20/tables/dt20_212.10.asp

National Center for Educational S (2020). Digest of educational statistics. Retrieved from https://nces.ed.gov/programs/digest/d20/tables/dt20_209.10.asp

Opper, I. M. (2019). Teachers matter: Understanding teachers' impact on student achievement. *Rand Corporation.* Retrieved from https://www.rand.org/content /dam/rand/pubs/research_reports/RR4300/RR4312/RAND_RR4312.pdf

Payscale (2022). 2022 state of the gender pay gap report. Retrieved June 21, 2022, from https://www.payscale.com/research-and-insights/gender-pay-gap/

PDK Poll (2019). Frustrations in the schools. Retrieved from https://pdkpoll.org /wp-content/uploads/2020/05/pdkpoll51-2019.pdf

Pham, L. D., Nguyen, T. D., & Springer, M. G. (2021). Teacher merit pay: A meta-analysis. *American Educational Research Journal, 58*(9), 527–566.

Reliability Index (2021). Top 100 UK cars. Retrieved June 20, 2022, from http:// reliabilityindex.com/top-100/

Sahlberg, P. (2011). *Finnish lessons: What can the world learn from educational change in Finland?* Teachers College Press.

Sarason, S. B. (1990). *The predictable failure of educational reform: Can we change course before it is too late?* Jossey-Bass education Series and the Jossey-Bass Social and Behavioral Science Series.

Urban, W. J. (1990). New directions in the historical study of teacher unionism. *Historical Studies in Education/Revue d'Histoire de l'Education,* 1–15.

Chapter 17

Amrhein, V., Greenland, S., & McShane, B. (2019). Scientists rise up against statistical significance. *Nature, 567,* 305–307. Retrieved August 27, 2022, from https://www.nature.com/articles/d41586-019-00857-9

Bergeron, P.-J. (2017). How to engage in pseudoscience with real data: A criticism of John Hattie's arguments in visible learning from the perspective of a statistician. *McGill Journal of Education/Revue des Sciences de l'Education de McGill, 52*(1), 237–246. Retrieved from http://mje.mcgill.ca/article/view/9475/7229

Blastland, M., & Dilnot, A. (2009). *The numbers game.* Gotham Books.

Brown, N. (2013). Book review: Visible learning. Retrieved from https:// academiccomputing.wordpress.com/2013/08/05/book-review-visible-learning/

Eriksson, K. (2012). The nonsense math effect. *Judgment and Decision Making,* *7*(6), 746.

Evans, D. (2012). He's not the messiah. *TES.* Retrieved from https://www.tes.com /news/tes-archive/tes-publication/hes-not-messiah

Glass, G. V. (1976). Primary, secondary, and meta-analysis of research. *Educational Researcher, 5*(10), 3–8.

Hattie, J. (2008). *Visible learning: A synthesis of over 800 meta-analyses relating to achievement.* Routledge.

Hattie, J. (2009). *Visible learning: A synthesis of over 800 meta-analyses relating to achievement.* Routledge.

Hattie, J. (2012). *Visible learning for teachers: Maximizing impact on learning.* Routledge.

Hattie, J. (2015). The applicability of visible learning to higher education. *Scholarship of Teaching and Learning in Psychology, 1*(1), 79.

Hattie, J., & Hattie, K. (2022). *10 Steps to develop great learners: Visible learning for parents.* Routledge.

Mansell, W. (2008). Research reveals teaching's Holy Grail. *TES.* Retrieved from https:// www.tes.com/news/tes-archive/tes-publication/research-reveals-teachings -holy-grail

Snook, I., O'Neill, J., Clark, J., O'Neill, A.-M., & Openshaw, R. (2009). Invisible learnings? A commentary on John Hattie's book: Visible Learning: A synthesis of over 800 meta-analyses relating to achievement. *New Zealand Journal of Educational Studies, 44*(1), 93.

Sperber, D. (2010). The guru effect. *Review of Philosophy and Psychology, 1*(4), 583–592.

Terhart, E. (2011). Has John Hattie really found the holy grail of research on teaching? An extended review of Visible Learning. *Journal of Curriculum Studies, 43*(3), 425–438.

Wasserstein, R. L., Schirm, A. L., & Lazar, N. A. (2019). Moving to a World Beyond "p<0.05." *The American Statistician, 73*(supp1), 1–19. Retrieved August 27, 2022, from https://www.tandfonline.com/doi/full/10.1080/00031305.2019.1583913

Zhao, Y. (2018). *What works may hurt: Side effects in education.* Teachers College Press.

Conclusion

Berliner, D. C. (2014). Exogenous variables and value-added assessments. *Teachers College Record, 116*(1), 1–31.

Harford, T. (2011). *Trial, error and the God complex.* TED Talk. Retrieved December 4, 2022 from https://www.ted.com/talks/tim_harford_trial_error _and_the_god_complex?language=en

Morris, Z. S., Wooding, S., & Grant, J. (2011). The answer is 17 years, what is the question: Understanding time lags in translational research. *Journal of the Royal Society of Medicine, 104,* 511–520.

Munro, C. L., & Savel, R. H. (2016). Narrowing the 17-year research to practice gap. *American Journal of Critical Care, 25*(3), 194–196.

Waldrop, M. M. (1992). *Complexity: The emerging science at the edge of order and chaos.* Touchstone Books.

Wheatley, M. J. (1992). *Leadership and the new science. Discovering order in a chaotic world.* Berrett-Koehler Publishers.

Index

About the Authors

Rick Ginsberg, Ph.D., is dean of the School of Education and Human Sciences at the University of Kansas. Previously he was director of the School of Education at Colorado State University. He currently serves as a co-chair of the Learn Coalition, promoting increased research funding for education. He previously was on and served as chair of the Kansas Professional Standards Board, served on the Kansas Continuing Legal Education Commission, was on the Board of Directors and former chair of the American Association of Colleges of Teacher Education (AACTE), and served on the Board of Directors of the Council for the Accreditation of Educator Preparation (CAEP). He is currently chairing the Kansas Board of Regents Educator Work Force Task Force. Previously he co-chaired the Kansas Department of Education Blue Ribbon Task Force on Bullying. He co-facilitated the formation of the Global Education Deans Forum (GEDF). He is the co-author or editor of four other books and over 90 refereed articles and book chapters. His work has been funded by over $4.5 million of federal and state grants. His recent study on the impact of social media on higher education leadership won the 2020 Neuner Award for Excellence in Scholarly-Professional Publication from the American Association of University Administrators. An earlier book was the National Library Association 1998 Learning Disabilities Recommended Book of the Year.

Yong Zhao, Ph.D., is a foundation distinguished professor in the School of Education and Human Sciences at the University of Kansas and a professor in educational leadership at the Melbourne Graduate School of Education in Australia. He previously served as the Presidential Chair, Associate Dean, and Director of the Institute for Global and Online Education in the College of Education, University of Oregon, where he was also a Professor in the Department of Educational Measurement, Policy, and Leadership. Prior to his role at the University of Oregon, Yong Zhao was university distinguished professor at the College of Education, Michigan State University, where he also served as the founding director of the Center for Teaching and Technology, executive director of the Confucius Institute, as well as the U.S.–China Center for Research on Educational Excellence. He is an elected member of the National Academy of Education and a fellow of the International Academy of Education. Yong Zhao has received numerous awards including the Early Career Award from the American Educational Research Association, Outstanding Public Educator from Horace Mann League of USA, and Distinguished Achievement Award in Professional Development from the Association of Education Publishers. He has been recognized as one of the most influential education scholars.